REA

ACPL ITE

DISCARDED

3 1833 00535 2296

Y0-BSM-474

WHO'S
WHO
IN
BOXING

JUN 0 5 '78

WHO'S WHO
IN
BOXING

Bob Burrill

ARLINGTON HOUSE New Rochelle, New York

Copyright © 1974 by Arlington House, New Rochelle, New York.

All rights reserved. No portion of this book may be reproduced without written permission from the publisher, except by a reviewer who may quote brief passages in connection with a review.

Library of Congress Catalog Card Number 73–13020

MANUFACTURED IN THE UNITED STATES OF AMERICA

Library of Congress Cataloging in Publication Data

Burrill, Bob.
  Who's who in boxing.

  1. Boxing—Biography—Dictionaries. I. Title.
GV1131.B87   796.8′3′0922   73–13020
ISBN 0–87000–232–5

2002594
FOREWORD

One of the great contributions to the continued interest in boxing is the record book, the recollection through statistics and biographical tidbits of the sport's fascinating past.

The records provide the ingredients for compassion and reminiscence as well as the necessary facts for fans, authorities and us old-timers. Of course, we don't all arrive at the same conclusions, interpreting the records. But we have an unbreakable basis for discussion and opinion of a sport we love.

Who's Who in Boxing contributes substantially to preserving boxing's timeless traditions and color, and adds a special flavor of its own with its profiles of promoters and managers in addition to history's outstanding fighters.

It all adds up to a healthy, substantial and interesting contribution to the grand old sport.

JACK DEMPSEY

June 1973

EDITOR'S NOTE

As every sports buff knows, the records of boxers are sometimes in dispute. Add to this the possibility of human error and you can see why the author is asking every reader of this work to pass on any corrections he might discover.

Beyond that, can you think of any significant omissions? These will normally fall into the gray "matter of opinion" area. But if sentiment does build for including a particular fighter or official in a revised edition, the author will want to.

If you have any suggestions or corrections, please write to the author in care of Arlington House, New Rochelle, N. Y. 10801. Since this volume is likely to become one of the established sources, you will be making a significant contribution to sports research. Everyone who helps will be given a credit line in the revised, enlarged, updated edition we hope to bring out in the later 1970s.

PREFACE

As Jack Dempsey points out in his foreword to this book, "One of the great contributions to the continued interest in boxing is the record book, the recollection through statistics and biographical tidbits of the sport's fascinating past." That, of course, is true of most sports. But none contains the intangibles of some boxing records and the picture they reflect.

Reasons for this are varied. In the early days when laws banned the sport, it was often a hide-and-hit event, and even oftener hastily kept records were either contradictory or lost. There has never been an overall regulation or commission to determine disputed champions, policy, penalties that would prevail in all states and nations. Occasions have found two, even three men recognized as world champions by as many commissions.

However, a legal blow that put boxing records into a groggy state for two decades was the "no decision" legislation. This ridiculous law, existing in many states from 1910 to 1930, disallowed an official decision if a bout lasted its scheduled distance. A knockout, foul, no contest, disqualification or act of God was officially recorded with the round it occurred in. But, lopsided or even, a fight going the distance you'll find recalled for posterity in your record books as ND (no decision).

This law was passed mainly to pacify antigambling factions siding with those opposing the legalizing of boxing. However, sideliners frustrated this objective. For the purpose of settling wagers, common practice was accepting the majority verdict of three designated boxing reporters at ringside with ND becoming more significant as "newspaper decision" than as "no decision."

But for historical boxing buffs ND is controversial, occasionally misleading and in some instances providing base for downright inaccurate conclusions. For example, a mediocre fighter with a knack for staying on his feet could boast a two- or three-year undefeated record, which not seldom included champions in nontitle ND fights. For many a champ was receptive to contests in ND states where his crown was comparatively safe. Even if the fight weren't at catchweights, it would call for a KO or disqualification for the title actually to change hands.

Some examples of the confusion NDs provide the records: of Jack Britton's 300 fights, 172 were ND; Harry Greb, 291 bouts, 166 ND; Benny Leonard, 115 of 209; Jack Dillon, 129 of 240.

Eventually, the ND law was scrubbed by all states, but not before it had mocked some phases of boxing research. This book, cognizant of this occasional possibility, has elaborated on such noteworthy ND series as the Gene Tunney–Harry Greb pairings with ringside postfight opinion.

In the Tunney-Greb instance, the cool statistics elude the reader in the dark. In their first fight, Tunney was subjected to a cruel beating (his only career loss), won decisions in two returns, and the fourth and fifth encounters are recorded as NDs, which, in the opinion of ringsiders, Tunney decisively won, a fact you will find noted in those and other consequential ND fights reported in this book.

Contributing to the confusion are the boxing commissions, often at variance with everything from world title recognitions to suspensions.

Today's worldwide boxing structure is foundationed on these associations: the WBA (World Boxing Association), formerly the long-established NBA (National Boxing Association), is generally regarded as the most influential; the New York State Athletic Commission, because of being a center of world fistic activity, entertains impact on its world champion recognition, suspensions and other rulings; the WBC (World Boxing Council), based in Manila, commands attention if disagreement with some rulings.

EBU (European Boxing Union) is the potent right hand of boxing in that area of the world; it is based in London and has a staunch membership in every boxing-minded European nation. The British Empire (Commonwealth) and British titles are determined with little contradiction, and the OBF (Oriental Boxing Federation) has set a respected example for establishing its undisputed Oriental champions and regulations.

All boxing commissions recognize the established weight divisions, pound limitations remaining constant. Oriental countries ignore the heavier classes, others disregard some of the junior classifications.

The basic eight classifications are heavyweight, 175 pounds and over; light heavy to 175; middle, 160 limit; welter, 147; light, 135; feather, 126; bantam, 118; fly, 112. Junior divisions: middle, 154; welter, 140; light, 130. Efforts to establish cruiserweight, junior light heavyweight and paperweight never graduated to tangible activity, nor did the 1920 Walker Law, which approved junior classifications for fly, bantam and feather in New York.

Weight classifications, regulations healthy or ill chosen, along with the participants themselves are consequential to a boxing history library. But no less important are the promoters and managers, the often flamboyant, sometimes shrewd, conniving, careless, always interesting personalities behind the big show. So far as I can determine, this marks the first such book in which they have been accorded detailed recognition; the first roundup of boxing promoter-manager activity ever published.

There is a reason. The happenings of these men are diversified, near and away from the ring and gym. An obituary never tells his story. It involves the accumulation and distillation of feature pieces, an occasional sport magazine story, numerous small newspaper clips, news columns unrelated to boxing, such as theater, hockey, investigations, stock market, politics—name it and it's likely a boxing promoter or manager has been there.

In the author's corner have been knowledgeable seconds, confirming or altering questionable detail, providing basic material, resurrecting long disregarded facts. My grateful acknowledgement to those who have provided assistance: Library of Congress, Minneapolis Public Library, *Chicago Tribune* Library, Dr. Albert Colson's private library, *Minneapolis Star-Tribune* Library. Record books: *Ring Boxing Encyclopedia, Everlast,* Tom Andrews'

Record Book. Magazines: *Ring, Sports Illustrated, Self Defense, Boxing Blade, Liberty.* Books: *Sugar Ray* by Ray Robinson and Dave Anderson, *The Heavyweight Champions* by John Durant, *The Real McCoy* by Robert Cantwell, *Sting Like a Bee* by Jose Torres, *Any Boy Can* by Archie Moore and Leonard Pearl, *Brown Bomber* by Barney Nagler. And special thanks to Vic Gold and William Lightbody.

ACCAVALLO, HORACIO B. 10/14/34, Argentina. 112 lbs. Ranks with top four as hardest-punching flyweight. Won over third of bouts by KO (33 of 84). First fight, Emilio Avila, KO 5, 9/21/56, Buenos Aires. First seven fights, 6 KO, 1 draw. Undefeated to 1959, Salvatore Burruni, lost 10. Won vacant South American fly title, Jupiter Mansilla, 15, 10/7/60, Manilla. Undefeated to 1967. Defended: Mansilla, 15, 5/10/61, Buenos Aires; Mansilla, 15, 9/7/63, Buenos Aires; Demetrio Carbajal, KO 11, 10/26/63, Buenos Aires; Nelson Alarcon, 12, 12/12/64, Buenos Aires. Won WBA fly title, Katsuyoshi Takayama, 15, 3/1/66, Tokyo. Nontitle, Kiyoshi Tanabe, KO by 6, 1967. Last fight, defended title, Hiroyuki Ebihara, 15, 8/12/67, Buenos Aires. Retired Oct. 1958. Recap: bouts 84, KO 33, decision 43, draw 6, lost decision 1, KO by 1.

AKINS, VIRGIL B. 3/10/28, St. Louis, Mo. Negro. 5'9". Amateur: 14 wins, 1 loss. First pro fight, Albert Adams, won 6, 3/11/48, St. Louis. To 1958, spotty record. Title elimination: Isaac Logart, KO 6, 3/21/58, NYC; won vacant world welter title, Vince Martinez, KO 4, 6/6/58, St. Louis. Lost title, Don Jordan, 15, 12/5/58, Los Angeles. Title return, Jordan, lost 15, 4/24/59, St. Louis. To 1966, several losses. Last fight, Rip Randall, lost 10, 3/20/62, Houston. Following day announced retirement, eye injury. Recap: bouts 92, KO 34, decision 26, draw 2, lost decision 28, KO by 2.

ALI, MUHAMMAD (Cassius Clay) B. 1/17/42, Louisville, Ky. Negro. 6'2", 210. Changed name to conform to Muslim religion. Amateur: 1960 National AAU light heavy title; National Golden Gloves heavy champ;

11

Olympic Games light heavy champ. Probably no man held scene as did Clay. Arrogant, boastful, ignoring conventions. Also able. After two-year exile, he mellowed. Some class him with greatest, others disdain his talent. Said Clay, "I started boxing because I thought it was fastest way for black people to make it." (Father was a fairly successful sign painter.) High school student when he won National AAU title in Toledo, shouted, "I am the prettiest and the greatest!" First pro, Tunney Hunsaker, won 6, 10/29/60, Louisville. Undefeated four years, including Billy Daniels, KO 7; Archie Moore, KO 4; Henry Cooper, KO 5; Doug Jones, won 10. Won world heavy title, Sonny Liston, KO 8 (Liston wouldn't come out for 8th), 2/25/64, Miami Beach. Defended: Liston, KO 1, 5/25/65, Lewiston, Me.; Floyd Patterson, KO 12, 11/22/65, Las Vegas; George Chuvalo, won 15, 3/29/66, Toronto; Cooper, KO 6, 5/21/66, London; Brian London, KO 3, 8/6/66, London; Karl Mildenberger, KO 12, 9/10/66, Frankfurt; Cleveland Williams, KO 3, 11/4/66, Houston; Ernie Terrell, NBA champ, won 15, 2/6/67, Houston; Zora Folley, KO 7, 2/22/67, NYC. Refused to serve in armed forces, maintaining Muslim religion prevented. Stripped of title, banned in U.S., faced jail. Vindicated by U.S. Supreme Court, 1970. Returned, Jerry Quarry, KO 3, Oscar Bonavena, KO 15. Title, Joe Frazier, lost 15, 3/2/70, NYC ($2½ million gate, including TV). 1971: Jimmy Ellis, KO 12; Buster Mathis, won 12; Jurgin Blin, KO 7. 1973: Ken Norton, lost 12, 3/31, San Diego; return, won 12, 9/10, Inglewood, Calif. Recap: bouts 35, KO 26, decision 7, lost decision 2.

ALLEN, TERRY (Edward Govier) B. 8/11/25, Islington, England. 5'3". First fight, Jim Thomas, won 6, 9/3/42, Islington. Undefeated 4 years. To title fight, 2 KO setbacks—Alec Murphy, 5/20/46, Haringey, Eng.; Rinty Monaghan, 3/11/47, London. World fly title, Monaghan, draw 15, 9/30/49, Belfast (earlier had beaten Monaghan, 10, 2/7/49, Haringey). Won world fly title, Honore Pratesi, 15, 4/25/50, Haringey. Lost title, Dado Marino, 15, 8/1/50, Honolulu. Won vacant British title, Vic Herman, 15, 6/11/51, Leicester. World title, Marino, lost 15, 11/1/51, Honolulu. Lost British title, Teddy Gardner, 15, 3/17/52, West Hartlepool. Won vacant British title, Eric Marsden, KO 6, 10/21/52, London. Defended: Marsden, won foul 5, 2/16/54, London. World title, Yoshio Shirai, lost 15, 10/27/53, Tokyo. Vacant European title, Nazzarino Gianelli, lost 15, 9/10/54, Milan (last fight). Announced retirement 9/20/54. Recap: bouts 76, KO 18, decision 42, won foul 2, draw 1, lost decision 10, KO by 3.

AMBERS, LOU (Louis D'Ambrosio) (Herkimer Hurricane) B. 11/8/13, Herkimer, N.Y. Italian. 5'6", 135. First fight, Frank Curry KO 2, 6/16/32, NYC. Undefeated in 47, lost 1. World light title, Tony Canzoneri, lost 15, 5/10/35, NYC. To mid-1936, undefeated 10 (Tony Scarpati KO 7, Brooklyn, died result of bout injury). Won world light title, Canzoneri, 15, 9/3/36, NYC. Lost nontitle 1936, Eddie Cool, 10; Jimmy McLarnin, 10. Defended: Canzoneri, won 15, 5/7/37, NYC; Pedro Montanez, won 15, 9/23/37, NYC. Lost title, Henry Armstrong, 15, 8/17/38. Regained title, Armstrong, 15, 8/22/39, NYC. Lost title, Lew Jenkins, KO by 3, 5/10/40, NYC. Last fight, Jenkins, KO by 7, 2/28/41, NYC. Coast Guard 1942. Hall of Fame 1964. Recap: bouts 102, KO 29, decision 59, draw 6, lost 6, KO by 2.

ANAYA, ROMERO B. Mexico. Early record not available. First recorded fight, Kazuyoshi, KO 5. Won world bantam title, Enrique Pinder, KO 3, 2/73, Panama City. Defended: Rogelio Lara, won 15, 6/73, Inglewood, Calif. Recap: bouts 6, KO 3, decision 3.

ANDREWS, TOM STORA B. 1869, Ontario. D. 12/1/41, Milwaukee, Wis. Promoter. A slender, gentle person, Tom Andrews looked more like a clergyman or small-town banker than Milwaukee's legendary fight promoter and dean of the area's sports authorities. Despite his overall sports knowledge, boxing was his first love, an inclination that was evident in his promotions, sports writing and publication of his annual *Andrews Record Book.*

The son of a blacksmith, he came to Milwaukee at age of one. As a youth he was an all-round athlete, played amateur football, basketball and baseball. He often recalled fondly that at he was a member of Milwaukee's Calumet Club football team that upset the U. of Wisconsin 27–0.

Starting his working years as a Western Union messenger, he finally obtained a job as a copy boy for the old *Evening Wisconsin,* earning his way through the ranks to the sports editor's desk.

His initial fight promotion was at the Standard Theatre in 1898, sharing a $180 profit with an associate. Young Andrews' promotions were successful and the Milwaukee Athletic Club hired him as a matchmaker. In 1927, he purchased Otto Borchert's interest in the Cream City Athletic Club, gained the all-important boxing franchise of the Milwaukee Auditorium. Andrews named himself president and matchmaker. Under his direction boxing prospered in Milwaukee and contributed to an era during which the Midwest graduated to one of the world's important boxing centers. He was 72 when he died in his Milwaukee home.

ANGOTT, SAMMY (Samuel Engotti) B. 1/17/15, Washington, Pa. Italian. 5′7″, 135. First fight, Tony Marengo, won 4, March 1935, NYC. To 1940, mostly impressive, won NBA light title, Davey Day, 10, 5/3/40, Louisville. (Nontitle, Fritzie Zivic, lost 10, 1940.) Won world light title, Lew

Jenkins, 15, 12/19/41, NYC. Defended: Allie Stolz, won 15, 5/15/42, NYC. Retired undefeated 11/13/42. Comeback, won NBA title, Slugger White, 15, 10/27/43, Hollywood. Lost title, Juan Zurita, 15, 3/8/44; retired again. To 1950, fair record, last fight Sonny Boy West, lost 10, 8/8/50, Detroit. Recap: bouts 125, KO 22, decision 72, draw 8, lost decision 22, KO by 1.

ANTHONY, TONY B. 2/6/35, New York, N.Y. 5'11", 170. National AAU welter champ 1953. Classy style prompted predictions of future champ; vulnerable jaw hesitated career. First pro fight, George Boddie, KO 2, 11/5/52, Cleveland. Eight straight KO to Miguel Mendevil, KO by 7, 1953. Undefeated to KOs by Jacques Royer-Crecy, 8, Willie Troy, 4, Bobby Boyd, 3. Undefeated 1956: 5 KO, 1 win, 1 draw. Light heavy title, Archie Moore, KO by 7, 9/20/57, Los Angeles. Undefeated 1958, including Yvon Durelle, KO 7. 1959: won three, lost three; last fight, Billy Hunter, KO by 7, 10/23/59, NYC. Recap: bouts 49, KO 30, decision 10, draw 1, lost 2, KO by 6.

APOSTOLI, FRED B. 2/2/14. Italian-American. 5'7", 160. Amateur: Golden Gloves middle championship, National AAU middle title. 1934, Pacific Coast junior welter title. First recorded pro fight, Freddie Steele, KO by 10, 4/1/35, Seattle, 6 wins, 1 KO. 1936, 7 wins incl. Paul Pirrone, Babe Risko, Lou Brouillard. 1937, Ken Overlin, lost 10, 7 wins included. Solly Krieger, won, KO; Marcel Thil, KO 10. 1938, Steele, KO 9; Glen Lee, won 12; Young Corbett, lost 10. Middle title claimed after win over Glen Lee, 10, 4/1/38, NYC. Defended: Young Corbett, KO 8, 11/18/38, NYC. Nontitle, lost twice to Billy Conn, 1939. Lost title, Ceferino Garcia, KO by 7, 10/2/39, NYC. 1940–48: won 26, lost 4. Navy 1943–45. Last fight, Earl Turner, lost 10, 12/1/48, Oakland, Calif. Recap: bouts 72, KO 31, decision 30, draw 1, lost decision 6, KO by 4.

ARAGON, ART (Arthur Anthony Aragon) (Golden Boy) B. 1928, Albuquerque, N. Mex. Mexican-American. 135. Sweetheart of Hollywood boxing fans. First fight, Frenchy Renee, won 4, 5/23/44, Los Angeles. Impressive first year, including Louis Salas, KO 1; only loss, Bert White, 5. Creditable early record, undefeated 1946. Impressive to 1951, mostly Hollywood, Los Angeles. Jimmy Carter, nontitle, won 10, 8/28/51. Light title, Carter, lost 16, 11/14/51, Los Angeles. Undefeated 1952, 5 KO, 1 dec. To 1958, wins included Carter, Don Jordan, Salas twice, Chuck Davey; KO by Carmen Basilio, 8, 1958. 1959: KO 6, won 2, lost 2. Last fight, Alvaro Gutierrez, KO by 9, Los Angeles. Recap: bouts 109, KO 61, decision 26, draw 4, lost decision 16, KO by 2.

14

ARCARI, BRUNO B. 1/1/72, Latina, Italy. First fight, Salvatore Colella, KO by 5, 12/11/64, Rome. 1965: undefeated. 1966: nontitle, Mario Consolati, KO by 9, return won Italian junior welter title, Consolati, foul 7, 12/7/66, Genoa. Defended: Efrem Donati, 12, 2/22/67, Genoa; Pietro Vargellini, KO 4, 9/16/67, Acqui Terme. Won European junior welter title, Johann Orsolics, KO 12, 5/7/68, Vienna. Defended: Des Rea, KO 6, 8/21/68, San Remo; Jose Torcida, KO 5, 12/1/69, Bologna. Won world junior welter title, Pedro Adigue, 15, 1/31/70, Rome. Defended: Rene Roque, won foul, 6, 7/10/70, Ligano; Joao Henrique, won 15, 3/6/71, Rome; Enrique Jana, KO 9, 6/26/71, Palermo; Domingo Corpas, KO 9, 10/9/71, Genoa; Henrique, KO 12, 6/10/72, Genoa; Everaldo Costa, 15, 12/2/72, Turin. Recap: bouts 55, KO 31, decision 19, won foul 3, KO by 2.

ARCHIBALD, JOEY B. 12/6/15, Providence, R.I. Irish. 5'4", 126. First fight, Ernst Kid Herbert, KO 4, 1932. Through 1934, 14 KO, 7 wins, 6 lost, mostly mediocre opposition. Impressive 1937, 7 KO, 4 wins, lost 2. Won vacant feather title, Mike Belloise, 15, 10/17/38, NYC. Nontitle, Pete Scalzo, KO by 2, 12/5/38. Defended: Leo Rodak, won 15, 4/18/39, Providence, R.I.; Harry Jeffra, won 15, 9/28/39, Washington, D.C. Lost title, Jeffra, 15, 5/20/40, Dayton, Ohio. Regained title, Jeffra, 15, 5/12/41, Providence. Lost title, Chalky Wright, KO by 11, 9/11/41, Washington, D.C. Lost 14 of last 17. Last fight, Doll Rafferty, KO by 3, 8/11/43, Milwaukee. Navy. Recap: bouts 106, KO 28, decision 32, draw 5, lost decision 32, lost foul 1, KO by 8.

ARIZMENDI, BABY (Alberto Arizmendi) B. 3/7/14, Torreon, Mexico. D. 12/31/63, Los Angeles, Calif. 5'5", 118–125. Early fights estimated 135, not recorded. First recorded fight, 1930, Babe Colima, lost, 10; return, draw, 10. Mex. bantam title, Kid Pancho, won 10, 1931, Mexico City. 1932–33, beat Henry Armstrong, Fidel LaBarba, Newsboy Brown, Speedy Dado, Eddie Shea twice. Won NY state version world feather title, Mike Belloise, 15, 8/30/34, NYC. Creditable record thru 1938. Welter title bout, Armstrong, lost 10, 1/10/39, Los Angeles. Series: Armstrong, won three, lost three; Lou Ambers, draw, lost, KO by; Brown, won two, lost. Other champs: Tony Canzoneri, lost; Sammy Angott, draw, lost; Jackie Wilson, KO by. Last fight, Roman Alvarez, lost 10, 8/21/42, Hollywood. Joined U.S. Navy. Recap: bouts 87, KO 8, decision 42, draw 11, lost decision 23, KO by 3.

ARMSTEAD, PAUL B. 3/3/37, Lufkin, Tex. 135. First fight, Harvey Price, KO 1, 4/9/55, Hollywood. Impressive early record: 1955, KO 5, dec. 1, lost 1; 1956, KO 4, dec. 2, KO by Billy Evans, 4 (won return in 1957). Won vacant Calif. light title, Lauro Salas, 12, 8/3/57, Hollywood. Defended: Jimmy

Hornsby, KO 10, 10/18/58, Hollywood; Emilio Flores, won 12, 1/26/62, Los Angeles; Jimmy Fields, won 12, 3/19/63, San Diego. Undefeated 1961–62. Michigan version of world light title, Kenny Lane, lost 15, 8/19/63, Saginaw. 1964: Joe Brown, won twice; Luis Molina, twice; Bobby Scanlon; lost, Percy Hayles. Overseas 1965: KO 1, dec. 2, draw 2, lost 1. 1967: two fights, lost Eddie Perkins, Ismael Laguna. Last fight, Gil King, lost 10, 12/30/70, Las Vegas. Recap: bouts 73, KO 14, decision 38, won disq. 1, draw 4, lost 14, KO by 2.

ARMSTRONG, HENRY (Henry Jackson) (Hurricane Henry) B. 12/12/12, Columbus, Miss. Negro. 5′6″, 165. Amateur: 62 bouts, won 58. Early ring name: Melody Jackson. Only fighter to hold three titles—feather, light, welter—simultaneously. First pro fight, Al Iovino, KO by 3, 7/27/31, Braddock, Pa. Spotty early record. 1937–38, approached peak, 36 KO, 4 wins. Won world feather title, Pete Sarron, KO 6, 10/29/37, NYC. Won world welter title, Barney Ross, 15, 5/31/38, NYC. Won world light title, Lou Ambers, 15, 8/17/38, NYC. Defended welter title: Ceferino Garcia, won 15, 11/25/38, NYC; Al Manfredo, KO 3, 12/5/38, Cleveland. (Vacated feather title, 1938.) Defended welter: Baby Arizmendi, won 10, 1/10/39, Los Angeles; Bobby Pacho, KO 4, 3/4/39, Havana; Lew Feldman, KO 1, 3/16/39, St. Louis; Davey Day, KO 12, 3/31/39, NYC; Ernie Roderick, won 15, 5/25/39, London. Lost light title, Lou Ambers, 15, 8/22/39, NYC. Defended welter title: Al Manfredo, KO 4, 10/9/39, Des Moines; Howard Scott, KO 2, 10/13/39, Minneapolis; Ritchie Fountaine, KO 3, 10/20/39, Seattle; Jimmy Garrison, 10, 10/24/39, Los Angeles; Bobby Pacho, KO 4, Denver; Garrison, KO 7, 12/11/39, Cleveland; Joe Ghnouly, KO 5, 1/4/40, St. Louis; Pedro Montanez, KO 9, 1/24/40, NYC; Paul Junior, KO 7, 4/26/40, Boston; Ralph Zanelli, KO 5, 5/24/40, Boston; Junior, KO 3, 6/21/40, Portland; Lew Jenkins, KO 6, 7/17/40, NYC (nontitle); Phil Furr, KO 4, 9/23/40. Lost title, Fritzie Zivic, 15, 10/4/40, NYC. Return title, Zivic, KO by 12, 1/17/41, NYC. Comeback. Four exhibition KOs, October 1941. Creditable closing record, KOs, Leo Rodak, Lew Jenkins, Al Davis, Mike Belloise; won, Zivic, Garrison, Sammy Angott. Last fight, Jack Silder, lost 10, 2/14/45, Oakland, Calif. Regarded as one of great champions. Ordained Baptist minister 1951. Hall of Fame 1954. Recap: bouts 175, KO 97, decision 47, ND 1, draw 8, lost decision 19, lost foul 1, KO by 2.

ATTELL, ABE B. 2/22/84, San Francisco, Calif. Jewish. 5′4″, 122. First fight, Kid Leonard, KO 2, 8/19/1900. Through 1901, 24 KO, 7 win, 2 draw, 1 loss. Vacant feather title, George Dixon, draw 20, 10/20/01, Cripple Creek, Colo. Won vacant world feather title, Dixon 15, 10/28/01, St. Louis. Nontitle, Harry Forbes, lost 15, 1901. Defended: Forbes, KO 5, 2/1/04, St. Louis;

Kid Goodman, draw 15, 2/22/05, Boston; Frankie Neil, won 20, 7/5/06, Los Angeles; Harry Baker, KO 5, 1/18/07, Los Angeles; Kid Solomon, won 20, 5/24/07, Los Angeles; Freddy Weeks, KO 4, 10/29/07, Los Angeles; Owen Moran, draw 25, 1/1/08, San Francisco; Moran, draw 23, 9/7/08, San Francisco; Frankie White, KO 8, 3/26/09, Dayton, Ohio; Forbes, KO 6, 2/28/10, NYC. Nontitle, Johnny Kilbane, KO by 4, 1/31/11, Cleveland. Lost title, Kilbane 20, 2/22/12, Vernon, Calif. Oliver Kirk, lost 6 (Attell claimed exhaustion); return, Kirk, KO 3, 3/19/13. Last fight, Sid Knott, W 6, Winnipeg, Man. Operated tavern. Hall of Fame 1955. Recap: bouts 166, KO 47, decision 43, won foul 1, draw 17, lost decision 7, KO by 3, ND 48.

BACKUS, BILLY B. Syracuse, N.Y. First fight, Randy Sanders, won 4, 3/9/62, Totowa, N.J. Rocky start, lost 7, draw 3 of 17. Inactive 1966. All KO 1967. Undefeated 1970, including winning world welter title, Joe Napoles, KO 4, 12/3/70, Syracuse, N.Y. Lost title, Napoles, KO by 4, 6/4/71, Los Angeles. Recap: bouts 47, KO 15, decision 17, draw 4, lost decision 10, KO by 1.

BAER, BUDDY B. 6/11/15, Denver, Colo. German-Jewish. 6'6½", 245. First fight, Tiny Abbott, KO 1, 9/22/34, Eureka, Calif. 11 straight KO first year. 1935: 11 KO, lost Babe Hunt, Ford Smith. 1936: 8 KO, 1 win, lost Andre Lenglet. Undefeated 1937, including Abe Simon, KO 3. Only 1938 fight, Gunnar Barlund, KO by 7. Comeback 1939-40: won 1, KO 8 including Nathan Mann, 7; Valentino Campolo, 1. 1941: Tony Galento, KO 7; Heavyweight title, Joe Louis, disq. 7, 5/23/41, Washington, D.C. (knocked Louis out of ring in first round). Army 1941. Title, Louis, KO by 1, 1/9/42, NYC. Younger brother of Max, both managed by Ancil Hoffman. After heart attack death of Max, Buddy toured nation for Eagles raising heart research funds. May have record percentage for one-round KOs: 23 of 43 KO in 55 fights. Recap: bouts 55, KO 43, decision 5, lost decision 4, disq. 1, KO by 2.

BAER, MAX (Maximilian Adelbert Baer) (Madcap Maxie) B. 2/11/09, Omaha, Nebr. D. 11/21/59, Hollywood, Calif., heart. German-Jewish. 6'2½", 220. Butcher. First fight, Chief Cariboo, KO 2, 1929. Several wins;

2 losses—Tiny Abbott, Les Kennedy. Frankie Campbell, KO 5, 8/25/30, San Francisco (Campbell died after fight. Baer talked of retiring). Ernie Schaaf, Eastern debut, lost 10, 12/19/30, NYC. Tom Heeney, KO 3, 1/16/31, NYC. Several wins, including Johnny Risko, King Levinsky, Schaaf, Tuffy Griffith. Max Schmeling, KO 10, 6/8/33, NYC. Won world heavy title, Primo Carnera, KO 11 (Primo down 11 times), 6/14/34, NYC. Lost title, Jim Braddock (probably biggest upset in ring history), 15, 6/13/35, NYC. Fight role in film *The Prizefighter and the Lady* with Myrna Loy. Two movies and weekly radio program canceled after fight because of Baer quip, "Jim can use title, he has five kids . . . I don't know how many I have. . . ." 1936–41, 30 fights, 20 KOs, KO by Lou Nova twice. Last fight, Nova, KO by 8, 4/4/41, NYC. Movies, radio, TV, referee, army. Hall of Fame 1968. Son, Max Jr., mediocre fighter, successful TV actor in "Beverly Hillbillies." Recap: bouts 79, KO 50, decision 15, lost decision 9, lost foul 1, KO by 3, ND 1.

BALDWIN, MATTY B. 1884, Boston, Mass. D. 10/1/18, Chelsea, Mass. Irish. 5′5″, 135. First fight, Kid Tirrell, KO 3, 1902. Creditable record to 1908, undefeated 1906–08 including Freddie Welsh, ND; Benny Yanger, won; Harlem Tommy Murphy, won; Kid Sullivan, won; Willie Moody, ND. Fought top rankers to 1914, never title chance: Abe Attell, ND; Jem Driscoll, ND, lost; Ad Wolgast, draw; Frankie Burns, ND; Welsh, lost twice; Joe Mandot, draw; Jack Britton, ND; Joe Shugrue, won. Series: Leach Cross, ND, lost foul, lost; Murphy, won, draw, lost; Owen Moran, ND, lost twice; Frank Adams, KO, won twice, draw, lost. Last fight, Welsh, lost 12, 10/27/14, Boston. Record sidelight: 49 draws in 185 fights; closest Jack (Twin) Sullivan, 40 draws in 137 fights. Recap: bouts 185, KO 22, decision 50, won foul 5, draw 49, lost decision 24, lost foul 1, ND 34.

BALLERINO, MIKE B. 1901, Bayonne, N.J. Italian. 5′4″, 126. First fight, Kid Ponso, KO 3, 1920. First two years fair, highlighted by Pancho Villa series: 2 draw, 2 ND, 8 lost. Creditable record through 1925, including Steve (Kid) Sullivan, 1 win, KO by 5, ND. Won junior light title, Sullivan, 12, 4/1/25, Phila. Lost title, Tod Morgan, KO by 10, 12/2/25, Los Angeles. To 1929, spotty. Last fight, Murray Fuchs, won 10, 1929. Recap: bouts 96, KO 8, decision 32, draw 14, lost decision 19, KO by 5, ND 18.

BARRY, JIMMY B. 3/7/70, Chicago, Ill. D. 1943, Chicago, Ill. Irish. 5′2″, 105–115. First fight, Fred Larson, KO 1, 1891. First year, 11 KO, 4 wins. Claimed world bantam title, Casper Leon, KO 28, 9/15/94, Lemont, Ill. Leon, draw 14, 3/30/95, Chicago (police stopped). Undisputed world title, Walter Croot, KO 20, 12/6/97, London (Croot died of brain injury). Nine more fights, never defended, retired undefeated. Recap: bouts 70, KO 39, decision 20, draw 9, no contest 2.

BARTFIELD, SOLDIER (Jacob Bartfield) B. 3/15/92, Lancyzn, Austria. Jewish. 5'7", 142–150. Described as the "man who fought them all, the famous, mediocre, big and small." First fight, George Alger, ND 10, 3/29/12, Brooklyn. Creditable first 5 years, 1917 undefeated. Series: Harry Greb, 5 ND, 1 lost; Ted Kid Lewis, 6 ND; Jack Britton, 4 ND, 1 lost; Mike O'Dowd, 2 ND, lost, draw; Benny Leonard, 3 ND; Bill Brennan, 3 ND; Mike Gibbons, 2 ND, 1 lost, Mickey Walker, 2 ND. Last fight, Sgt. Sammy Baker, KO by 2, 2/19/25, Brooklyn. Recap: bouts 167, KO 18, decision 11, won foul 2, draw 8, lost decision 13, KO by 4, ND 111.

BARTOLO, SAL B. 11/5/17, Boston, Mass. Italian. 126. First fight, Art Nadeau, KO 3, 4/3/37, Boston. To 1943, active, hard campaigner. Joey Archibald, won 10, 3/26/43; Willie Pep, lost 10, 4/9/43. World feather title, Pep, lost, 15, 6/8/43, Boston. Maritime service. Won NBA feather title, Phil Terranova, 15, 3/10/44, Boston. Defended: Terranova, won 15, 5/5/44, Boston; Willie Roache, 15, 12/15/44, Boston; Spider Armstrong, KO 6, 5/3/46, Boston. Lost title, Willie Pep, KO by 12, 7/7/46, NYC. Last fight, Paulie Jackson, won 10, 1/25/49, Salem, Mass. Recap: bouts 97, KO 16, decision 58, draw 5, lost decision 16, KO by 2.

BASILIO, CARMEN B. 4/2/27, Canastota, N.Y. Italian. 5'6½", 147. Onion picker, wire factory worker. Marine Corps 1945–47. Amateur: 14 bouts, won 11. First pro fight, Jimmy Evans, KO 3, 11/24/48, Binghamton, N.Y. Up-down to 1958: Ike Williams, won; Billy Graham, won, draw; welter title, Kid Gavilan, lost 15, 9/15/53, Syracuse. Undefeated to 1955. Won world welter title, Tony DeMarco, KO 12, 6/10/55, Syracuse. Defended: DeMarco, KO 12, 11/30/55, Boston. Lost welter title, Johnny Saxton, 15, 3/14/56, Chicago. Regained welter title, Saxton, KO 9, 9/12/56, Syracuse. Defended: Saxton, KO 2, 2/22/57, Cleveland. Won middle title, Ray Robinson, 15, 9/23/57, NYC. Vacated welter title. Lost middle title, Robinson, 15, 3/25/58, Chicago. For vacated NBA title, Gene Fullmer, KO by 14, 8/28/59, San Francisco. NBA middle title, Fullmer, KO by 12, 6/29/60, Salt Lake City. Middle title, Paul Pender, lost 15, 4/22/61, Boston. Retired 4/25/61. Hall of Fame 1969. Recap: bouts 78, KO 26, decision 29, draw 7, lost decision 14, KO by 2.

BASS, BENNY B. 12/4/04, Kiev, Russia. Jewish. 5'3½", 130. First fight, Young Kansas, KO 3, 1923. To mid-1927, impressive record, beat Babe Herman, Joey Glick, Red Chapman, foul. Won vacant world feather title, Chapman, 10, 9/12/27, Phila. Lost title, Tony Canzoneri, 15, 2/10/28, NYC. Won junior light title, Tod Morgan, KO 2, 12/19/29, NYC. Lost title, Kid Chocolate, KO by 7, 7/15/31, Phila. Fair record for remaining career, Johnny Jadick, won; Eddie Shea, won; Henry Armstrong, KO by 4. Last fight, Tommy Spiegel, lost 10, 5/7/40, Phila. Recap: bouts 198, KO 59, decision 79, won foul 2, draw 6, lost decision 16, lost foul 10, KO by 2, ND 23, no contest 1.

BASSEY, HOGAN (Okon Bassey Asuque) (Kid) B. 6/3/32, Calabar, Nigeria. First recorded fight, Dick Turpin, won 12, 1949, Lagos, Nigeria. 1949–59, fights in Nigeria, England, France. Impressive record: Nigerian, British Empire titles. Won vacant world bantam title, Cherif Hamia, KO 10, 6/24/57. Paris. Defended: Ricardo Moreno, KO 3, 4/1/58, Los Angeles. Lost title, Davey Moore, KO by 13, 3/18/59, Los Angeles. Title return, Moore, KO by 11, 8/19/59, Los Angeles. Retired. 1963, named physical education director of Nigeria. Recap: bouts 68, KO 20, decision 35, draw 1, lost decision 6, lost foul 2, KO by 4.

BATTALINO, BATTLING (Christopher Battalino) B. 2/18/08, Hartford, Conn. Italian. 5'6", 126. First fight, Archie Rosenberg, KO 2, 1927. To title, undefeated in 22, lost 1. Won world feather title, Andre Routis, 15, 9/23/29, Hartford. Defended: Kid Chocolate, won 15, 12/12/30, NYC; Fidel LaBarba, won 15, 5/22/31, NYC; Irish Bobby Brady, won 10, 7/1/31, Jersey City; Freddie Miller, won 10, 7/23/31, Cincinnati; Earl Mastro, won 10, 11/4/31, Chicago. 1932, outgrew, relinquished title. Fair lightweight record. Billy Petrolle, KO by 12, lost 10; Barney Ross, lost 10; Howard Scott, lost twice. Last fight, Dick Turcotte, lost 10, 1/30/40, Hartford. Recap: bouts 88, KO 24, decision 34, draw 3, lost decision 24, lost foul 1, KO by 1, no contest 1.

BECERRA, JOE (Jose Becerra Covarrubias) B. 4/15/36, Guadalajara, Jalisco, Mexico. 5'5". First fight, Ray Gomez, KO 4, 8/30/53, Guadalajara. Impressive five years in Mexico. First U.S. bout, Dwight Hawkins, KO by 4, Los Angeles, 11/6/57. To 1959, prestige in U.S. Won bantam title, Alphonse Halimi, KO 8, 7/8/59, Los Angeles. Defended: Halimi, KO 9, 2/4/60, Los Angeles; Kenji Yonekura, won 15, 5/23/60, Tokyo. Upset nontitle, Elroy Sanchel, KO by 8, 8/30/60, Juarez, Mexico. Retired after fight. Recap: bouts 78, KO 42, decision 29, draw 2, lost decision 3, KO by 2.

BELANGER, ALBERT (Frenchy) B. 5/17/06, Toronto, Ontario. French-Canadian. 5'4", 112. Outstanding amateur and early pro record 1925–26. Upset Newsboy Brown, 10, 1927. Won vacant NBA world fly title, Frankie Genaro, 10, 11/28/27, Toronto. Defended: Ernie Jarvis, won 10, 12/8/27, Toronto. Lost title, Genaro, 10, 2/6/28, Toronto. Return nontitle, lost 10, 10/15/28, Toronto. Canadian fly title, Steve Rocco, lost 10, 6/5/28, Toronto.

Won Canadian title, Rocco, 10, 1/2/29, Toronto. American title, Izzy Schwartz, lost 12, 3/12/29, Toronto. Genaro, lost 10, 1930, Toronto. Inactive 1931. Last fight, Frankie Wolfram, KO by 7, 1932, Toronto. Recap: bouts 62, KO 13, decision 24, draw 7, lost decision 15, lost foul 1, KO by 2.

BELLOISE, MIKE B. 2/18/11, New York, N.Y. Italian. 125. First fight, Jimmy Hughes, KO 3, 1932. Impressive three years. For N.Y. feather title recognition, Baby Arizmendi, lost 15, 8/30/34, NYC. Everette Rightmire, KO 14, 4/3/36, Chicago. N.Y. recognized Belloise champ. Lost title, Joey Archibald, 15, 10/17/38, NYC. Henry Armstrong, lost 1936, 1937, KO by 4, 1944. Spotty record 1938–42. Chester Reco, KO by 7, 3/3/42, NYC. Announced retirement after fight, but returned same year, won four straight. Fair record to Armstrong, KO by 4 in 1944. Last fight, Tommy Steelhouse, KO by 5, 8/26/47, Elmira, N.Y. Recap: bouts 126, KO 19, decision 65, draw 13, lost decision 15, KO by 14.

BENJAMIN, JOE B. 9/7/99, Stockton, Calif. Jewish. Outstanding amateur flyweight. Fought pro from bantam to light. First fight, Jimmy Fox, won 10, 1917. Undefeated first year including Frankie Burns, won; Eddie Camp, ND. Impressive 1919–21 including Benny Valgar, won 12; Joe Welling, ND twice; only loss, Benny Leonard, 4. 1922: lost, Johnny Dundee, Phil Salvadore, return Salvadore, won. 1923: only loss, Johnny O'Donnell, 4, won return 1924. Last fight, Ace Hudkins, lost 10, 4/8/25, Vernon, Calif. Retired, Hollywood film job. Marines, World War II. Recap: bouts 68, KO 15, decision 26, won foul 1, draw 5, lost decision 8, lost foul 2, KO by 1, ND 10.

BENVENUTI, NINO B. 4/26/38, Trieste, Italy. Amateur: 1960 Olympic welter champ. First pro, Ben Ali Allala, won 6, 1/20/61, Trieste. Undefeated to mid-1966, won vacant Italian middle title, Tommaso Truppi, KO 11, 3/1/63, Rome. Defended: Franco Fiori, KO 3, 8/30/63, Priverno; Fabio Bettini, KO 2, 7/30/64, San Remo; Truppi, KO 5, 2/12/65, Bologna. Won vacant European middle, Luis Folledo, KO 6, 10/15/65, Rome. Defended: Jupp Elze, KO 14, 5/14/66, Rome; Pascal DiBenedetto, KO 10, 10/21/66, Rome. Won world middle title, Emile Griffith, 15, 4/17/67, NYC. Lost title, Griffith, 15, 9/29/67, NYC. Regained title Griffith, 15, 3/4/68, NYC. Defended: Don Fullmer, won 15, 12/14/68, San Remo; Fraser Scott, won disq. 7, 10/4/69, Naples; Luis Rodriguez, KO 11, 11/22/69, Rome; Tom Bethea, KO 8, 5/23/70, Umago, Italy. Lost title, Carlos Monzon, KO by 12, 11/7/70, Rome. Title, Monzon, KO by 3, 5/8/71, Monte Carlo. Recap: bouts 90, KO 35, decision 42, won foul 5, draw 1, lost decision 4, KO by 3.

23

BERG, JACK (Judah Bergman) (Kid; Whitechapel Windmill) B. 6/28/09, London, England. Jewish. 5'9", 145. First fight, Young Johnny Gordon, KO 2, 6/8/24, London. Only losses in seven years, Johnny Cuthbert twice in 1925, won return, KO 11; Billy Petrolle, draw, KO by 5, 1928, defeated Petrolle, 10, 1930. Won junior welter title, Mushy Callahan, KO 10, 2/18/30, London. Lost title, Tony Canzoneri, KO by 3, 4/24/31, Chicago. Won British light title, Harry Mizler, KO 10, 10/29/34, London. British Empire light title, Laurie Stevens, lost 12, 1/11/36, Johannesburg. Lost British title, Jimmy Walsh, KO by 9, 4/24/36, Liverpool. Active to 1941, moderate success. British army. Last fight, Johnny McDonald, KO 5, 5/19/45, Coventry. Enlisted RAF. Recap: bouts 197, KO 59, decision 89, won foul 14, draw 9, lost decision 18, KO by 8.

BERLENBACH, PAUL (Astoria Assassin) B. 2/18/01, New York, N.Y. German. 5'10½", 170. Olympic heavy wrestling champ, AAU light heavy wrestling champ, 1920. Amateur boxing: AAU national heavy champ. Pro, first fight, Jim Roberts, KO 1, 10/4/23, NYC. Ten consecutive KOs. Jack Delaney, KO by 4, 3/14/24, NYC. Won world light heavy title, Mike McTigue, 15, 5/30/25, NYC. Defended: Jimmy Slattery, KO 11, 9/11/25, NY; Jack Delaney, won 15, 12/11/25, NYC; Young Stribling, won 15, 6/10/26, NYC. Lost title, Delaney, 15, 6/16/26, Brooklyn. 1927, KO by McTigue, Delaney. 1928, wrestled. Comeback as boxer, 1931, 2 KO. Last fight, Carl Knowles, lost 10, Oct. 1933, Atlanta. Broke at gambling tables. Retired, into business. Recap: bouts 49, KO 30, decision 7, draw 3, lost decision 4, KO by 3, ND 1, no contest 1.

BERNSTEIN, JACK (John Dodick) B. 11/5/99, New York, N.Y. D. 12/26/45, Yonkers, N.Y. Jewish. 5'4½", 130. First fight, Young West, ND 4, 1914. Through 1922, spotty record. 1923 undefeated to junior light title, won from Johnny Dundee, 15, 5/30/23, NYC. Lost title, Dundee, 15, 12/17/23, NYC. To 1931 mostly trial horse, lost Sammy Mandell, Rocky Kansas, Sid Terris, Bruce Flowers, Joe Glick. Last fight, Johnny Gaito, lost 6, 11/10/31. Yonkers. Recap: bouts 107, KO 17, decision 48, draw 7, lost decision 22, KO by 1, ND 12.

BETHEA, WAYNE B. 3/27/32, Dillon, S.C. 6', 200. Rugged trial horse, fought top heavies. First fight, Rue Williams, KO 3, 8/12/54, NYC. Harold Carter series: KO 7, 1954; draw one, lost two, 1955. 1956: upset Ezzard Charles, won Jimmy Slade, Zora Folley lost, return 1957 lost. Only KO by, Sonny Liston, 1, 1958. Upset Ernie Terrell, 10, 1960; Eddie Machen lost. 1961–63: spotty record, including loss to Cleveland Williams, Karl Mildenberger twice, Henry Cooper. European campaign, won 4, draw 2, lost 3. Last fight, Ernie Knox, KO 9, 10/14/63, Baltimore. Recap: bouts 50, KO 11, decision 17, draw 4, lost 17, KO by 1.

BETTINA, MELIO B. 11/18/16, Bridgeport, Conn. Italian. 5'10", 175–180. First bout, Joe Gargiso, KO 1, 10/6/34, NYC. 1934 to title 1939, 50 bouts: KO 19, won 23, draw 2, no decision 1, lost 4, KO by 1, Frank Zamoris, won return. Vacant NY light heavy title, Tiger Jack Fox, KO 9, 2/3/39, NYC. Lost title, Billy Conn, 15, 7/13/39, NYC. Title return, Conn, lost 15, 9/25/39, Pittsburgh. Vacant NBA light heavy title, Anton Christoforidis, lost 15, 1/13/41, Cleveland. Through 1942, 3 KO, 10 win, no defeat. Army 1942. 1943–1948, good record marred by Gus Lesnevich, KO by 1, 5/23/47, NYC. Last fight, Johnny Flynn, KO by 6, 12/21/48, Rochester, NY. Grueling, crowd pleaser, some regarded underrated. Manager James V. Grippo was hypnotist, claimed his talent played important role in fights. Recap: bouts 99, KO 36, decision 46, draw 3, lost decision 10, KO by 3, ND 1.

BLACKBURN, JACK (Charles Henry Blackburn) B. 1883, Versailles, Ky. D. 4/24/42, Chicago, Ill. Negro. 5'10", 135. First fight, Kid Miller, KO 8, undated, Indianapolis. To 1904 undefeated. Early career studded with name fighters: ND—Joe Gans twice, Joe Grim, Phila. Jack O'Brien; draw—Sam Langford three, Mike (Twin) Sullivan. To 1909 only loss Gans, 15, 1904. Served 1909–1913 in prison for manslaughter in Phila. Resumed career 1914, creditable six years including ND—Gunboat Smith, Harry Greb, Young Ahearn twice. Undefeated to last two fights, Panama Joe Gans, KO by 4, and last fight, Ray Pelkey, KO by 2, 3/9/23, Oakland, Calif. Retired as boxer, became outstanding trainer of Joe Louis, Bud Taylor, Sammy Mandell. Recap: bouts 103, KO 22, decision 15, won foul 1, draw 12, lost decision 1, KO by 2, ND 50.

BLOOM, PHIL (Ring Gorilla) B. 10/24/94, London, England. 5'7", 140. First fight, Walter Hennessey, KO 3, 1912. Undefeated to 1916 including ND —Benny Leonard twice, Jack Britton twice, Johnny Dundee twice, Leach Cross, Ted Kid Lewis. Majority fights ND. 1916, Leonard, KO by 8; ND— Freddie Welsh, Dundee. Series: Leonard, ND six, KO by two; Dundee, ND three; Joe Welling, won one, ND three, draw, lost; Irish Patsy Cline, ND four, lost foul; Joe Welling, won, ND three, draw, lost; Steve Latzo won, ND, lost. Rugged campaigner, fought six world champs—Leonard, Britton, Dundee, Lewis, Welsh, Rocky Kansas—never title chance. Last fight, Harry Galfund, lost 12, 9/24/23, Brooklyn. Located Hollywood, worked movie industry. Recap: bouts 172, KO 15, decision 27, won foul 1, draw 11, lost decision 18, lost foul 1, KO by 3, ND 96.

BOGASH, LOU (Luigi Bogassi) B. 2/24/01, Fantina, Italy. 5'5", 160. First fight, Billy Murphy, KO 2, 1916. Creditable early years, undefeated 1920 including Jack Britton, draw. 1921: 5 KO, 8 won, Mike O'Dowd, draw; Soldier Narfield, won, draw; lost—Jock Malone, Pal Reed. New England middle title, Jack Delaney, lost 15, 2/13/22, Bridgeport. 1922: Mickey Walker, won; Mike McTigue, draw; Tommy Loughran, ND. 1923: Jimmy Darcy, KO, won; Malone, won, lost; Harry Greb, ND. Series: Frank Moody, won, KO by 12, return, won; Tiger Flowers, won foul, ND one, lost 2. Undefeated 1926. Last fight, Tom Kirby, lost 8, 5/27, Boston. Recap: bouts 107, KO 23, decision 42, won foul 2, draw 10, lost decision 12, KO by 1, ND 17.

BOGS, TOM B. 11/21/44, Copenhagen, Denmark. 165. Outstanding amateur to 1964 Tokyo Olympics, eye injuries caused withdrawal. Pro 1965; undefeated in 12—6 KO, 5 dec., 1 win foul. 1966–69: sensational undefeated record. Won European light heavy title, Lothar Stengel, KO 1, 9/12/68, Copenhagen. Defended: Piero del Papa, 15, 1/28/69, Copenhagen. Resigned title to return to middles. Won European middle title, Juan Carlos, 15, 9/11/69, Copenhagen. Defended: Luigi Patruno, KO 5, 12/7/69, Aarhus, Denmark. 1970: Don Fullmer, draw 10; Emile Griffith, lost 10. Defended middle title: Les McAteer, KO 11, 4/2/70, Aarhus; Chris Finnegan, 15, 8/27/70, Copenhagen. Lost European title, Carlos Duran, 15, 12/4/70, Rome. Impressive 1971, including Fullmer, won. World middle title, Carlos Monzon, KO by 5, 8/19/72, Copenhagen. 1973, Regained vacant European middle title, Fabio Bettini, 10. Mike Quarry, won 10. Recap: bouts 76, KO 26, decision 41, won foul 1, draw 1, lost decision 4, KO by 3.

BONAVENA, OSCAR B. 9/25/42, Buenos Aires, Argentina. First fight, Lou Hicks, KO 1, 1/3/64, NYC. First year: 7 KO, 1 win. 1965: Zora Folley, lost 10; returned to Argentina, 6 straight KO to South America heavy title, Gregorio Peralta, won 12, 9/4/65, Buenos Aires. 1966: Joe Frazier, lost 10; 7 KO, 7 won including George Chuvalo. Jimmy Ellis, lost 12, 1967. Undefeated, including Folley, to N.Y. version of world heavy title, Frazier, lost 15, 12/10/68, Phila. 1969–71: 8 KO, won, lost disq., KO by Muhammad Ali, 15, 1970. Recap: bouts 53, KO 36, decision 9, won disq. 1, draw 1, lost decision 3, KO by 1, lost disq. 2.

BORKORSOR, VENICE B. Thailand. 111. First fight, Lugnakorn Chaiari, KO 7, 3/4/70, Rajuri Prov. 1970 to title, undefeated: 7 KO, 3 won. WBC fly title, Betulio Gonzalez, KO 10, 9/29/72, Bangkok. Won world fly title, Erbito Salvarria, 15, 3/73, Bangkok. Recap: bouts 13, KO 9, decision 4.

BOUTTIER, JEAN-CLAUDE B. 10/13/43, Vitry, France. 1965–68: undefeated in 35, including 19 KO. 1969–70, creditable record. 1971: undefeated, including European middle title, Carlos Duran, won 15, 6/10/71, Paris. Defended: Bunny Sterling, KO 14, 12/20/71, Paris. World middle title, Carlos Monzon, KO by 12, 6/17/72, Paris. Won disq., 1972: Jose Chirino, 4; Emile Griffith, 7. 1973: Antonio Aquilar, KO 9; Joe DeNucci, KO 9. Recap: bouts 64, KO 38, decision 20, won disq. 2, lost decision 3, KO by 1.

BOWKER, JOE (Tommy Mahon) B. 7/20/80, London, England. D. 10/30/55, London, England. 5'3½", 122. 1901: won 115-lb. novice tourney, 64 entries. First pro fight, Jack Guyon, won 6, 1/21/01, London. Undefeated, won British bantam title, Andy Tokell, 20, 5/25/03. Won world bantam title, Frank Neil, 20, 10/17/04, London. Outgrew division. Mediocre success as feather. Last fight, Charlie Ward, KO 15, 10/9/19, London. Recap: bouts 51, KO 8, decision 32, draw 1, lost decision 4, KO by 4, ND 2.

BOYD, BOBBY B. 10/25/33, Chicago, Ill. 5'11", 160. First fight, Len Salvo, won 4, 3/3/52, Chicago. Impressive early record: from 1953, 8 KO, 4 wins, to KO by Willie Troy (9), Moses Ward (3). 1955: upset Gene Fullmer, 10; KO Tony Anthony, 3; only loss, Milo Savage (return, KO 10, 1956). 1957: won seven including Willie Vaughn twice, Rocky Castellani, Charley Joseph; only loss, Rory Calhoun, KO by 2. Spotty record through 1959. Inactive 1960. 1961: KO two. Last fight, George Price, KO by 9, 5/16/61, Houston. Recap: bouts 67, KO 25, decision 28, lost decision 5, KO by 9.

BRADDOCK, JIM (James J. Braddock) (Cinderella Man) B. 12/6/05, New York, N.Y. Irish. 6'2", 192. First fight, Walter Westman, KO 3, 1926. 15 fights in 1926, undefeated, KO 11. 1927: won 8, KO 5, ND 5. 1928 highlight, Corn Griffin, KO 3. Light heavy title, Tommy Loughran, lost 15, 7/18/29, NYC. Record spotty to 1933. Broke both hands in bout with Abe Feldman (NC 6, 9/25/33, NYC). Discouraged, retired. Broke, wife, three children. Occasional dock worker, on relief. After nine months, fight with promising young Corn Griffin—semifinal to Baer-Carnera heavy title—upset Griffin, KO 2, 6/14/34, NYC. John Henry Lewis, won 10, 11/16/34, NYC. Art Lasky, won 15, 3/22/35, NYC. Won world heavy title in greatest upset, Max Baer, 15, 6/13/35, NYC. (Gained "Cinderella Man" tag—from docks and relief line to heavy title.) Toured, refereed, exhibitions, radio, stage. Over Max Schmeling's protests, title, Joe Louis, KO by 8, 6/22/37, Chicago. Floored Louis round 1 for 2 count, lost from that point. Tommy Farr, won 10. Last fight, Red Burman, exh., 5, 3/26/38, Charlotte, N.C. Boxing manager, referee; army captain; now driving truck for construction firm, visitations for Eagles on Heart Fund. Living NYC. Recap: bouts 84, KO 26, decision 25, draw 3, lost 19, KO by 2, ND 7, no contest 2.

BRADY, WILLIAM A. B. 6/19/63, San Francisco, Calif. D. 6/16/45. Manager. "The Lord is always good to the honest gambler" was the chosen philosophy of Bill Brady. He is considered an authority on the subject.

The only man to manage two world heavy champions, he also produced 260 plays, including a Pulitzer Prize winner, and won in a session with Broadway gambling prince Arnold Rothstein, cutting cards at $15,000 a cut.

Brady experienced success as a playwright and sometime actor, but the potential of the boxing box office intrigued him. His first champion was James J. Corbett, whom he guided to the historic John L. Sullivan upset.

His Corbett experience involved the occasion when three men were making Sullivan's life miserable by their consistant challenges, prompting John L. finally to announce that he would defend against the first to post a $10,000 guarantee. Brady was on the spot with the money the next morning.

Three months after the match was announced, Brady starred his fighter in a N.Y. play, *Sport McAllister,* and the month following his 21st-round KO over Sullivan, Corbett was featured in *Gentleman Jack* on an Elizabeth, N.J., stage. Bob Fitzsimmons doubled up Corbett with his solar-plexus punch, relieved him of the title, and when Jim lost by a foul to Tom Sharkey, Brady became disenchanted.

Meanwhile, he began to entertain some enthusiasm for a young burly heavy named James J. Jeffries. "Make me manager of Jeffries and I'll arrange a title fight with Fitz," Brady assured the fighter's manager, Bill Delaney. Brady had actually arranged the fight before making the offer to Delaney, who went along with the proposition, demoting himself.

After Jeff gained the title, relations between Delaney and Brady tensed and they finally split, but not before the producer had featured his new champion in a stage play.

Brady liked to keep several balls in the air at the same time. In 1899, while promoting the Jeffries-Sharkey event at Coney Island, he opened *King John* with Robert Mantell the same night.

After his rift with Delaney, he hung up the gloves, turned full time to the stage and stock market.

Brady had one urge to explore boxing's rainbow again. In 1920, he and London promoter C. B. Cochran visualized rich possibilities in a Jack Dempsey–Georges Carpentier fight. They posted the purse, but arrangements became entangled to a point where Brady threw up his hands, leaving the gate wide open for Tex Rickard. Brady sat in a $50 seat the night of July 2, 1921, at Boyle's Thirty Acres surveying boxing's first million-dollar gate ($1,-789,238).

In 1929, Brady lost $1 million in the stock market crash and broke a leg. While recuperating he passed time by reading plays. He came across *Street Scene,* which sparked the same glimmer he had at first sight of Corbett and Jeffries. Promissory notes, other loans put the play on the stage where it experienced 600 performances, won a Pulitzer Prize, and regained Brady his millionaire status.

BRATTON, JOHNNY B. 9/9/27, Little Rock, Ark. 145 lbs. First fight, Doyle Hirt, won 4, 6/12/44, Chicago. Impressive early career. Rushed into fast company, Gene Spencer, won twice, lost once; Beau Jack, KO by 8; Sammy Angott, lost 10. Upset Joe Brown 1948 (KO 4). Ike Williams, lost 10, 1949. Five straight KO to Williams return, KO by 8, 1950. Lost, Holly Mims twice, 1950. Bounced back, 3 successive KO: Leslie Felton, 3; Sammy Mastrean, 3; Bobby Dykes, 1. Vacant NBA world welter title, Charley Fusari, won 15, 3/14/51, Chicago. Lost title, Kid Gavilan, 15, 5/18/51, NYC. (World title recognized by NBA and N.Y. Commission; not internationally accepted by Charles Humez, European champion. Some records refer to championship as American title. When Humez moved to middle class, Gavilan, winner over Billy Graham, was recognized as complete world champ.) Return, nontitle, Gavilan, draw, 1951. 1953, undefeated to title, Gavilan, lost 15, 11/13/53, Chicago. Lost last three fights, Johnny Saxton, Chico Varcona, Del Flanagan (last fight—KO by 9, 3/17/55, St. Paul). Recap: bouts 86, KO 32, decision 27, draw 3, lost decision 21, KO by 3.

BRENNAN, BILL (William Schenck) B. 6/23/93, Chicago, Ill. D. 6/15/24. 6', 195. First fight, Al Goodale, KO 1, 1914. Undefeated through late 1917, lost Battling Levinsky. Jack Dempsey, KO by 6, in 1918, dislocated ankle, unable to continue. Harry Greb, ND 3, lost 1; Billy Miske 2 ND, lost 1. Undefeated early 1919–late 1920. World heavy title, Dempsey, KO by 12, 12/14/20, NYC. Through 1922, something of trial horse: Miske, ND, KO by 4; Bob Martin, won, ND; Luis Firpo, KO by 12. Last fight, Miske, KO by 4, 11/7/22, Omaha. Opened cafe NYC. Fatally shot. Recap: bouts 117, KO 64, decision 5, draw 3, lost decision 4, KO by 4, ND 37.

BRISCO, BENNY B. 2/8/43, Atlanta, Ga. 160. Colorful, completely bald, constant threat to champ. First fight, Sam Samuel, won 4, 9/10/62, Phila. Undefeated first 3 years. 1965: spotty. 1966: Undefeated. 1967: 4 straight KO;

Carlos Monzon draw; Luis Rodriguez, lost twice. 1970 to mid-1972: all KO; lost, Luis Vinales; return, KO 7. World middle title, Monzon, lost 15, 10/11/72, Buenos Aires. North American middle title, Art Hernandez, KO 3, 1973. Recap: bouts 56, KO 37, decision 7, draw 1, lost decision 10, lost disq. 1.

BRITT, JIMMY (James Edward Britt) B. 10/5/79, San Francisco, Calif. D. 1/29/40, San Francisco, Calif. 5'6", 133. First recorded fight, Toby Irwin, won 15, 2/18/02, San Francisco. Undefeated first year. 1904: fought 3 champs—Young Corbett, won 20; Battling Nelson, won 20; Joe Gans, lost foul 5, 10/31/04, San Francisco. (Britt claimed title when Gans couldn't make weight, recognized by several authorities.) Return bout Nelson, advertised as title fight, KO by 18, 9/9/05, Colma, Calif. Terry McGovern, ND, 1906; Nelson, won, 1907. (Nelson lost title bout, Gans, foul 42, 1906.) Return, Gans, KO by 6 (Britt broke wrist), 9/9/07, San Francisco. 1908–09: Nelson, ND; Packey McFarland, KO by 6; Johnny Summer won, lost; last fight, Summers, KO by 9, 7/31/09, London. Success in vaudeville. Recap: bouts 23, KO 3, decision 10, draw 1, lost decision 1, lost foul 2, KO by 4, ND 2.

BRITTON, JACK (William J. Breslin) (Boxing Marvel) B. 10/14/85, Clinton, N.Y. D. 3/27/62, Miami, Fla. Irish. 5'8", 144. First fight, Johnny Earle, won 6, 1905. Steve Kinney, KO by 5, 1905. Undefeated in 48 to mid-1909, then Kid Farmer, lost foul 3, return, KO 7. 1912 to Ted Lewis in 1915, undefeated 63, lost foul 1. Britton-Lewis series, 1915–21, longest series top-ranked boxers in history, 20: 1915—lost 2, ND 1; 1916—won 2, ND 2, won welterweight title, 20, 4/24, New Orleans; 1917—ND 4, lost title 20, 6/25, Dayton, Ohio; 1918—ND 4; 1919—won title, KO 9, 7/28, Canton, Ohio, ND 1; 1921—won, 15, 2/7, NYC. Defended title: Benny Leonard, won foul 13, 6/26/22, NYC. Lost title, Mickey Walker, 15, 11/15/22, NYC. Never another title chance, mostly impressive through 1930. Last fight, Young Bobby Buffalo, won 8, 5/8/30. Boxing instructor, operated gas station, fight manager. Hall of Fame 1960. Recap: bouts 325, KO 21, decision 77, won foul 1, draw 20, lost decision 25, lost foul 2, KO by 1, ND 177, no contest 1.

BROAD, KID (William M. Thomas) B. 3/5/78, Cornwall, England. D. 6/11/47, New York, N.Y. 5'5", 133. First fight, Peter Lacey, won 10, 1/1/98, NYC. Englishman, but never fought in Eng. Trial horse. Undefeated first year. Creditable early record including Joe Bernstein, KO, won; Young Corbett, KO, lost; George Dixon and Terry McGovern, lost. 1902–06: Abe Attell, draw, lost; Corbett, lost; Benny Yanger, draw, ND, lost; Leo Houck, lost three. Inactive 1907–08. Last fight, George Frasier, draw 6, 2/1/09, Lorain, Ohio. Unique draw record, 16, almost 25 percent. Recap: bouts 67, KO 5, decision 11, won foul 2, draw 16, lost decision 20, lost foul 1, KO by 3, ND 9.

BROUILLARD, LOU (Lucien Brouillard) B. 5/23/11, Eugene, Quebec. French. Early record vague, pro 1928, claims 64 fights, 44 KO, 16 decisions, lost 4. First recorded fight, Al Palladino, KO 1, 1/30/31, Worcester, Mass. 12 straight wins, including welter champ Young Jack Thompson and Paul Pirrone. Won world welter title, Thompson, 15, 10/23/31, Boston. Lost title, Jackie Fields, 10, 1/28/32, Chicago. Won N.Y. Commission middle title, Ben Jeby, KO 7, 8/9/33, NYC. Lost title, Vince Dundee, 15, 10/30/33, Boston. Two more chances at middle crown: Marcel Thil, lost foul 4, 1/20/36, Paris; Thil, lost foul 6, 2/15/37, Paris. To 1940, lost 9 of 18. 1942, Army. Recap: bouts 140, KO 66, decision 43, won foul 1, draw 3, lost decision 24, lost foul 2, KO by 1.

BROWN, AL (Alphonse Theo Brown) (Panama Al Brown) B. 7/5/02, Panama. D. 4/11/51, NYC, buried Panama City. 5'11", 118. First fight, Jose Moreno, won 6, 1922, Panama. Undefeated to 1925 when lost to Johnny Russo, 10. Spotty record to late 1927, then undefeated in 17 bouts to bantam title, Vidal Gregorio, 15, 6/18/29, NYC (elimination tourney). Defended: Knud Larsen, won 10, Copenhagen, 8/28/29, Copenhagen; Eugene Haut, won 15, 10/4/30; Nick Bensa, won 10, 2/11/31, Paris; Pete Sanstol, won 15, 8/25/31, Montreal; Haut, won 15, 10/27/31, Montreal; Kid Francis, won 15, 7/10/32, Marseilles, France (riot over decision); Emile Pladner, KO 1, 9/19/32, Toronto; Dom Bernasconi, won 12, 3/18/33, Milan; Johnny King, won 15, 7/3/33, London; Young Perez, won 15, 2/19/34, Paris. Lost title, Baltazar Sangchilli, 15, 6/1/35, Valencia. Following years, mostly creditable. Last fight, Mike Belloise, won 10, 3/13/44, Balboa. Recap: bouts 156, KO 58, decisions 62, won foul 3, ND 2, draw 12, lost decision 15, lost foul 2, KO by 2.

BROWN, JACKIE B. (date unknown), Ancoats, Manchester, England. 5'5", 120. First fight, Dick Manning, won 6, 3/23/26, Manchester. To early 1929, mediocre, won Northern English title, George Greaves, 20, 2/12/29, Manchester. Won British flyweight title, Bert Kirby, KO 3, 10/13/29, West Bromwich. Lost fly title and Lonsdale Belt, Kirby, KO by 3, 3/30/30. Regained British title, Belt, Kirby, won 15, 2/2/31. Manchester. Won European flyweight title, Emile Degand, 15, 6/15/31, London. Defended: Vincenzo Savo, won 15, 7/6/31, Manchester. British flyweight title, Jim Maharg, won foul 8, 9/19/32, Manchester. Won world fly title, Young Perez, KO 13,

10/31/32, Manchester. Defended: Valentin Angelmann, won 15, 6/12/33, London; Angelmann, won 15, 9/11/33, Manchester; Ginger Foran, won 15, 12/11/33, Manchester; Angelmann, draw 15, 6/18/34, Manchester. Lost world, European, British titles, Benny Lynch, KO by 2, 9/8/35, Manchester. Fought to 1939, fair success, never another title chance. Last fight, Benny Jones, won 10, 7/24/39, Manchester. Never U.S. visit. Recap: bouts 129, KO 36, decision 58, won foul 3, draw 7, lost decision 17, lost foul 4, KO by 4.

BROWN, JOE (Old Bones) B. 5/18/26, Baton Rouge, La. 5'7½". First fight, Leonard Caeser, lost 5, 1/13/46, New Orleans. Return bouts with Caeser in 1946: draw, 6, won 8. Undefeated 1949. Spotty record to 1956. Won world light title, Wallace (Bud) Smith, 15, 8/24/56, New Orleans. Defended: Smith, KO 11, 2/13/57, Miami Beach; Orlando Zulueta, KO 15, 6/19/57, Denver; Joe Lopes, KO 11, 12/4/57, Chicago; Ralph Dupas, KO 8, 5/7/58, Houston; Kenny Lane, won 15, 7/23/58, Houston; Johnny Busso won 15, 2/11/59, Houston; Paulo Rosi, KO 9, 6/3/59, Washington, D.C.; Dave Charnley, KO 6, 12/2/59, Houston; Cisco Andrade, won 15, 4/28/60, Los Angeles; Charnley, won 15, 4/18/61, London; Bert Somodio, won 15, 10/28/61, Quezon City, Philippines. Lost title, Carlos Ortiz, 15, 4/21/62, Las Vegas. Fought to 1970, mostly lost. Last fight, Ramon Flores, won 10, 4/24/70, Tucson. Recap: bouts 130, KO 47, decision 57, draw 12, lost decision 2, lost foul 1, KO by 9, no contest 2.

BROWN, NEWSBOY (David Montrose) B. 1904, Russia. Jewish. 5'1", 112–118. First recorded fight, Earl Puryear, ND 10, 1924. In second year, 1925, fought three champs—Frankie Genaro, won; Cpl. Izzy Schwartz, won; Fidel LaBarba, draw. 1926: undefeated. 1927: won 7 including Genaro return, 10. Lost for vacant American flyweight title to Schwartz, 15, 12/16/27, NYC. 1929–30: undefeated, including win over Midget Wolgast. Won Orient bantam title, Cris Pineda, 12, 3/19/32, Manila. Series: Baby Arizmendi, won, lost twice; Ernie Peters, won four; Speedy Dado, KO two, lost. Recap: bouts 66, KO 8, decision 38, draw 6, ND 2, lost decision 11, KO by 1.

BUCHANAN, KEN B. 6/28/45, Edinburgh, Scotland. First fight, Brian Tonks, KO 2, 9/20/65, London. Undefeated to 1970; won British lightweight title, Maurice Cullen, KO 11, 2/19/68, London. Vacant European light title, Miguel Velezquez, lost 15, 1/29/70, Madrid. Won British light title, Brian Hudson, KO 5, 5/12/70, London. Won world light title, Ismael Laguna, 15, 9/26/70, San Juan. Defended: Ruben Navarro, won 15, 2/12/71, Los Angeles; Laguna, won 15, 9/13/71, NYC. 1972: 2 KO, 1 dec.; lost title, Roberto Duran, KO by 13, 6/26/72, NYC. 1973: British light title defense, Jim Watts, won 15. Frank Otero, won 10, 5/29/, Miami Beach. Recap: bouts 49, KO 17, decision 30, lost decision 1, KO by 1.

BUCKLEY, JOHNNY B. 1893. D. 8/6/63, Boston, Mass. Manager. Johnny Buckley was cut from the cloth that cloaked an era of colorful fight managers, the 1920s and 30s. He handled gladiators of all shapes and sizes, and in those days of active small fight clubs, promoters could anticipate that a call to Buckley would provide talent for a four-round curtain raiser to a main event. His roll call could produce near champions and champs. Most prominent was Jack Sharkey, with whom he shared more than a million dollars.

Ernie Schaaf, top-ranking heavy for years, was guided by Buckley to several substantial paydays. Two of his charges, Lou Brouillard and Paul Pender, were middle champs.

Damon Runyon, whose name for Buckley was "Stout John," observed that the Buckley-Sharkey relationship "remains unique and peculiar among fighters who have won the heavyweight championship, in that Sharkey has stuck to his original manager. . . . Stout John and Sharkey have had many picturesque arguments but so far their differences have had no effect on their partnership arrangement. . . ."

When his fighters weren't making headlines, Buckley was providing copy for sports and other pages. He was charged with allowing his Boston building to be utilized for gambling purposes, including eight phones registered in his name; suspended in all NBA states for rule infractions while seconding Schaaf against Young Stribling in Chicago; suspended six months by the Mass. Commission for allowing posting of a false weight for his fighter, Andy Callahan, in a title bout with middle champ Vince Dundee; target of a 13-state alarm for clubbing his brother-in-law. From as distant as Paris his activity prompted a $250 fine for "unbecoming conduct to the referee," involving his continuing protest of the ref's actions against his fighter, Norman Hayes, fighting Claude Milazzo.

However, Stout John was once respectfully called a "fighter's manager," meaning that his loyalty, ability and connections could gain the capacity for his charge in the ring and at the box office.

He was 70 when he died at St. Elizabeth's Hospital, Boston.

BUFF, JOHNNY (John Lesky) B. 6/12/88, Amboy, N.J. D. 1/14/55, East Orange, N.J. Polish. 5'3", 112–118. First fight, Johnny Rosner, won 8. Mostly impressive, first three years: beat Pete Herman, Midget Smith; Pal Moore, ND. Won American flyweight title, Frankie Mason, 15, 2/11/21, New Orleans. Defended: Abe Goldstein, KO 2, 3/30/21. NYC. Won world bantam title, Pete Herman, 15, 9/23/21, NYC. Defended bantam: Jack Sharkey, won 15, 10/10/21, NYC. Lost both titles following year. Bantam, Joe Lynch, KO by 14, 7/10/22, NYC; flyweight, Pancho Villa, KO by 11, 9/14/22. Never recovered status for another title fight. Last fight Johnny

Hamm, KO by 2, 6/15/26, Pittsburgh. Recap: bouts 94, KO 13, decision 15, draw 4, lost decision 9, KO by 7, ND 45, no contest 1.

BUGNER, JOE B. 3/13/50, Hungary. 6'1", 220. First fight, Paul Brown, KO by 3, 12/18/67, London. 1968: Undefeated, 10 KO, 1 win. 1969–70: won 19, including Brian London, KO 5; only loss, Dick Hall, 8. Won European, British, British Commonwealth titles, Henry Cooper, 15, 3/15/71, London. Lost titles, Jack Bodell, 15, 9/27/71, London. Undefeated 1972, won European title, Jurgen Blin, KO 8, 10/10/72, London. 1973: KO 1, win 1; lost, Muhammad Ali, 12, Las Vegas; lost, Joe Frazier, 12, 7/2/73, London. Recap: bouts 48, KO 27, decision 14, won foul 1, draw 1, lost 4, KO 1.

BURNS, FRANKIE B. 6/24/89, Jersey City, N.J. Irish. 5'5½", 118. First fight, Clarence Burns, won 4, 3/10/08, NYC. Undefeated four years. World bantam title, Johnny Coulon, lost 20, 2/25/12, New Orleans. To 1917, only loss to Eddie Campi, return bout, draw, 1913. Bantam title, Kid Williams, draw 20, 12/6/15, New Orleans. Title, Pete Herman, lost 20, 11/5/17, New Orleans. Return nontitle, Herman, ND. Undefeated 1916. Johnny Kilbane, KO by 5, 1919. Undefeated to last fight, Packey O'Gatty, ND 8, 7/2/21, Jersey City. (First fight on radio, a prelim to Dempsey-Carpentier.) Laundry business, later opened tavern, Jersey City. Recap: bouts 170, KO 33, decision 17, draw 10, lost decision 3, lost foul 1, KO by 1, ND 105.

BURNS, TOMMY (Noah Brusso) B. 6/17/81, Hanover, Ontario. D. 5/10/55, Vancouver, British Columbia. German-Canadian. 5'7", 175. First fight, Fred Thornton, KO 5, 1900, Detroit. 1900–05: KO 23, decision 5, draw 7, lost 3 (Mike Schreck, Jack O'Brien, Twin J. Sullivan). Won world heavy crown, Marvin Hart, 20, 2/23/06, Los Angeles. Jim O'Brien, Jim Walker, KO both 1, same night, 3/28/06, in exhibitions, San Diego. Defended: Jim Flynn, KO 15, 10/2/06, Los Angeles; Jack O'Brien, draw 20, 11/28/06, Los Angeles; Jack O'Brien, won 20, 5/8/07, Los Angeles; Bill Squires, KO 1, 7/4/07, Colma, Calif.; Gunner Moir, KO 10, 12/2/07, London. 1908: 6 KO —Jack Palmer, Jem Roche (in 1:28 of 1st, fastest for heavy title fight, 3/17/08, Dublin), Jewey Smith, Bill Squires (2), Bill Lang. Lost title, Jack Johnson, 14, 12/26/08, Sydney, Australia. Last fight, Joe Beckett, KO by 7, 7/16/20, London. Took minister's vows 12/25/48. Hall of Fame 1960. Recap: bouts 60, KO 36, decision 10, draw 8, lost decision 4, KO by 1, ND 1.

BURRUNI, SALVATORE B. 4/11/33, Alghero, Italy. Amateur champ Italy 1954–56. Melbourne Olympic Games 1956, eliminated second series. First pro fight, Maurice Sevelle, KO 4, 4/3/57, Milan. Undefeated first year.

Won vacant Italian flyweight title, Giacomo Spano, 12, 9/27/58, Alghero. Defended: Salvatore Manca, won 12, 5/27/59, Milan; Spano, won 12, 12/23/59, Alghero; Angelo Rampin, won 12, 7/10/60, Alghero; Manca, won 12, 10/30/60, Cagliari. Won European title, Risto Luukkonen, 15, 6/29/61, Alghero. Defended: Derek Lloyd, KO 6, 8/14/61, San Remo; Mimun Ben Ali, won 15, 6/30/62, St. Vincent; Rene Libier, won 15, 7/5/63, Alessandria; Walter McGowan, won 15, 4/24/64, Rome. Won world fly title, Pone Kingpetch, 15, 4/23/65, Rome. Defended: Rocky Gattellari, KO 13, 12/2/65, Sydney, Australia. Lost title, McGowan, 15, 6/14/66, London. Won European bantam title, Mimun Ben Ali, 15, 1/10/68, Naples. Defended: Franco Zurlo, won 15, San Benedetto del Tronto, Italy; Pierre Vetroff, KO 8, 4/9/69, Reggio Calabria, last fight. Retired Aug. 1969. Recap: bouts 110, KO 31, decision 68, draw 1, lost decision 8, KO by 2.

BUSSO, JOHNNY B. 6/4/34, Poughkeepsie, N.Y. 5'9", 132. First fight, Rudy Rosco, won 4, 1953. Only defeat first year, Tony Marciano, 10, return KO 5; 8 KO, 15 bouts. Creditable record to 1957, undefeated 1956. 1957–59: Carlos Ortiz, won, lost; Joe Brown, won, 1958. World light title, Brown, lost 15, 2/11/59, Houston. To 1961, three straight KO by, Kenny Lane 6, Battling Torres 2, Len Matthews 1. Last fight, Joey Donovan, lost 10, 4/24/61, NYC. Recap: bouts 49, KO 15, decision 21, draw 1, lost decision 8, KO by 4.

BYGRAVES, JOE B. 5/26/31, Jamaica, West Indies. Negro. 185. First fight, Don Maxwell, KO 1, 2/12/53, Liverpool. Impressive early start marred by 2 KO by Joe Crickman, won return 1954. Henry Cooper, lost 8, 1955. Won vacant British Empire heavy title, Kitione Lave, 15, 6/26/56, London. Defended: Cooper, KO 9, 2/19/57, London; Dick Richardson, draw 15, 5/27/57, Cardiff. Lost title, Joe Erskine 15, 11/25/57, Leicester. Spotty record to 1964: lost, Willie Pastrano, Roy Harris; KO by Ingemar Johansson. Last fight, George Chuvalo, lost 10, 12/7/65, London. Recap: bouts 69, KO 22, decision 18, draw 1, lost decision 18, lost foul 3, KO by 7.

CALHOUN, RORY (Herman Calhoun) B. 9/29/34, McDonough, Ga. 5' 9", 168. First fight, John Gibson, won 4, 9/13/54, Brooklyn. Undefeated 1954–55 to Spider Webb, lost 10, 1956. 1957: Bobby Boyd, KO 2; Joey Giambra, draw, lost; won Rocky Castellani, Charley Cotton; Joey Giardello, lost. 1958–59: Tiger Jones, won, lost; Dick Tiger, won, draw; Spider Webb, KO by 4. Spotty record to last fight, Jim Ellis, KO by 1, 1/11/62, Louisville. Popular TV fighter. Recap: bouts 61, KO 21, decision 24, draw 2, lost decision 9, KO by 5.

CALLAHAN, MUSHY (Vincent Morris Scheer) B. 11/3/05, New York, N.Y. Jewish. 5'8½", 140. First fight, Davey Barnes, KO 1, 1924, San Pedro, Calif. 1924–25 undefeated, including Ace Hudkins, win, draw. Won junior welter title, Pinkey Mitchell, 10, 9/21/26, Vernon, Calif. 1927–30: didn't defend. Lost title, Jack (Kid) Berg, KO by 10, 2/18/30, London, last fight. In army. Recap: bouts 60, KO 18, decision 25, draw 4, lost decision 10, KO by 2, ND 1.

CALLURA, JACKIE B. 9/24/17, Hamilton, Ontario. 5'6½". First fight, Red Casson, won 6, 1936. Record spotty, 3 years. First name win, Freddie Miller, 10, 1939. Won 13, lost 1, 1931. 1940–43: creditable record. Won NBA feather title, Jackie Wilson, 15, 1/18/43, Providence, R.I. Return title bout, Wilson, won 15, 3/18/43, Boston. Nontitle, Phil Terranova, KO by 3, 1943. Lost title, Terranova, KO by 8, 8/16/43, New Orleans. Title, Terranova, KO by 6, 12/27/43, New Orleans. Downhill record, lost 7 of 9, 1946–47. Last

37

fight, Humberto Sierra, KO by 2, 6/4/47, Miami. Recap: bouts 100, KO 13, decision 43, won foul 1, draw 10, lost decision 27, KO by 6.

CAMPI, EDDIE (Eddie de Campus) B. 7/4/93, San Francisco, Calif. D. 1919, Hollister, Calif. Irish-French. 5'4", 116. Regarded as a perfectionist. Verge of two title chances. First fight, Johnny Perry, KO 2, 1908. First loss, Jimmy Fox, 1910, return bouts, 2 draw, won, 1911. Frankie Burns series: won 2, ND, draw. Elimination to meet champ Johnny Coulon, KO by 12, Kid Williams, who KO'd Coulon. Elimination to fight Williams, Pete Herman, lost 20; Herman beat Williams. Won over Coulon, 1916. To 1919, creditable record. Last fight, Lee Johnson, won 4, 2/16/18. Killed in a hunting accident. Recap: bouts 101, KO 19, decision 44, draw 8, lost decision 5, KO by 2, ND 22, no contest 1.

CANZONERI, TONY B. 11/6/08, Slidell, La. D. 12/9/59, New York, N.Y. Italian. 5'4", 122–126. Moved to Brooklyn. Amateur: 95 lbs., won N.Y. State bantam title 1924. First pro fight, James Gardner, KO 1, 1/17/25, NYC. Undefeated first year, first loss, Davey Abad, 1926. Bantam title, Bud Taylor, draw 10, 3/26/27, Chicago; return bout, lost 10, 6/24/27, Chicago. Won world feather title, Benny Bass, 15, 2/10/28, NYC. Lost feather title, Andre Routis, 15, 9/28/28, NYC. Lightweight title, Sammy Mandell, lost 10, 8/2/29, Chicago. Won lightweight title, Al Singer, KO 1, 11/14/30, NYC. Won junior welter title, Jack (Kid) Berg, KO 3, 4/24/31. Defended junior welter: Cecil Payne, won 10, 7/13/31, Los Angeles; Phillie Griffin, won 10, 10/29/31, Newark. Lost junior welter title, Johnny Jadick, 10, 1/18/32, Phila. Title, Jadick, lost 10, 7/18/32, Phila. Regained title, Battling Shaw, 10, 5/21/33, New Orleans. Light title, defended: Berg, won 15, 9/10/31, NYC; Kid Chocolate, won, 15, 11/20/31; Billy Petrolle, won 15, 11/4/32, NYC. Lost junior welter, light title, Barney Ross 10, 6/23/33, Chicago. Title, Ross, lost 15, 9/12/33, NYC. Won vacant light title, Lou Ambers, 15, 5/10/35, NYC. Defended: Al Roth, won 15, 10/4/35, NYC. Lost title, Ambers, 15, 9/3/36, NYC. Title, Ambers, lost 10, 5/7/37, NYC. To 1939, never another title chance, creditable record; last fight, Al Davis, KO by 3, 11/1/39, NYC. Regarded by many as one of all-time greats. Acting, screen, stage. Opened restaurant. Hall of Fame 1956. Recap: bouts 181, KO 44, decision 94, draw 1, lost decision 27, lost foul 1, KO by 1, ND 3.

CAREY, WILLIAM F. B. 9/14/78, Hoosick Falls, N.Y. D. 2/24/51, Indio, Calif. Promoter. One of boxing's most improbable combinations featured William F. Carey and James J. Johnston, who guided Madison Square Garden's destiny during the depression days of the early 1930s. Carey was a highly successful businessman, builder of railroads and the Panama Canal;

Johnston, a flamboyant character from boxing's ranks who was sometimes fondly, more often appropriately called the "Boy Bandit."

Carey was mainly a contractor. His exposure to fistic activity was inspired by association with Tex Rickard while building the second Madison Square Garden. Much of his contracting reputation was gained laying tracks for the railroads, during which activity he established the reputation of an astute negotiator. He brought this talent to boxing in 1930 when he announced from behind Tex Rickard's former desk that he had obtained one-year leases for Garden-sponsored boxing at both Yankee Stadium and the Polo Grounds, only major outdoor stadiums in New York City.

This maneuver stifled any outdoor competition that could have formulated from Humbert J. Fugazy or Jack Dempsey, and others aspiring to rake in the jackpot created by the Rickard destiny. The big blue chip was the heavy title vacated by Gene Tunney following his last defense (Tom Heeney, KO 11, 7/26/29, NYC).

In 1930 the ball parks provided the sites for four major events including the Max Schmeling–Jack Sharkey showdown for the vacated title (Schmeling won on foul, 4, 6/12/30), grossing $711,668.

Carey was officially named Garden president in a surprise announcement at a banquet sponsored for him by N.Y. newsmen March 1929, in appreciation of treatment accorded the press at the Sharkey–Young Stribling fight in Miami, a sidecar Garden promotion.

For months, Carey unofficially assuming the late Rickard's position, had been confronted with the question of devoting adequate time from his other duties to cudgel the Garden responsiblities. Pressure from his fellow directors and others associated with boxing prodded the conclusion that he could handle the job. Too, he enjoyed public association and never entertained an aversion to personal publicity.

When Carey officially assumed the Garden front office, he was asked how he intended to acquire the successful technique that Rickard had displayed. "How did you learn engineering?" the newsman asked. "Engineering," replied Carey.

Despite the depression years Carey kept the Garden lights burning brightly. From 1930 to his resignation in mid-1933, he promoted some 90 headliners, more than one event a month, including such classics as Baer-Schaaf, Hudkins-Rosenbloom, LaBarba-Graham, Mandell-Singer, Singer-McLarnin, Chocolate-LaBarba, McLarnin-Petrolle, Wolgast-Genaro, Braddock-Schaaf, Loughran-Baer, Loughran-Schaaf, Battalino-LaBarba, McLarnin-Petrolle,

Loughran-Uzcudun, Walker-Uzcudun, Leonard-McLarnin, Carnera-Schaaf.

He resigned June 1933, recommending his assistant, John Kilpatrick, as his successor. Kilpatrick was named president.

In 1936, N.Y. Mayor Fiorello LaGuardia persuaded Carey to accept appointment as commissioner of the much criticized Department of Sanitation, an assignment he held for nine years.

The former Garden president, builder of railroads and a canal, related a story that typified his personality as he was closing a $1 million contract for NYC snow-removal equipment: Never one to carry cash, he stopped at a drugstore soda counter, ordered a malted milk, received his check—20 cents. "I found two Indian head pennies in my pocket." Commissioner Carey washed dishes to reimburse the management.

Never losing his interest in boxing and its people, he retired to his ranch in Indio, Calif., where he died at 72 after a lengthy illness.

CARNERA, PRIMO (The Ambling Alp) B. 10/26/06, Sequals, Italy. D. 6/29/67, Sequals, Italy. 6'5¾", 260. Carpenter's apprentice. Circus strongman, wrestler. Discovered by Leon See, Paris promoter. First bout, Leon Sebilo, KO 2, 9/12/28, Paris. 1928–29: 11 KOs. To U.S. 1930. Big Boy Peterson, KO 1, 1/24/30, NYC. Involvement with nightclub owner and alleged racketeer Bill Duffy, followed by series of KOs and ballyhoo. Won heavyweight title, Jack Sharkey, KO 6, 6/29/33, Long Island City, N.Y. Defended: Paolino Uzcudun, won 15, 10/22/33, Rome; Tommy Loughran, won 15, 3/1/34, Miami. Lost title, Max Baer, KO by 11 (floored 11 times), 6/14/34, NYC. Joe Louis, KO by 6, 6/25/35, NYC. Italian army 1943, aiding U.S. forces. Last fight, Luigi Musina, lost 10, 5/13/46, Milan. Wrestler, referee. Death by cancer occurred exactly 34 years after he became heavy champ. Recap: bouts 99, KO 66, decision 18, won foul 2, lost decision 5, lost foul 1, KO by 6, no contest 1.

CARPENTIER, GEORGES (Orchid Man) B. 1/12/94, Lens, France. 5'11½", 175. Fought in every division, flyweight through heavyweight. First fight, C. Bourgois, won 4, 2/24/07. French welter title, R. Eutache, KO 15, 6/15/11, Paris. Europe welter title, Young Joseph, KO 10, 10/23/11, London. French middle title, Frank Klaus, lost foul 19, 6/24/12, Dieppe. Spotty record through 1914. Aviation lieutenant World War I, 1915–16. Won light heavy title, Battling Levinsky, KO 4, 10/12/20, Jersey City. Heavy title, Jack Dempsey, KO by 4, 7/2/21, Jersey City, first million-dollar gate—$1,789,-238. Lost light heavy title, Battling Siki, KO by 6, 9/24/22, Paris. Gene

Tunney, KO by 15. Last fight, Jack Walker, exh. 4, 1/11/27, Paris. Retired, entertainer. Hall of Fame 1964. Recap: bouts 106, KO 51, decision 30, won foul 4, draw 5, lost decision 6, lost foul 1, KO by 8, ND 1.

CARRUTHERS, JOHNNY B. 7/5/29, Paddington, Australia. Outstanding amateur, Olympics, 1948. First pro fight, Ted Fitzgerald, KO 3, 8/15/50. Leichhardt, Australia. Sparkling record to 1954. Won Australian bantam title, Elley Bennett, KO 15, 5/14/51, Sydney. Won world bantam title, Vic Toweel, KO 1, 11/15/52, Johannesburg. Defended: Toweel, KO 10, 3/21/53, Johannesburg; Henry Gault, won 15, 11/13/53, Sydney; Chamrern Songkitrat, won 12, Bangkok. Retired, undefeated 5/16/54. Opened tavern, refereed. Comeback after 7 years (1961). KO 2, lost 2, KO by 1. Last fight, Jimmy Cassidy, lost foul 7, 6/18/62, Wellington. Recap: bouts 25, KO 13 decision 8, lost decision 2, lost foul 1, KO by 1.

CARTER, JIMMY (James W. Carter) B. 12/15/23, Aiken, S.C. 5'7", 132. First fight, Clifton Bordies, won 4, 3/14/46, Newark. To 1951: mostly impressive. Won world light title, Ike Williams, KO 14, 5/25/51, NYC. Defended: Art Aragon, won 15, 11/14/51, Los Angeles; Lauro Salas, won 15, 4/1/52, Los Angeles. Lost title, Salas, 15, 5/14/52, Los Angeles. Won back title, Salas, 15, 10/15/52, Chicago. Defended: Tommy Collins, KO 4, 4/24/53, Boston; George Araujo, KO 13, 6/12/53, Boston; Armand Savoie, KO 5, 11/11/53, Montreal. Lost title, Paddy DeMarco, 15, 3/5/54, NYC. Regained title, DeMarco, KO 15, 11/17/54, San Francisco (first fighter to hold same world title 3 times). Lost title, Wallace (Bud) Smith, 15, 6/29/55, Boston. Title, Smith, lost 15, 10/19/55, Cincinnati. To 1960, mediocre record. Last fight, Luis Garduno, lost 10, 4/1/60, Mesa, Ariz. Recap: bouts 126, KO 32, decision 51, draw 10, lost decision 30, KO by 3.

CASTILLO, CHUCHU (Jesus Castillo Aguillera) B. 6/17/44, Mexico. First fight, Amulfo Daza, won 8, 8/10/62, Oaxaca, Mex. Rocky record to Mexican title, beat Joe Medel, 12, 4/29/67, Mexico City. World bantam title, Lionel Rose, lost 15, 12/7/68, Los Angeles. Bantam title, Ruben Olivares, lost 15, 4/19/70, Los Angeles. Won world bantam title, Olivares, KO 14, 10/17/70 Los Angeles. Lost title, Olivares, 15, 4/3/71, Los Angeles. Won N. American title, Rafael Herrera, 12, 8/23/71, Los Angeles. Recap: bouts 48, KO 19, decision 17, won foul 1, draw 2, lost decision 5, KO by 4.

CERDAN, MARCEL B. 7/22/16, Sidi Bel-Abbes, Algeria. D. 10/27/49, Azores, in an airplane crash. French. First fight, Marcel Bucchanieri, won 6, 11/4/34, Meknes, Morocco. Spectacular record, 109 victories, 1 KO by,

1 lost (won return), 2 lost foul. 9 fights U.S. and Canada, others overseas. Won French middle title, Omar Kouidri, 12, 2/21/38, Casablanca; won Inter-Allied middle title, Joe Di Martino, KO 1, 2/20/44, Algiers. Defended French middle title, Assana Diouf, KO 3, 11/30/45, Paris. Won European middle title, Leon Fouquet, KO 1, 2/2/47, Paris. Lost European title, Cyrille Delannoit, 15, 5/23/48, Brussels; regained title, Delannoit, won 15, 7/10/48, Brussels. Won world middle title, Tony Zale, KO 12, 9/21/48, Jersey City. Lost title, Jake LaMotta, KO by 10, 6/16/49, Detroit. Hall of Fame 1962. Recap: bouts 113, KO 66, decision 43, lost decision 1, lost foul 2, KO by 1.

CERDAN, MARCEL, JR. B. 12/4/43, Casablanca, Morocco. 145 lbs. Son of late Hall of Fame middle champ Marcel Cerdan, killed in plane crash, Azores, 1949. Early fights prompted speculation of unprecedented father and son holding world championships. First pro fight, Jack Vandriessche, lost 6, 12/4/64, Casablanca, followed by early sensational career. After first fight, six years undefeated in Europe, mostly France, including 11 KO. Only loss, first U.S. fight, Donato Paduano, lost 10, NYC, 1970. Returned to France: KO 2, decision 5, draw 1 to Pietro Gasparri, lost 10, 1971. Won 1, lost 2, 1972. Retired 1973. Recap: bouts 61, KO 15, decision 38, won foul 1, draw 2, lost decision 5.

CERVANTES, ANTONIO B. (date not available), Cartagena, Colombia. First fight, Juan Martinez, won 6, 1964, Cerete. Undefeated first four years. 1968–69: won 12, lost 1, KO by Cruz Marcano, 6, 12/29/68. Undefeated, including Rufolfo Gonzales, KO 8, 1970, to junior welter title, Nicolino Loche, lost 15, 12/12/71, Buenos Aires. 1972: KO 2, won 1; 1973: won 1. Recap: bouts 54, KO 18, decision 31, draw 2, lost decision 2, KO by 1.

CHANEY, GEORGE (KO) B. 1893, Baltimore, Md. Irish. 5'1½", 126. First fight, Willie Williams, KO 1, 1/2/10, Baltimore. Impressive early KO record. 1914–16 undefeated to feather title fight, Johnny Kilbane, KO by 3, 9/4/16, Cedar Point, Ohio. Creditable nine more years: Johnny Dundee, ND three, lost, lost foul; Lew Tendler, ND, KO by; Rocky Kansas, ND twice, lost; Phila. Pal Moore, KO; Benny Valger, ND; Willie Ritchie, ND; Abe Attell, lost. Last fight, Danny Kramer, KO by 1, 8/10/25, Phila. Recap: bouts 181, KO 86, decision 23, lost decision 3, lost foul 6, KO by 8, ND 55.

CHARLES, EZZARD B. 7/7/21, Lawrenceville, Ga. Negro. 6', 182. Outstanding welter, middle amateur 1937–39, undefeated. First pro fight, Medley Johnson, KO 3, 3/15/40, Middletown, Pa. First loss, Ken Overlin, 10, 6/9/41, Cincinnati. Overlin, draw 10, 3/2/42, Cincinnati. Kid Tunero, lost

10, 5/13/42, Cincinnati. Joey Maxim, won twice, 1942. Army 1942–1943. Jimmy Bivins, lost 10, 1943; Lloyd Marshall, KO by 8, 1943; won from both in returns. 1946: Archie Moore, won 2, decision, and KO 8. Vacant NBA heavyweight title, Joe Walcott, won 15, 6/22/49, Chicago. Defended: Gus Lesnevich, KO 7, 8/10/49, NYC; Pat Valentino, KO 8, 10/14/49, San Francisco; Freddy Beshore, KO 14, 8/15/50, Buffalo; Joe Louis (NBA, New York titles), won 15, 9/27/50, NYC; Nick Barone, KO 11, 12/5/50, Cincinnati; Lee Oma, KO 10, 1/12/51, NYC; Walcott, won 15, 3/7/51, NYC; Maxim, won 15, 5/30/51, Chicago. Lost title, Walcott, KO by 7, 7/18/51, Pittsburgh. Title, Walcott, lost 15, 6/5/52, Phipadelphia. Title, Rocky Marciano, lost 15, 6/17/54, NYC. Title, Marciano, KO by 8, 9/17/54, NYC. 1955–56, spotty; last fight, Dick Richardson, disq. 2, 10/2/56, London. Announced retirement. Referee, public appearances. Comeback 1958: 6 fights, KO by 2, lost 2. Last comeback fight, Alvin Green, lost 10, 9/1/59, Oklahoma City. Illness, 1960; benefit banquet, 1969. Hall of Fame 1970. Recap: bouts 122, KO 58, decision 38, draw 1, lost decision 17, lost foul 1, KO by 7.

CHIONOI, CHARTCHAI (Laemfapha) B. 10/10/42, Bangkok, Thailand. Undetailed record 1959: 6 KO, 2 decision, 1 draw, 2 lost. Won Orient fly title, Primo Famiro, 12, 9/22/62, Manila. Lost title, Hiroyuki Ebihara, 12, 12/31/62, Tokyo. Orient fly title, Takeshi Nakamura, lost 12, 7/8/63, Osaka. Won world fly title, Walter McGowan, KO 9, 12/30/66, London. Defended: McGowan, KO 7, 9/19/67, London; Puntif Keosuriya, KO 3, 7/26/67, Bangkok; Bernabe Villacampo, won 15, 11/10/68, Bangkok. Lost title, Elfren Torres, KO by 8, 2/23/69, Mexico City. Regained title, Torres, 15, 3/20/70, Bangkok. Lost title, Erbito Salvarria, KO by 2, 12/7/70 Bangkok. Recap.: bouts 58, KO 27, decision 16, draw 1, lost decision 12, KO by 2.

CHIP, GEORGE (George Chipulonis) B. 8/25/88, Scranton, Pa. D. 11/6/60, New Castle, Pa. Lithuanian. 5'8", 158. First fight, George Gill, KO 2, 1909. 1909–10: won 24, KO by Buck Crouse 3. Jack Dillon, 1910–18, one of longest series in boxing history: 12–10 ND, lost 1, draw 1. Harry Greb, 3 ND, 1915–17. Tommy Gibbons, ND 2, lost 2, 1918–19. Mike Gibbons, ND 3, 1917–19. Crouse, KO by 1, ND 3, 1910–15. Won world middle title, Frank Klaus, KO 6, 10/11/13, Pittsburgh. Defended: Klaus, KO 5, 12/23/13, Pittsburgh. Lost title, Al McCoy, KO by 1, 4/6/14, Brooklyn. McCoy, return nontitle, ND 10, 4/6/15, NYC. Title, Johnny Wilson, ND 10, 1/17/21, Pittsburgh. Last fight, Frank McGuire, ND 8, Lancaster, Pa., 4/24/22. Recap: bouts 155, KO 34, decision 3, won foul 1, draw 3, lost decision 10, lost foul 3, KO by 3, ND 97, no contest 1.

CHOCOLATE, KID (Eligio Sardinias) (The Cuban Bon Bon) B. 1/6/10, Cerro, Cuba. 5'6", 126. Newsboy to one of Cuba's greatest, most colorful boxers. Undefeated, 100 amateur bouts. Pro: Cuba, 21 bouts, 21 KO. First U.S. fight, Eddie Ennos, KO 3, 8/1/28, NYC. To mid-1930 undefeated 45 bouts including Al Singer, Fidel La Barba. First U.S. loss, Jack (Kid) Berg, 10, 8/7/30, NYC. Lost 2 more 1930, La Barba, 10, and Battling Battalino, 15, latter for world feather title. Won junior light title, Benny Bass, KO 7, 7/15/31, Phila. Won N.Y. feather title, Lew Feldman, KO 12, 10/13/32, NYC. Defended feather: La Barba, won 15, 12/9/32, NYC; Seaman Watson, won 15, 5/19/33, NYC. Lost junior light title, Frankie Klick, KO by 7, 12/26/33, Phila. To 1938 mostly successful, last fight, Nicky Jerome, draw 10, 12/18/38, Havana. Boxing instructor, Cuba, received government pension until Castro regime. Hall of Fame 1959. Recap: bouts 162, KO 64, decision 82, draw 6, lost decision 8, KO by 2.

CHOYNSKI, JOE B. 11/8/68, San Francisco, Calif. D. 1/25/43, Cincinnati, Ohio. Jewish. 5'10½", 168. Amateur 1884, Pacific Coast champion 1887. First pro, George Bush, KO 2, 11/14/88, San Francisco. Jim Corbett, three successive: 1889, no contest (stopped by police); KO by 27; lost 4. Exh. John L. Sullivan, 1891. Bob Fitzsimmons, draw, 1894 (stopped by police). Tom Sharkey, lost 8, 1896, draw, 1898, KO by 2, 1900; Peter Maher, KO by 6, 1896, won, 1900, KO 2, 1903; Jim Jeffries, draw 20, 1897. Kid McCoy, lost 20, draw 6, 1899, KO by 4, 1900. Jack Johnson, KO 3, 1901. Joe Walcott, KO by 7, 1900. Last fight, Jack Williams, ND 6, 11/24/04, Phila. Rugged meet-anybody type, never experienced clear shot at title. Athletic instructor at Pittsburgh A.C. 15 years. Business San Francisco, Chicago. Recap: bouts 79, KO 25, decision 22, won foul 3, draw 6, lost decision 4, KO by 10, ND 8, no contest 1.

CHRISTOFORIDIS, ANTON B. 5/26/18, Messina, Greece. 5'10", 175. First bout, Taddel, KO 4, 1934. Spotty record—campaigning in Europe until Lou Brouillard fight, which he won 10, Paris, 1939. To U.S. 1940, 6 win, 2 KO, lost 10 to Jimmy Bivins, won return 10. Won vacant NBA light heavy title, Melio Bettina 15, 1/13/41, Cleveland. Lost title, Gus Lesnevich, 15, 5/22/41, NYC. Ceferino Garcia, won 10, 1941. Ezzard Charles, KO by, 1942, lost Jimmy Bivins, 15, Lloyd Marshall, 10, 1943. Joined U.S. Navy 1943. 1946: 2 KO; Steve Belloise, KO by 10. Last fight, Anton Raadik, KO by 8, 2/18/47, Chicago. Recap: bouts 74, KO 14, decisions 36, won foul 1, draw 8, lost decision 12, KO by 3.

CHUVALO, GEORGE B. 9/12/37, Toronto, Ontario. 6', 180. First fights, four straight KO in Jack Dempsey heavyweight novice tourney, 1958. Impressive record to Canadian heavy title, James J. Parker, KO 1, 9/15/58,

Toronto. First US fight, Pat McMurty, lost 10, NY, 1959. Defended title, Yvon Durrelle, KO 12, 11/17/59, Toronto; lost title, Bob Cleroux, 12, 8/17/60, Toronto; regained title, Cleroux, 12, 11/23/60, Toronto; lost Cleroux, 12, 8/8/61, Toronto. Inactive 1962. Undefeated 1963. To US 1964, Zora Folley, lost; 4 straight KO, including Doug Jones, 11. 1965: Floyd Patterson, lost 10; 4 straight KO to WBA heavyweight title, Ernie Terrell, lost 15, 11/1/65, Toronto. Oscar Bonavana, lost 10, 1965. World heavyweight title, Muhammad Ali, lost 15, 4/29/66, Toronto. 12 straight KO to Joe Frazier, KO by 4, 1967. Regained Canadian title, Jean-Claude Roy, 12, 6/5/68, Regina, Canada. Defended: Roy, won 12, 6/5/69, Regina. Five straight KO to Buster Mathis, lost 12, 1969; 6 straight KO, including Jerry Quarry, 7, to George Foreman, KO by 3, 1970; 4 straight KO to 1971, Jimmy Ellis, lost; Cleveland Williams, won. 1972: KO 4, including defending Canadian heavy title, Tommy Burns, KO 1, 8/10/72. Recap: bouts 92, KO 64, decision 9, draw 1, lost decision 15, lost disq. 1, KO by 2.

CLABBY, JIMMY B. 7/14/90, Norwich, Conn. D. 1/18/34, Calumet City, Ill. Irish. 5'8½", 158. First fight, Billy Smith, KO 2, 1906. Tireless, hard hitter, "spoiler," never chance at title, regarded underrated. Mike Gibbons, won, ND 3; George Chip, won, ND 2; Eddie McGoorty won, won foul, draw; Mike (Twin) Sullivan, ND 2; Al McCoy, ND, Les Darcy, lost 2. Last fight, Morrie Schlaifer, KO by 2, 7/31/23, Chicago. Recap: bouts 155, KO 40, decision 37, won foul 2, draw 20, lost decision 16, lost foul 1, KO by 4, ND 34, no contest 1.

COCHRANE, FREDDIE (Red) B. 5/6/15, Elizabeth, N.J. Irish. 5'7½", 145. First fight, Steve Petronick, won 4, 6/4/33. Elizabeth, N.J. Rocky start, dubious distinction. To title: 103 fights, lost 30. Won world welter title, Fritzie Zivic, 15, 7/21/41, Newark. Zivic, lost 10, nontitle, 1942. Joined U.S. Navy. 1945: started with 5 straight KO, then twice KO by Rocky Graziano, 10 each time, NYC. Lost title, Marty Servo, KO by 4, 2/1/46, NYC. Recap: bouts 116, KO 26, decision 46, draw 9, lost decision 30, KO by 5.

COFFEY, JIM (The Roscommon Giant) B. 7/4/91, County Roscommon, Ireland. D. 10/20/59, Dublin, Ireland. 6'1", 210. First fight, Al Benedict, KO 8, 1912. Impressive first four years, KOs—Jack (Twin) Sullivan, 5; Arthur Pelkey, 2; Jim Flynn, 9; Gunboat Smith, 1. NDs—Battling Levinsky, 3; Carl Morris, Charley Weinert. 1915–16: bouts 15, KOs 11; KO by Frank Moran twice; NDs Smith, Morris. To 1918 only defeat Bartley Madden, KO by 7. Last fight, Joe Jennette, ND 4, 11/22/18, New Haven. Unique record: Out of 62 bouts, won only 1 decision, lost none, but involved in 38 KOs. Recap: bouts 62, KO 34, decision 1, draw 1, KO by 4, ND 22.

COFFROTH, JIMMY (James W.) (Sunny Jim) D. 2/7/49. Promoter. When California was the world's dominant boxing center in the 1890s and early 1900s, Coffroth was the man behind the promoter's desk. In later years, even after Tex Rickard was scoring with his Jack Dempsey presentations, syndicated sports columnist Warren Brown provided a column lead with, "As a personal nomination for the No. 1 fight promoter who has come over the horizon I shall have to submit the name of Jimmy Coffroth." Brown added, "While it is a popular thing to acclaim Rickard, the fact remains that Tex needed a Jack Kearns first and a Jack Dempsey always. Coffroth needed just Jim Coffroth."

Before boxing was legislated out of California in 1910, Coffroth sponsored the majority of the nation's major fights, including Jim Jeffries' fights with Jim Corbett, Bob Fitzsimmons, Jack Monroe and such memorables as Gans-Nelson, Britt-Nelson, Britt-Gans, Nelson-Young Corbett, McGovern-Corbett, Neil-Forbes, Neil-Attell, Fitzsimmons-Sharkey, Ketchel-Papke and Ketchel-Johnson.

He attained one promotional feat that probably never will be duplicated, two championship fights, two days apart at two different locations: feather champ Abe Attell–Owen Moran, draw 23, Labor Day (9/7/08) at San Francisco. Two days later, Mexican Labor Day (9/9/08), Battling Nelson defended light title against Joe Gans, KO 21 at Colma, Calif.

Sunny Jim also entertained his promotional gimmicks such as the 23-round fight between Attell and Moran. He explained the 23-round billing as a conversation piece to achieve more publicity, which it did.

Popular with the press, Coffroth gained a reputation as a "square shooter". That endorsement followed him when he parted paths with boxing as it was legislated out of California in 1910. He devoted full effort to his second love, race-track promotion, where he again experienced success, becoming one of the sport's outstanding personalities.

His return to boxing was prompted by World War I when fistic events became a financially successful stimulant for army and navy funds. President Wilson named Coffroth chairman of the boxing division of the War Charities Board, and his promotions realized more funds than any other of the board's units.

After the war, he returned to semiretirement at his Tijuana race track, his flowers and books on his expansive San Diego estate. But he always indulged his interest in boxing, never missing a major fight.

Recalled is a classic and typical story of Sunny Jim, an admirer of Dempsey from Jack's early days.

He came to Philadelphia for Dempsey's title defense against Gene Tunney, wagering heavily on the champion. But he found many respected opinions leaning toward Tunney to author the upset. He was nearly convinced to hedge his early money by wagering on Tunney until a long-time associate, Jim Hussey, posed a question: "If a guy had you down in an alley, beating the hell out of you, who would you holler for, Dempsey or Tunney?" Convinced, Jim invested more money, and, like Dempsey, lost, too. But he was more fortunate than Jack the second time around, betting heavily on Tunney.

From that point Coffroth's interest in boxing waned and he returned to his flowers, books and race track.

COHEN, NESSIM (Max) B. 1/12/41, Morocco. Only name boxer born in Morocco. First fight, Lucien Poelger, won 6, 1/13/64, Paris. Creditable early record. Undefeated in 1970, including French middle title, Pascale DiBenedetto, draw 12, 6/12/70, Marseilles. Won vacant title, Fabio Bettini, 12, 6/4/71, Marseilles. Lost title, Bettini, 15, 11/4/71, Perpignan. Emile Griffith, lost 1971. Undefeated 1972—4 KO, 4 dec. 1973: Emile Griffith, draw 10. Recap: bouts 43, KO 12, decision 15, won disq. 1, draw 6, lost decision 7, lost disq. 1, KO by 1.

COHEN, ROBERT B. 11/15/30, Algeria. 5'3½". First fight, Gauche, KO 2, 9/12/51, Paris. 1951–54 impressive, only 1 loss. Won French bantam title, Maurice Sandeyron, 15, 11/6/53, Paris. Won European bantam title, John Kelly, KO 3, 2/27/54, Belfast. Relinquished French title 3/17/54. Won vacant world bantam title, Chamrern Songkitrat, 15, 9/19/54, Bangkok, Thailand. Defended: Willie Toweel, draw 13, 9/3/55, Johannesburg, South Africa. Lost title, Mario D'Agata, KO by 8, 6/29/56, Rome. Last fight, Peter Lock, lost 10, 7/13/59, Ndola, Rhodesia. Recap: bouts 43, KO 14, decision 22, draw 3, lost decision 2, KO by 2.

COKES, CURTIS B. 6/13/37, Dallas, Tex. Negro. First fight, Manual Gonzales, won 6, 3/24/58, Midland, Tex. Gonzales series: lost, 1959; won, 1961; WBA title, won 15, 8/24/66, New Orleans. Won vacant world welter title, Jean Josselin, 15, 11/28/66, New Orleans. Defended: Francois Pavilla, KO 10, 5/19/69, Dallas; Charles Shipes, KO 8, 10/2/67, Oakland, Calif; Willie Ludick, KO 5, 4/16/68, Dallas; Ramon La Cruz, won 15, 10/21/68, New Orleans. Lost title, Jose Napoles, KO by 13, 4/18/69, Los Angeles. Title, Napoles, KO by 10, 6/29/69, Mexico City. Retired 3/3/70. Returned as middle later in year, KO 1, won 2, draw 1, lost 2. Recap: bouts 77, KO 30, decision 30, draw 4, lost decision 10, KO by 3.

COLLINS, MIKE (Michael E.) D. 10/2/44, Superior, Wis. Promoter. From his days as the "Boy Promoter" to the era when he was called the "Old Grey Fox," Collins manipulated hard and successfully to gain recognition as the Midwest's greatest fight promoter.

As a young promoter in Hudson, Wis., 1912, Collins anticipated the financial potential of a sport that was outlawed in neighboring Minnesota with its populated Minneapolis–St. Paul area.

Building an arena and scheduling special trains from Minnesota's Twin Cities, Collins built Hudson to a boxing center of some national consequence. Capacity crowds saw such fighters as Mike and Tom Gibbons, Ad Wolgast, Mike O'Dowd, Leach Cross, Freddie Welsh, Billy Miske, Jock Malone, Jack Dillon, Fred Fulton, Carl Morris, Eddie McGoorty, Pal Brown and Al Palzer.

Collins' Hudson promotions weren't smaller-city exhibits of a name fighter versus a pliable unknown. Mike Gibbons avenged a New York defeat by Eddie McGoorty in Hudson (3/2/15), drawing a $25,000 gate, a big payday in those times; Mike O'Dowd defeated Soldier Bartfield (11/12/15); and Fulton, one of Mike's heavy contenders, was KO'd 4 by Palzer (5/22/14)— to name some of the attractions that would have warranted metropolitan billing.

When Minnesota legalized boxing in 1915, Collins turned his head to greener acres and set up ring in Minneapolis.His name and promotional talents were familiar. Boxing flourished through the 1920s, a time when Minnesota law stipulated no decision fights. Collins booked champs from almost every division with considerable area favorites to provide interesting opposition, Billy Petrolle, Dick Daniels, the Gibbons boys, O'Dowd, Otto von Porat, King Tut, Fulton, Johnny Ertle, Malone.

A low point in Mike's career was service as matchmaker of the financially ill-fated Dempsey-Gibbons title fight in the little town of Shelby, Mont. (Dempsey, dec. 15, 7/4/23). A promotion designed to draw national attention to the area, it broke the community. Dempsey and Jack Kearns, demanding their payday before the fight, emptied the till.

Collins was a sometime manager, handling the affairs of Tom Gibbons, Fulton, Ertle, Daniels, Malone.

He founded the *Boxing Blade* in 1919, a comparatively successful publication which established the junior welter division. With his eye ever on the box office, Collins announced that the fans would elect the champion. Eligibility to vote was determined by a subscription to the *Blade*. Pinkey Mitchell was proclaimed champion in 1922. Collins sold the publication in 1926 for $40,-

48

000. However, it failed to survive the upcoming lean years, and Midwest boxing experienced the same troubled times.

Collins semiretired, but had always found it harder to hold a buck than to make it. He revived his *Blade* in the late 1930s, and a local theater operator financed his return as a promoter, competing with another franchise. Both Collins' ventures experienced indifferent success.

At outbreak of World War II, Collins was employed as personnel manager of Butler Shipyards, Superior, Wis., and accorded a citation for duties by Maritime Commission. After lengthy illness he died at Superior.

CONLEY, FRANKIE (Francesco Conte) B. 10/4/90, Platania, Italy. D. 8/21/52, Kenosha, Wis. 5'5½", 118. First fight, Kid Hertz, won 6, 8/11/06, Kenosha, Wis. Undefeated to Ad Wolgast, lost 8, 9/10/07, Milwaukee; returns, draw twice. To 1911 undefeated to Charley White, ND twice. World vacant bantam title, advertised, not recognized, Monte Attell, KO 42, 2/22/10, Los Angeles. ND bouts with Owen Moran, White; beat Joe Mandot, 10; drew with Abe Attell. World bantam title, Johnny Coulon, lost 20, 2/26/11, New Orleans. Return title bout, Coulon, lost 20, 2/3/12, Vernon, Calif. 1913–15 creditable including Frankie Mason, KO 3. Inactive 1916–18. Last fight, Jimmy Hanlon, KO by 2, 1919. Recap: bouts 81, KO 15, decision 22, draw 10, lost decision 7, KO by 4, ND 21, no contest 2.

CONN, BILLY (The Pittsburgh Kid) B. 10/8/17, Pittsburgh, Pa. Irish. 6'½", 175–182. First fight, Dick Woodwer, lost 4, 1935, Fairmont, W. Va. Lost 5, 1935. Undefeated in 23 in 1936 including Fritzie Zivic, won 10. 1937–38: 12 won, 3 lost, beaten by Young Corbett, 10, then won rematch, 10. Lost to Solly Krieger, 12, then won rematch, 12. Lost to Teddy Yarosz, 12, then beat him twice. Title, NY State light heavy, Melio Bettina, won 15, 7/13/39, NYC. Defended: Bettina, won 15, 9/25/39, Pittsburgh; Gus Lesnevich, won 15, 11/17/39, NYC; Lesnevich, won 15, 6/5/40, Detroit. 1940–41: 4 won, 5 KO, including Bob Pastor, 13. Heavy title bout, Joe Louis, KO by 13, 6/18/41, NYC (some scorecards had Conn leading, overconfident). Army (ETO) 1942–45. Title, Louis, KO by 8, 6/19/46, NYC. Last appearance, Louis, exh. 6, 12/10/48, Chicago. Hall of Fame 1965. Recap: bouts 74, KO 14, decision 50, lost decision 8, KO by 2.

CONTEH, JOHN B. 5/27/51, Liverpool, England. 170. Outstanding amateur: 1970 ABA middle champ, Commonwealth Games Gold Medalist, 1971 ABA light heavy champ. First pro fight, Okaca Boubekeur, KO 1, 10/18/71, London. Undefeated first year, 1972—KO 10, lost 1. EBU light heavy title, Rudi Schmidtke, KO 12, April 1973, Wembley, England. British, Empire light heavy titles, Chris Finnegan, won 15, London. Recap: bouts 20, KO 14, decision 5, lost decision 1.

COOPER, HENRY B. 5/3/34, London, England. Probably most beloved of English fighters; 17-year career, British heavy titleholder nearly 11 yrs., longer than any previous pugilist. Only fighter to win three Lonsdale belts. First fight, Henry Painter, KO 1, 9/14/54, London. First year: four KO wins. 1956: three straight KO, including Brian London, 1, KO by Peter Bates, 5. 1957: rocky year, including British Empire title, Joe Bygraves, KO by 9, 2/19, London; European title, Ingemar Johansson, KO by 5, 5/19, Stockholm; British title, Joe Erskine, lost 15, 9/17, London. Comeback 1958, including Zora Folley, won 10. 1959, won British and Empire titles, Brian London, 15, 1/12/59, London. Defended: Gawie de Klerk, KO 5, 8/26/59, Porthcawl, Wales; Erskine, KO 12, 11/17/59, London; Erskine, KO 5, 3/21/61, Wembley; Erskine, KO 9, 4/2/62, Nottingham; Dick Richardson, KO 5, 3/26/63, London. 1963: Muhammad Ali, KO by 5, London. Won vacant European title, Brian London, 15, 2/24/64, Manchester. European title declared vacant by EBU 9/64 for failure to defend against Karl Mildenberger. World title, Ali, KO by 6, 5/21/66, London. Floyd Patterson, KO by 4, 1966. Defended British and Empire titles: Johnny Prescott, KO 10, 6/15/65, London; Jack Bodell, KO 2, 6/13/67, Wolverhampton; Billy Walker, KO 6, 11/7/67, London. European title, Mildenberger, won disq. 8, 9/18/68, London. Defended Empire title: Piero Tomasoni, KO 5, 3/14/69, Rome. Defended British title: Jack Bodell, W 15, 3/24/70, London. Last fight, lost European, Empire and British titles, Joe Bugner, 15, 3/16/71, London. Recap: bouts 55, KO 27, decision 11, won foul 1, won disq. 1, draw 1, lost decision 5, lost foul 1, KO by 8.

CORBETT, JAMES J. (Gentleman Jim) B. 9/1/66, San Francisco, Calif. D. 2/18/33, Bayside, N.Y. Irish. 6'1", 187. Amateur, 1880, won Olympic A.C. championship 1885. In 1885–86 assumed name of Jim Dillon, fought two professionals in Salt Lake City, Frank Smith, KO 2; Don McDonald, draw. Turned pro 1886. (Fought amateurs, not uncommon at the time.) First all-pro fight 1889, Joe Choynski, police interrupting, 4; met again twice that year, KO 27, won 4. A 4–1 underdog, won heavyweight title from John L. Sullivan, KO 21, 9/7/92, New Orleans (first championship fight with padded gloves, under Queensberry rules). Defended: Charley Mitchell, KO 3; Peter Courtney, KO 6 (first motion picture of fight, 2-minute rounds); Jim McVey, KO 3; Tom Sharkey, draw 4. Several exhibitions. Lost title, Bob Fitzsimmons, KO 14, 3/17/97, Carson, Nev. Tom Sharkey, lost foul 9. Title, Jim Jeffries, KO by 23, 5/11/1900, New York. Kid McCoy, KO 5, 8/30/1900. Title, Jeffries, KO by 10, 8/14/03, San Francisco. Retired. Corbett marked turning point in ring history, replacing mauling sluggers with new school of faster, scientific boxers. In several stage plays during and after boxing career. Played to capacity houses on a tour of England following his victory over Mitchell. On Broadway, *Cashel Byron's Professional,* 1895. Successful film made, *Gentleman Jim,* starring Errol Flynn, based on Jim's life. Authored book, *Roar of the Crowd,* 1925. Hall of Fame 1954. Recap: bouts 33, KO 9, decision 11, draw 6, lost decision 1, lost foul 1, KO by 3, ND 2.

CORBETT, YOUNG (William H. Rothwell) B. 10/4/80, Denver, Colo. D. 4/10/27, Denver, Colo. 5'2½", 133. First fight, Bert Carter, won 3, 1897. Creditable early three-year record: Kid Broad, KO by 4, 1901; won rematch, 10; 5 wins, 2 by KO. Won feather title, Terry McGovern, KO 2, 11/28/01, Hartford, Conn. Vacated, too heavy for class. 1902–04: undefeated in 23, lost to Jimmy Britt, 20; Battling Nelson, KO by 10. Nelson, KO by 9, 1905. To 1910: won 27, KO by 5, lost 2. Last fight, Willie Beecher, KO by 4, 10/20/10, NYC. Hall of Fame 1965. Recap: bouts 71, KO 15, decision 43, draw 5, lost decision 6, KO by 2.

CORBETT, YOUNG, III (Ralph Capabianca Giordano) B. 5/27/05, Naples, Italy. 5'7½", 147. First fight, Terry McGovern, won 4, 9/28/19, Fresno, Calif. Up-down early career: lost French King, Jack McCarthy, Tommy Herman; Young Jack Thompson, draw; Sgt. Sammy Baker, won, lost; beat Sam Langford, Jackie Fields, Ceferino Garcia, Joey Glick; Bucky Lawless, KO. Won world welter title, Fields, 10, 2/22/33, San Francisco. Lost title, Jimmy McLarnin, KO by 1, 5/29/33, San Francisco. Fought back to title chance: beat Mickey Walker, Billy Conn (lost return), Fred Apostoli, Glen Lee. Middleweight title bout, Apostoli, KO by 8, 11/18/38, NYC. Won last four fights. Last fight, Sheik Rangel, won 10, 8/20/40, Fresno, Calif. Police force. Recap: bouts 104, KO 33, decision 20, draw 12, lost decision 6, KO by 8, no decision 25.

COULON, JOHNNY (Chicago Spider) B. 2/12/89, Toronto, Ontario. Irish-French. 5', 110. One of boxing's great little men. First fight, Young Bennie, KO 6, 1/18/05, Chicago. Undefeated to mid-1907, then lost Kid Murphy, 10. Won U.S. bantam title, Murphy, 10, 1/8/08. Defended: Murphy, won 10, 1/29/08, Peoria, Ill.; Cooney Kelly, KO 9, 2/20/08, Peoria. Murphy, won 5, 2/11/09, NYC; Earl Denning, KO 9, 1/30/10, New Orleans; Jim Kendrick, won 10, 2/19/10, New Orleans; won vacant world title, Kendrick, KO 19, 3/6/10, New Orleans. Defended: Denning, won 5, 12/19/10, Memphis; Frankie Conley, won 20, 2/26/11, New Orleans; Conley, won 20, 2/3/12, Vernon, Calif.; Frankie Burns, won 20, 2/18/12, New Orleans; Kid Williams, ND 10, 10/18/12, NYC. Lost title, Williams, KO by

3, 6/9/14, Vernon, Calif. Undefeated to 1917, then lost to Pete Herman, 3. Army instructor 1918–19. Last fight, Charles Ledoux, KO by 6, 3/16/20, Paris. Active postboxing career: referee, vaudeville, gymnasium. Hall of Fame 1965. Recap: bouts 96, KO 24, decision 32, draw 4, lost decision 2, KO by 2, ND 32.

CRIQUI, EUGENE (Wounded Wonder) B. 8/15/93, Paris, France. 5'4½", 122. First fight, Gouguillon, won 4, 1910, Paris. Outstanding record to 1916. French army World War I. 1917–19: won 25, lost 1, Pal Moore, KO by 14, all in France. 1920–22: undefeated. Won French bantam title, Billy Matthews, 17, 12/2/22, Paris. Won world feather title, Johnny Kilbane, KO 6, 6/2/23, NYC. Lost title, Johnny Dundee, 15, 7/26/23, NYC. Returned to Paris. 1923–28: won 2, lost 3, KO by 1. Last fight, Benny Carter, won 10, 3/19/28, Paris. Recap: bouts 115, KO 40, decision 54, draw 8, lost decision 11, KO by 2.

CROSS, LEACH (Dr. Louis C. Wallach) B. 2/12/86, New York, N.Y. D. 9/7/57, New York, N.Y. Jewish. 5'7½", 135. Dentist. First fight, Bob Waters, KO 2, 1906. First year: 2 setbacks, KOs by Jack Doyle, Frankie Madden. To mid-1909: undefeated including Packey McFarland, ND twice; Young Erne, ND twice; Jem Driscoll, ND; Young Otto, KO 5. Dick Hyland, KO by 4, 1909. To 1921 fought division's best, never title chance: Hyland, return ND; Joe Rivers, won twice, ND; Jack Britton, ND twice; Battling Nelson, ND; Willie Ritchie, ND; Ad Wolgast, won, ND; Johnny Dundee, ND; Freddie Welsh, lost. Last fight, Frankie Maxwell, won 12, 11/7/21, NYC. Retired. Practiced dentistry Hollywood. Built hotel, "Cross Arms." Lost finances in 1929 stock market crash. Resumed dental practice in NYC, served as boxing judge. Recap: bouts 154, KO 25, decision 16, won foul 2, draw 2, lost decision 5, lost foul 1, KO by 4, ND 99.

CRUZ, CARLOS TEO B. 11/4/37, Dominican Republic. D. 2/15/70, Dominican Republic. First fight, Juan Jiminez, lost 8, 10/23/59, Santo Domingo. Early record spotty. To U.S. Dec. 1962: Candy Padilla, won 6. Mediocre, left U.S. Undefeated in 1965, 1 loss 1966, undefeated 1967, 1968: won world lightweight title, Carlos Ortiz, 15, 6/20/68, Santo Domingo. Defended: Hidemori Tsujimoto, won 10, 12/19/68, Tokyo. Lost title, Mando Ramos, KO by 11, 2/16/69, Los Angeles. Last fight, Benito Juarez, won 10, 2/15/70, San Juan. Killed with family in airplane crash. Recap: bouts 31, KO 19, decision 9, lost decision 3.

DADE, HAROLD B. 10/9/24, Chicago, Ill. D. 7/17/62, Los Angeles, Calif. Negro. 5'5". First fight, Ceferino Robleto, won 4, 12/18/42, Hollywood. To 1947 impressive. Won world bantam title, Manuel Ortiz, 15, 1/6/47, San Francisco. Lost title, Ortiz, 15, 3/11/47, Los Angeles. To 1955 fought name fighters: Lauro Salas, Charles Riley, Sandy Saddler, Willie Pep, Kid Chocolate. Never another title chance. Last fight, Paul Jorgensen, KO by 4, 3/29/55, Houston. Recap: bouts 77, KO 9, decision 32, draw 6, lost decision 23, lost foul 2, KO by 5.

D'AGATA, MARIO B. 5/29/26, Arezzo, Italy. Amateur five years, 110 bouts. First pro, Salardi, won 6, 10/14/50, Siena, Italy. To 1953: active, successful. Won Italian bantam title, Gianni Zuddas, foul 9, 9/26/53, Arezzo. Defended: Luigi Fasulo, KO 4, 1/23/54, Naples; Zuddas, won 12, 4/10/54, Milan. Stripped of title Dec. 1954 for not defending. Undefeated 1955, won vacant European title, Andre Valignat, foul 5, 10/29/55, Milan. Won world bantam title, Robert Cohen, KO 6, 6/29/56, Rome. Lost title, Alphonse Halimi, 15, 4/1/57, Paris. Lost European title, Piero Rollo, 15, 10/12/58, Cagliari. Last fight, Federico Scarponi, lost 12, 7/19/62, Rome. Retired 8/1/62. Recap: bouts 67, KO 24, decision 27, won foul 4, draw 3, lost decision 8, KO by 1.

DARCY, LES (James Leslie Darcy) B. 10/31/95, Woodville, New South Wales, Australia. D. 5/24/17, Memphis, Tenn. 5'6", 158. 1911 tournament fights unrecorded. First fight, "Guvnor" Balsa, 1910. Brief, sensational career, untimely death probably deprived of recognition as outstanding champion. Eddie McGoorty, KO 15, 7/31/15, Sydney (recognized for world middle title in Australia). Jimmy Clabby, won twice, 1915, 1916. Return, McGoorty, KO 8. Goerge Chip, KO 9 in last fight, 9/30/16, Sydney. Accused of draft evasion for leaving Australia 1917 for U.S., denied boxing matches. Joined National Guard, Tennessee, with approval of governor; died American soldier, 5/24/17, Memphis, of mental breakdown, fever. Hall of Fame 1957. Recap: bouts 39, KO 20, decision 14, won foul 1, lost decison 3, lost foul 1.

DE JESUS, ESTEBAN B. 8/2/51, Carolina, Puerto Rico. 135 lbs. First fight, El Tarita, KO 2, 2/10/69, San Juan. Undefeated 1969–70. First career loss, Antonio Gomez, 10, 1971. First U.S. fight, George Foster, KO 8, 4/10/72, NYC. Nontitle, upset light champ Roberto Duran, 10, 11/17/72, NYC.Won North American light title, Ray Lampkin, 12, 4/73, San Juan. Recap: bouts 34, KO 19, decision 14, lost decision 1.

DELANEY, JACK (Ovila Chapdelaine) (Bright Eyes) B. 3/18/1900, St. Francis, Quebec. D. 11/27/48, Katonah, N. Y. French-Canadian. 5'11½", 175. First fight, Tom Nelson, KO 2. To 1925, outstanding record, Tommy Loughran, won, draw; Paul Berlenbach, KO; Tiger Flowers, KO twice; world light heavy title, Berlenbach, lost 15, 12/11/25, NYC. Won title, Berlenbach 15, 6/16/26, Brooklyn. Never defended title, entering heavy ranks. Spotty record as heavy, losing Jimmy Maloney, Johnny Risko, Tom Heeney, KO by Jack Sharkey. Last fight, Leo Williams, KO 1, 4/21/28, Hartford. Retired, business. Recap: bouts 86; KO 42, decision 27, won foul 1, draw 3, lost decision 7, KO by 3, ND 2, no contest 1.

DELMONT, AL (Alfredo Delmonti) B. 7/4/85, Naples, Italy. 5'2", 115. Undefeated 5 of 12 active years, never KO by, never title chance. First fight, Ben Locke, won 3, 1902. Impressive first two years. Undefeated 1904–06. Only loss 1907, Owen Moran, 20. Upset Joe Bowker 1909. Pal Moore, ND, lost; Johnny Kilbane, lost, 1910. Undefeated 1911. One loss 1912. Undefeated 1913. Series, Johnny Lynch: KO one, won five, draw three; Jimmy Walsh: won one, lost three, draw five, Joe Wagner: KO one, won three, draw one. Last fight, Young McAuliffe, won 15, 10/25/13, Bridgeport. Recap: bouts 154, KO 38, decision 55, won foul 1, draw 35, lost 11, ND 14.

DEMARCO, PAT (Paddy) B. 2/10/28, Brooklyn, N.Y. Italian. 5'6", 132. First fight, Sal Giglio, won 4, 3/20/45, Jersey City. Promising early record: lost Willie Pep; KO by Sandy Saddler, in rematches beat Saddler twice. Won world light title from Jimmy Carter, 15, 3/5/54, NYC. Lost title, Carter, KO by 15, 11/17/54, San Francisco. To 1959: rocky record. Last fight, Benny Medina, KO by 7, 11/3/59, Fresno, Calif. Recap: bouts 102, KO 8, decision 67, draw 3, lost decision 17, KO by 7.

DEMARCO, TONY (Leonardo Liotta) B. 1/14/32, Boston, Mass. 5'5½", 145. Italian. First fight, Meetor Jones, KO 1, 10/21/48, Boston. Hit peak 1953–55: 10 KO, 5 win, 1 draw. Won world welter title, Johnny Saxton, KO 14, 4/1/55, Boston. Lost title, Carmen Basilio, KO by 12, 6/10/55, Syracuse. Title bout, Basilio, KO by 12, 11/30/55, Boston. Virgil Akins, KO by twice, 1957 and 1958. 1959: KO 1, win 1. 1960: Denny Moyer, KO by 2. 1961: Don Jordan, KO by 2; last fight, Stefan Redl, won 10, 2/6/62, Boston. Retired. Recap: bouts 71, KO 33, decision 25, draw 1, lost decision 5, KO by 7.

DEMPSEY, JACK (John Kelly) (The Nonpareil) B. 12/15/62, County Kildare, Ireland. D. 11/2/95, Portland, Oreg. 5'8", 150. First fight, Ed McDonald, won 21, 4/7/83, Long Island, N.Y. Undefeated in 55, 1883–88. Won welter and middle titles, George Fulljames, KO 22, Great Kills, N.Y. Defended: George LaBlanche, KO 13, 1886. Johnny Reagen, 12/13/87, KO 45, Long Island—first ring became water-submerged, then moved several miles to finish bout amid nearly four hours of snow and cold. George La-Blanche, KO by 32, 8/27/89, San Francisco, but LaBlanche disqualified for illegal punch and Dempsey kept title. Defended: Billy McCarthy, won 28, 2/18/90, San Francisco. Lost title, Bob Fitzsimmons, KO by 13, 1/14/91, New Orleans. 1893: Mike Keogh, won 4. 1894: McCarthy, draw. Last fight, Tommy Ryan, lost 3, 1/18/95, Coney Island, N.Y. Benefit held June 8, last public appearance. After death, some N.Y. admirers visited Oregon to see his grave, found no trace. A Portland reporter, named McMahon, conducted a search, found the plot, wrote a poem, "The Nonpareil's Grave," which was widely published and became something of a classic. Recap: bouts 68, KO 8, decision 42, draw 12, lost decision 1, won disq. 1, KO by 1, ND 3.

DEMPSEY, JACK (William Harrison Dempsey) (Manassa Mauler) B. 6/24/95, Manassa, Colo. Scotch-Irish. 6'1", 189. Worked way from poverty to top. First recorded fight, Young Herman, draw 6, 8/17/14, Ramona, Colo. 1914–19: 49 KO; KO by 1, Jim Flynn, 1917; lost: Jack Downey, 1915; Willie Meehan, 1918. Won world heavy title, Jess Willard, KO 3 (Jess down 7 times in 1st round), 7/4/19, Toledo, Ohio. Defended: Billy Miske, KO 3, 9/6/20, Benton Harber, Mich.; Bill Brennan, KO 12, 12/14/20, NYC; Georges Carpentier, KO 4, 7/2/21, Jersey City (first million-dollar gate); Tom Gibbons, won 15, 7/4/23, Shelby, Mont.; Luis Firpo, KO 2 (Firpo down 7 times, Jack 2), 9/14/23, NYC. Lost title, Gene Tunney, decision 10, 9/23/26, Philadelphia. Jack Sharkey, KO 7, 7/21/27, New York. Title, Tunney, lost 10, 9/22/27, Chicago, in famous "long count" battle. 1931–40: several fights and exhibitions against mediocre opponents, no losses. Last fight, Ellis Bashara, KO 2, 7/29/40, Charlotte, N.C. Boxing's symbol during Golden Age of Sports. Dempsey, Kearns and Rickard put boxing into big business. Unpopular as champion, Dempsey became one of history's most popular after losing title. Referee. Lt. Comdr., Coast Guard, World War II. Restaurateur. Hall of Fame 1954. Recap: bouts 81, KO 49, decision 10, won foul 1, draw 8, lost decision 6, KO by 1, ND 6.

DE OLIVEIRA, MIGUEL B. 10/29/48, Brazil. First fight, Alvacir Doria, won 4, 6/16/68, Sao Paulo. Undefeated 30 straight: 19 KO, 10 decision, 1 draw, all in Sao Paulo. 1972: 5 KO, 1 decision. WBA junior middle title, Koichi Wajima, draw 15, 1/73. Undefeated career. Recap: bouts 37, KO 24, decision 11, draw 2.

DILLON, JACK (Ernest Cutler Price) (Jack the Giant Killer) B. 2/2/91, Frankfort, Ind. D. 8/7/42, Chattahoochee, Fla. Scotch-Irish. 5'7½", 158. Started fighting 1908: KO 3, won 1, draw 2, 1909–1914: lost 3—Ray Bronson, Eddie McGoorty, Frank Klaus; Battling Levinsky (fighting as Barney Williams), ND 10, 1913; Battling Levinsky, won 12, 4/14/14, Butte, Mont. Claimed vacant light heavy title and won recognition by beating Al Norton, 10, 5/28/14, Kansas City. Levinsky, 5 return fights: won 1, draw 1, 2 ND, lost title decision 12, 10/24/16, Boston. Continued to 1923, fighting several heavies. Urged to retire. Last fight, Joe Walters, ND 10, 1/12/23, Bicknell, Ind. Hall of Fame 1959. Recap: bouts 240, KO 60, decision 31, draw 15, lost decision 6, ND 127, NC 1.

DIXON, GEORGE (Little Chocolate) B. 7/29/70, Halifax, Nova Scotia. D. 1/6/09, New York, N.Y. Negro, 5'3½", 87–122. Estimates indicate 800 fights, including barnstorming. First recorded fight, Young Johnson, KO 3, 11/1/86, Halifax. Undefeated through 1888. Tommy Kelly, draw 9, 5/10/88, Boston, claimed world bantam title.* George Wright, lost foul, 1, 1889. To 1896: undefeated. Defended bantam title: Nunc Wallace, KO 18, 7/27/90, London; Johnny Murphy, won 40, 10/23/90, Providence, R.I. Recognized as feather champ after beating Cal McCarthy, 22, 3/31/91, Troy, N.Y. Defended: Abe Willis, KO 5, 7/28/91, San Francisco; Fred Johnson, KO 14, 6/27/92, Coney Island; Jack Skelly, KO 8, 9/6/92, New

---

*Bantam title is a birth without record. Charley Lynch, American champion in mid-1800s, invaded England, several fights, Simon Finightly, KO 43, claimed title. Returned to U.S., retired. Title dormant until 1870s when several claims were submitted. George Dixon was generally regarded as champ. Outgrew, relinquished title 1892. To contribute to confusion, there was continued dispute over weight, starting at 105, graduating to 112, 115, finally 118.

Orleans. Lost feather title, Solly Smith, 20, 10/4/97, San Francisco. Smith broke arm in losing fight, Dave Sullivan, 5, 9/26/98, Coney Island, and Dixon regained title, Sullivan, KO 10, 11/11/98, NYC. Lost title, Terry McGovern, KO by 8, 1/9/1900, NYC. For vacant title, Abe Attell, lost 15, 10/28/01, St. Louis. (McGovern unable to make weight, vacated title, Attell claimed.) To 1906: downwind record. Last fight, Monk Newsboy, lost 15, 12/10/06, Providence, R.I. Hall of Fame 1956. Recap: 158, KO 30, decision 55, won foul 1, draw 38, lost decision 21, KO by 4, ND 9.

DONOVAN, ARTHUR B. 8/10/91, New York, N.Y. Referee. Likened to Tex Rickard, Jack Kearns, and others who contributed milestones to boxing without donning the gloves. Donovan was *the* third man in the ring. He officiated 14 heavy title bouts; Ruby Goldstein trails a distant second with 7.

Donavan was born to boxing. His father Mike, in boxing's Hall of Fame, was the first middle champ, later boxing instructor for over three decades at N.Y. Athletic Club, where among his charges was Teddy Roosevelt. Art succeeded his father at NYAC as boxing instructor, retiring in 1965 after a fruitful 50 years. His own son Arthur carried on the tradition of greatness, but not in the ring. Art Jr. anchored the pro football Baltimore Colts' defensive line in the 1950s; the all-pro entered the Hall of Fame in Canton, Ohio, in 1968.

Meanwhile, Art Sr. was established as the third man in the ring and as an international personality. He recalls officiating 16 Joe Louis fights, including the two Max Schmeling sessions. His fame as a referee was preceded by an inconspicuous tenure with the gloves. He experienced his lumps as a fighter, indirectly occasioned by his joining the Merchant Marine. Entering at only 117 pounds, he attended Fort Schuyler for training, then took his first cruise to England. There some cadets boarded, suggested a boxing tournament. Art, playing the rude host, belted one Englishman over the side. On another occasion, he avenged the insult of a mammoth matey by decking him. Recalling the episode to Red Smith, Art said that "a big English mate slapped me in an argument. He was about 250 pounds and with a black mustache but him being English I couldn't take that. I hit him a hook and flattened him." Encouraged by his comrades, Donovan turned pro. Posterity, however, has failed to retain his boxing record. But his record as referee par excellence will linger.

At 82, in August '73, the retired referee and boxing instructor was looking for work. "Doing nothing is treacherous," he said.

DONOVAN, MIKE (Professor) B. 9/27/1847, Chicago, Ill. D. 3/24/18, New York, N.Y. Irish. 148. First fight, Billy Crowley, lost foul 92, 1886. Mostly a bare-knuckle fighter, but regarded as first middle champion under Marquis of Queensberry rules. Reasoning: Tom Chandler defeated Dooney Harris, 23, bare knuckles, San Francisco, gained recognition as middle champ. George Rooke challenged Chandler 1872, was ignored, title passed to Rooke who lost to Donovan in 2 rounds (stopped by police), March 1881, NYC. Donovan beat George Burke, leading challenger, 4, Sept. 1881, NYC, Queensberry rules. Never defended again, fought overweight bouts. Boxing instructor 1888. Urged to return, fight Nonpareil Jack Dempsey, draw, 11/15/88, Brooklyn. Again, W. C. McClellan, KO 1, May 1891, NYC. Exhibition tour with John L. Sullivan, retired three times. Undefeated career, except two lost on fouls. Son Arthur, famous referee. Hall of Fame 1971. Recap: bouts 33, KO 2, decision 22, draw 7, lost foul 2.

DOWNEY, BILL (William Bryan Downey) B. 9/7/96, Columbus, Ohio. Irish-German. 5'6", 165. First fight, Jimmy Albright, KO 2, 2/2/14, Columbus. Undefeated to 1918, then lost to Jack Britton. Undefeated to world middle title dispute, Johnny Wilson, lost foul 7, 7/4/21, Cleveland. Boxing commission wouldn't recognize verdict, claimed Downey KO winner. Press, public ignored commission ruling. Title, Harry Greb, lost 10, 12/3/23, Pittsburgh. Jock Malone series: won, draw, ND four, lost two. To 1925: ND two, lost two. Last fight, Ted Moore, ND 10, Canton, Ohio. Recap: bouts 118, KO 18, decision 19, draw 14, lost decision 8, lost foul 1, ND 57, no contest 1.

DRISCOLL, JEM B. 12/15/81, Cardiff, Wales. D. 1/31/25, Cardiff, Wales. 5'6", 126. Despite his amazing record and recognition as one of history's greatest feathers, never a title chance. First fight, Billy Lucas, won 4, 1901. Undefeated 13 years, except for foul loss to Freddie Welsh, to his last fight. Before coming to U.S. 1908: George Dixon, KO, won; Joe Bowker, KO, won; Welsh, ND; Owen Moran, ND. In U.S., immediate success, handily beating Marty Balwin first ND bout. In other ND, reporters gave vote over Abe Attell, Leach Cross, Tony Marto, Tom Langdon. Returned home, Welsh, lost foul 10, 1910, Cardiff. England feather title, Moran, draw 20, 1/27/13, London. British army World War I, 1914–18. Returned 1919, Peddler Palmer, won; Francis Rossi, draw. Last fight, Charles Ledoux, KO by 16, 10/20/19, London. Hall of Fame 1956. Victim of pneumonia. Recap: bouts 71, KO 27, decision 25, won foul 1, draw 6, lost foul 1, KO by 1, ND 10.

DUNDEE, JOE (Samuel Lazzaro) B. 1902, Italy. 5'7", 147. First fight, Little Jeff, lost 4, 3/14/19, Baltimore. Mostly impressive to 1926: Lew Tendler, draw 10; Tommy Freeman, KO 4; Mickey Walker, KO 8. Won world welter title, Pete Latzo, 15, 6/3/27, NYC. Nontitles: Young Jack Thompson, KO by 2; Johnny Indrisano, lost 10; Al Mello, lost twice in 10. Lost title, Jackie Fields, foul 2, 7/25/29, Detroit. Last fight, Mike Lichtenstein, won 10, 2/16/31, Baltimore. Recap: bouts 123, KO 23, decision 62, won foul 1, draw 11, lost decision 13, lost foul 2, KO by 5, ND 4, no contest 2.

DUNDEE, JOHNNY (Joseph Corrara) (The Scotch Wop) B. 11/22/93, Sciacca, Italy. D. 4/22/65, E. Orange, N.J. 5'4½", 124. One of boxing's fabulous fighters, 320 fights. Top featherweight and lightweight over two decades. First, Harry Smith, won 4, 1910, NYC. To 1921: for feather title, Johnny Kilbane, draw 10, 4/29/13, Vernon, Calif.; Pal Moore, Freddy Welsh, Lew Tendler, Benny Leonard, ND fights. Won first title, junior light, George Chaney, foul 5, 11/18/21, NYC. Defended: Jack Sharkey, won 15, 7/8/22, NYC; Elino Flores, won 15, 2/2/23, NYC. Lost title, Jack Bernstein, 15, 5/30/23, NYC. Regained title, Bernstein, 15, 12/27/23, NYC. Lost title, Kid Sullivan, 10, 6/20/24, NYC. Won world feather title, Eugene Criqui, 15, 7/26/23, NYC. Outgrew, resigned feather title 1924. To lights, only fair success to 1932: lost Rocky Kansas, Sid Terris, Joey Glick, Tod Morgan, Tony Canzoneri, Al Foreman, A natural, great feather, reporters say Dundee was too late, too light for lights. Last fight, Al Dunbar, lost 10, 1932, Brooklyn. Hall of Fame 1957. Recap: bouts 320, KO 19, won decision 93, won foul 1, draw 18, lost decision 29, KO by 2, ND 158.

DUNDEE, VINCE (Vincent Lazzaro) B. 1904, Italy, D. 7/27/49, Glendale, Calif. 5'8", 147. First fight, Mickey White, won 4, 9/19/23, Baltimore. Johnny Hayes, won 8, 12/5/25, NYC. Andy DiVodi lost 8, 1926. 1927: undefeated in 4. 1928: won 7, lost 2 to Jackie Fields. 1929–31: mostly success. 1932: undefeated in 15. Middle title, Ben Jeby, draw 15, 3/17/33, NYC. Won N.Y. Commission middle title, Lou Brouillard, 15, 10/30/33, Boston. Defended: Andy Callahan, won 15, 12/8/33, Boston; Al Diamond, won 15, 5/1/34, Paterson, N.J. Lost title, Teddy Yarosz, 15, 9/11/34, Pittsburgh. 1935: won 3, lost 1 to Freddie Steele, KO by 3. 1937: won 3, KO 2, lost 2 to Billy Conn, Honeyboy Jones. Last fight, Jones, lost 10, 6/15/37, Pittsburgh. Recap: bouts 150, KO 27, decision 85, draw 13, lost decision 18, KO by 1, ND 5, no contest 1.

DUPAS, RALPH B. 10/14/35, New Orleans, La. 5'8½", 145. First fight, Jitterbug Smith, draw 4, 8/7/50, New Orleans. Impressive first years, 1951–53, outstanding return wins: three losses, Fred Monforte, Jose Vasquez, Brian Kelly, won all returns. 1954, only loss, Paddy DeMarco, Frankie Ryff; 1955 returns, dec. both. Kenny Lane, won 1955, lost 1956 return. Undefeated 1957, including Vince Martinez, Johnny Busso, Joe Miceli, Gaspar Ortega, to light title, Joe Brown, KO by 8, 5/7/58, Houston. 1959–62: lost, won returns, Rudell Stitch, Del Flanagan, Gus Sumlin; won, Lane, Joey Giardello, Virgil Akins. World welter title, Emile Griffith, lost 15, 7/13/62, Las Vegas. Won WBA jr. middle title, Denny Moyer, 15, 4/29/63, New Orleans. Defended: Moyer, won 15, 4/29/63, Baltimore. Lost title, Sandro Mazzinghi, KO by 13, 12/2/63, Sydney. 1964: won one, KO by twice, including Emile Griffith, 3; last fight, Willie Ludick, KO by 2, 9/12/64, Johannesburg. Recap: bouts 130, KO 17, decision 84, won foul 1, draw 6, lost 15, lost foul 1, KO by 6.

DUPREE, JIMMY B. 4/27/41, Millerville, S.C. 175. First fight, Joe Reynolds, won 4, 10/2/61, NYC. Early career, mostly impressive. Undefeated 1969–70: 7 KO, 1 dec., including Paul Johnson (KO 9), Johnny Persol (KO 7), Eddie Jones (KO 10)—all had earlier defeated him. WBA light heavy title, Vincente Rondon, KO by 6, 2/27/71, Caracas. Won North American light heavy title, Ray White, 12, 7/10/71, Santa Monica. Defended: Joe Burns, 12, 8/30/71, Tampa. Lost title, Mike Quarry, disq. 5, 10/30/71, Anaheim. 1972: 3 KO; Eddie Jones, won, KO by 7. 1973: 1 KO, 1 draw. Recap: bouts 49, KO 23, decision 15, draw 3, lost decision 2, lost disq. 1, KO by 5.

DURAN, CARLOS (Juan) B. 6/13/36, Buenos Aires, Argentina. Became naturalized Italian. 145–155 lbs. First fight, Roberto Gallardo, KO 2, 11/58, Mar del Plata, Argentina. 1958–59 undefeated. Vacant Argentine middle title, Farid Salim, lost 15, 1/20/60, Buenos Aires. Undefeated, 1961–62 to upset, Paolo Cottini, KO by 3. Undefeated to Nino Benvenuti, lost 10, 1964. Won Italian middle title, Bruno Santini, 12, 7/22/66, Turin, Italy. Defended: Fabio Bettini, KO 10, 8/18/66, San Remo; Mario Lamagna, 12, 5/19/67, Naples; Tommaso Truppi, KO 3, 8/16/67, San Remo. Won vacant European middle title, Luis Folledo, KO 12, 11/17/67, Turin. Defended: Wally Swift, won disq. 10, 3/26/68, London; Jupp Elze, KO 15, 6/12/68, Cologne; Johnny Pritchett, won disq. 13, 2/20/69, Milan; Hans-Dieter Schwartz, KO 14, 6/25/69, Montecatina Terme, Italy. Lost title, Tom Bogs, 15, 9/11/69, Copenhagen. Regained title, Bogs, 15, 12/4/70, Rome. Lost title, Jean-Claude Bouttier, 15, 6/9/71, Paris. Defended Italian title: Lucian Sarti, draw 12, 2/5/72, Padua. Won EBU jr. middle title, Jose Hernandez, 12, 7/5/72, San Remo. Defended 1973: Jacques Kechichian, won disq. 15; Hans Orsolics, 15. Lost title, Kechichian, KO by 9, 7/5/73. Retired next day. Recap: bouts 83, KO 22, decision 36, won foul 4, won disq. 3, draw 8, lost decision 7, KO by 2, no contest 1.

DURAN, ROBERTO B. 6/16/51, Panama City, Panama. Undefeated to 1971, including four straight KO in 1969, six straight KO in 1971. All fights Panama and Mexico to Benny Huertas, KO 1, 9/13/71, NYC. Won world lightweight title, Ken Buchanan, KO 13, 6/26/72, NYC. Lost nontitle, Esteban de Jesus, 10, 11/17/72, NYC. Defended: Jimmy Robertson, KO 5, 2/15/73, Panama City. Recap: bouts 30, KO 24, decision 5, lost decision 1.

DURELLE, YVON B. 10/14/29, Baie Ste. Anne, New Brunswick. 5'9", 170–185. First fight, Sonny Ramsey, KO 2, 8/48, Chatham, N.B. Impressive early record 1948–49, foul only loss; Cobey McCloskey only 1950 loss, return KO 6, 1951. Lost two, 1951–52, Roy Wouters, Hurley Sanders; won Sanders return. Undefeated to Canadian light heavy title, Gordon Wallace, won 12, 9/8/53, Sydney. Lost title, Doug Harper, 12, 11/17/53, Calgary. Regained title, Harper, 12, 6/7/54, Newcastle, N.B. Defended: Wallace 12, 9/27/54, Bathhurst, N.B.; Billy Fifield, KO 1, 7/28/55, Moncton, N.B. 1955, three KO by: Floyd Patterson 5, Jimmy Slade 7, Yolande Pompey 7. Won British Empire light heavy title, Wallace, KO 2, 5/30/57, Moncton. Defended: Mike Holt, KO 9, 7/16/58, Montreal. World light heavy title, Archie Moore, KO by 11, 12/10/58, Montreal. Return title, Moore, KO by 3, 8/12/59, Montreal. Undefeated to Canadian heavy title, George Chuvalo, KO by 12, 11/17/59, Toronto. Announced retirement, became wrestler 1961, Returned to boxing 1963, two KO; last fight, Phonse LaSaga, KO 1, 3/24/63, Three Rivers. Returned to wrestling. Recap: bouts 105, KO 44, decision 38, lost decision 10, lost foul 3, KO by 9, no contest 1.

DYKES, BOBBY B. 9/8/28, San Antonio, Tex. First fight, Lauro Salas, lost 4, 1944, Corpus Christi. Undefeated 1947, including 14 KO. 1948–50: 24 KO; Lester Felton, won, lost; Frankie Abrams, KO, won, lost; Ray Robinson, lost. 1951, 1st fight, Johnny Bratton, KO by 1; won balance, including Joey Giardello. American middle title, Kid Gavilan, lost 15, 2/4/52, Miami. Creditable record to 1957, including Kid Gavilan, won 1955. Undefeated 1957. Last fight, Gordon Pouliot, KO 3, 3/30/57, Fort Lauderdale. Recap: bouts 109, KO 26, decision 57, draw 7, lost 17, KO by 2.

EBIHARA, HIROYUKI B. 3/26/40, Tokyo, Japan. First fight, Kazuhiko Kurihara, KO 4, 9/20/59, Tokyo. Only one defeat in five years. Won world flyweight title, Pone Kingpetch, KO 1, 9/18/63, Tokyo. Lost title, Kingpetch, 15, 1/23/64, Bangkok, Thailand. WBA title, Horacio Accavallo, lost 15, 7/16/66, Buenos Aires. Rematch for title, Accavallo, lost 15, 8/13/67, Buenos Aires. Won vacant WBA flyweight title, Jose Severino, 15, 3/30/69, Sapporo, Japan. Lost title, Bernabe Villacampo, 15, 10/20/69, Tokyo, last fight. Retired 10/21/69. Recap: bouts 69, KO 34, decision 29, draw 1, lost 5.

ELLIS, JIMMY B. 2/24/40, Louisville, Ky. First fight, Arley Seifer, KO 3, 4/19/61, Louisville, starting as middle. First year, only loss, Holly Mims, 10; return, won 10, 1962. Undefeated 1963. Spotty 1964. Undefeated 1965–68. Won WBA heavy title, Jerry Quarry, 15, 4/27/68, Oakland, elimination final to fill title vacated by Muhammad Ali suspension for refusing draft order. Defended: Floyd Patterson, 15, 9/14/68, Stockholm. Inactive 1969. World title, Joe Frazier, KO by 5, 2/16/70, NYC. 1971: George Chuvalo, won 10; Ali, KO by 12. Undefeated 1972, 8 straight (4 in '72) to Ernie Shavers, KO by 1, 6/18/73, NYC. Recap: bouts 46, KO 22, decision 16, lost decision 5, KO by 3.

ELORDE, FLASH (Gabriel Elorde) B. 4/25/35, Bogo, Cebu, Philippines. First fight, Kid Gonzaga, KO 4, 6/16/51, Cebu City. Early record mostly impressive. Won Orient bantam title, Horishi Hiroguchi, 12, 10/18/52,

63

Tokyo. Defended: Akiyoshi Akanauma, draw 12, 11/18/52, Tokyo. Lost title, Larry Bataan, 12, 5/20/53, Manila. Orient feather title, Shigeji Kaneko, lost 12, 6/29/54, Tokyo. Won Filipino bantam title, Tommy Romulo, 12, 8/18/54, Manila. Filipino light title Leo Alonzo, lost 12, 6/15/55, Manila. World feather title, Sandy Saddler, KO by 13, 1/18/56, San Francisco. Won Filipino light title, Romulo, 12, 3/16/57, Manila. Orient light title, Onsap Laempapha, lost 12, 6/23/57, Bangkok. Defended Filipino light title: Alonzo won 12, 10/23/57, Manila; Javallana Kid, won 12, 5/3/58, Manila. Won Orient light title, Hirosha Okawa, 12, 3/1/58, Tokyo. Defended: Hisao Kobayashi, won 12, 9/12/58, Tokyo; Kelichi Ishaikawa, KO 6, 11/15/58, Manila; Takeo Sugimori, won 12, 2/6/59, Tokyo; Hisao Koayshi, won 12, 10/7/59, Tokyo; Sakuji Shinozowa, won 12, 10/17/60, Manila; Somkait Katmuangon, KO 2, 3/10/62. Manila. Lost Orient title, Tervo Kosaka, 12, 4/30/62, Tokyo. Regained, Kosaka, 12, 8/4/62, Cebu City. Defended: Tsunstomi Miyamoto, KO 9, 6/1/63, Manila; Rene Barrientos, won 12, 2/27/65, Manila. Lost Orient title, Yoskiaki Numata, 10, 6/9/66, Tokyo. Won world junior light, Harold Gomes, KO 7, 3/16/60, Manila. Defended: Gomes, KO 1, 8/17/60, San Francisco; Joe Lopes, won, 15, 3/19/61, Manila; Sergio Caprari, KO 1, 12/16/61, Manila; Auburn Copeland, won 15, 6/23/62, Manila; Johnny Bizzarro, won 15, 2/16/63, Manila; Love Allotey, won disq. 11, 11/16/63, Manila; Kosaka, KO 12, 7/27/64, Tokyo; Kosaka, KO 15, 6/5/65, Manila; Suh Kang II, won 15, 12/4/65, Manila. Lost title, Yoskiaki Numata, 15, 6/15/67, Tokyo. World light title, Carlos Ortiz, KO by 14, 2/15/64, Manila; Ortiz, KO by 14, 11/14/66, NYC. Inactive 1968. 1969–71: lost 3 of 7. Recap: bouts 111, KO 27, decision 49, won foul 1, draw 2, lost decision 28, KO by 4.

ERNE, FRANK B. 1/8/75, Zurich, Switzerland. D. 9/17/54, New York, N.Y. 5'5¾", 133. First fight, J. L. Sullivan Jr., won 2, 1/7/94, Buffalo. 1894–98: undefeated in 21, lost 2. World light title, Kid Lavigne, draw 20, 9/28/98, Coney Island. Won world light title, Lavigne, 20, 6/3/99, Buffalo. Defended: Jack O'Brien, draw 25, 12/4/99, Coney Island; Joe Gans, KO 12, 3/23/1900, NYC. World welter title, Rube Ferns, KO by 9, 9/23/01, Fort Erie, Ontario. Nontitle, Terry McGovern, KO by 3. Welter title, Rube Ferns KO by 9, 9/23/01, Fort Erie. Lost light title, Joe Gans, KO by 1, 5/12/02, Fort Erie. Last fight, Charley Watson, won 10, March, Paris. Recap: bouts 40, KO 10, decision 11, won foul 1, draw 12, lost decision 2, KO by 4.

ERTLE, JOHNNY (Kewpie) B. 3/21/96, Dunafaldyar, Austria. 4'11", 112–116. Located in St. Paul, home of manager Mike McNulty. First fight, La Scotte, KO 3, 10/31/13, St. Paul. To mid-1915 undefeated, then lost Pal Moore, 8. Kid Williams, won foul 5, 9/10/15, claimed bantam title, not generally recognized. Williams, draw, 1917. Undefeated mid-1915 to mid-1918 when lost to Pal Moore, 15. Through 1923 spotty record. Last fight, Carl Tremaine, lost 12, 5/7/23, Columbus, Ohio. Recap: bouts 79, KO 14, decision 4, won foul 2, draw 3, lost decision 8, KO by 3, ND 45.

ESCOBAR, SIXTO B. 3/23/13, Barcelona, Puerto Rico. 5'4", 118. First fight, Ramon Rodriguez, KO 6, 1931. Creditable foreign record. To U.S. 1934: Bobby Leitham, KO 7; Joey Archibald, won 10; won NBA bantam title, Baby Casanova, KO 9, 6/26/34, Montreal. Defended: Eugene Huat, won 15, 8/8/34, Montreal. Lost title, Lou Salica, 15, 8/26/35, NYC. Regained title, Salica, 15, 11/15/35, NYC. Won world bantam title, Tony Marino, KO 13, 8/13/36, NYC. Defended: Indian Quintana, KO 1, 10/13/36, NYC. Lost title, Harry Jeffra, 15, 9/23/37, NYC. Regained world bantam title, Jeffra, 15, 2/20/38, San Juan. Defended: KO Morgan, won 15, 4/2/39, Puerto Rico. 1939, vacated title because of weight. Last fight, Jeffra, lost 10, 12/2/40, Baltimore. In U.S. Army. Recap: bouts 64, KO 21, decisions 21, draw 4, lost decision 18.

FAMECHON, JOHNNY B. 3/28/46, France. Member of famous clan of Australian fighting Famechons. First fight, Sammy Lang, draw 3, 6/7/61, Melbourne. Impressive record to 1965. Won Australian feather title, Domenico Chilorio, 15, 2/19/65, Melbourne. Defended: Max Murphy, KO 7, 9/24/65, Melbourne; Chilorio, won 15, Melbourne. Won British feather title, Johnny O'Brien, KO 11, 11/24/67, Melbourne. Defended: Billy McGrandle, KO 12, 9/13/68, Melbourne. Won world feather title, Joe Legro, 15, 1/21/69, London. Vacated British title. Defended: Fighting Harada, won 15, 7/28/69, Sydney; Harada, KO 14, 1/6/70, Tokyo. Lost title, Vicente Saldivar, won 15, 5/9/17, Rome. Retired. Recap: bouts 68, KO 20, decision 36, won foul 1, draw 6, lost decision 5.

FARR, TOMMY B. 3/12/14, Clydach Vale, Wales. First fight, Jack Jones, won 6, 12/18/26, Tonypandy. To 1937: fights in Wales, London, outstanding record. Won Welsh light heavy title, Randy Jones, 15, 7/22/33, Tonypandy. Defended: Charley Bundy, won 15, 9/13/34, Trealaw; Jim Wilde, KO 7, 9/14/36, Swansea. British light heavy title, Eddie Phillips, lost 15, 2/4/35, Mountain Ash. Won British Empire heavy title, Ben Foord, 15, 3/15/37, London. U.S. fighters fought overseas: Tommy Loughran, won 10; Bob Olin, won 10, Max Baer, won 12. World heavy title, Joe Louis, lost 15, 8/30/37, NYC. Lost four successively in U.S., Jim Braddock, Baer, Lou Nova, Red Burman. Retired 1940. Comeback after 10 years. Won Welsh heavy title, Dennis Powell, KO 6, 7/7/51, Shrewsbury. Won 7, lost 2 to last fight, Don Cockell, KO by 7, 3/9/53, Nottingham. Recap: bouts 104, KO 23, decision 48, draw 11, lost decision 18, lost foul 1, KO by 3.

FELTON, LESTER B. 3/6/29, Detroit, Mich. Middle. Brilliant early career. First fight, Jimmy Root, won 4, 3/4/47, Detroit. Undefeated first two years, 10 KO, 15 dec. 1st loss, Bobby Dykes, 1949, won return 1950. Upset Kid Gavilan, 10, 1949; Carmen Basilio, 10, 1951. Nontitle, lost four champs, Ike Williams, Johnny Bratton, Joe Brown, Johnny Saxton, 1950–52. Never title chance. 1953: dec. 4, KO 1, lost 1. 1954–57, five fights: lost dec. three, KO by two. Series, Dykes: dec. two, lost one. Last fight, Rocky Castellani, KO by 3, 6/6/57, Youngstown. Recap: bouts 78, KO 21, decision 38, won disq. 1, draw 3, lost 13, KO by 2.

FERNS, JIM (Rube Ferns) (The Kansas Rube) B. 1/20/74, Pittsburg, Kans. D. 6/11/52, Pittsburg, Kans. 5'8½", 145. First fight, Jack Dougherty, KO 2, 1896. To 1900: creditable early record. Won world welter title, Mysterious Billy Smith, foul 21, 1/15/1900, Buffalo. Matty Matthews, 3 successive fights: nontitle, won 15; lost title, 15, 10/16/1900, Detroit; regained title, KO 10, 5/24/01, Toronto. Defended: Frank Erne, KO 9, 9/23/01, Fort Erie, Ont. Lost title, Joe Walcott, KO by 5, 12/18/01, Fort Erie. 1902–06: KO by two, lost three. Two with Matthews: lost 1, KO 1. Last fight, Cal Delaney, KO 3, 2/22/06, Grand Rapids. Recap: bouts 53, KO 31, decision 9, won foul 1, draw 1, lost decision 8, KO by 3.

FIELDS, JACKIE (Jacob Finkelstein) B. 1907, Chicago, Ill. Jewish. 5'7½", 130–45. Amateur: Olympic feather title 1924 Paris Olympic Games, youngest athlete, 17, to win Gold Medal. 54 bouts, 51 wins. First pro, Joe Sales, won 4, 9/8/24, Los Angeles. Undefeated until lost to Jimmy McLarnin, KO by 2, 11/12/25. To 1929 fought top fighters: Sammy Mandell, ND 10; Louis (Kid) Kaplan, lost 10; Mushy Callahan, won 10; Vince Dundee, won 10; Young Jack Thompson, won 10, Sgt. Sammy Baker, KO 2. Won NBA welter title, Thompson, 10, 3/25/29, NYC. Defended: Joe Dundee, won foul 2, 7/25/29, Detroit. Lost title, Thompson, 15, 5/9/30, Detroit. Won world welter title, Lou Brouillard 10, 1/28/32, Chicago. Lost title, Young Corbett III, 10, 2/22/33, San Francisco. Last fight, Young Peter Jackson, won 10, 5/2/33, Los Angeles. In U.S. Army. Public relations director, Tropicana Hotel, Las Vegas. Recap: bouts 84, KO 28, decision 41, won foul 1, draw 2, lost decision 8, KO by 1, ND 2, no contest 1.

FINNEGAN, CHRIS B. 6/5/44, Hayes, England. 170. Olympic champ 1968, Mexico City. First pro fight, Mick Fleetham, KO 3, 12/9/69. London. Impressive early career. European middle title, Tom Bogs, lost 15, 8/27/70, Copenhagen. Won British and Empire light heavy titles, Eddie Avoth, KO, 15, 1/24/71, London. European light heavy title, Conny Velensek, draw 15, 5/5/71, Berlin. Undefeated 1971. Won European title, Velensek, 15, 2/1/72,

Nottingham. Defended: European title, Jan Lubbers, KO 8, 6/6/72. World title, Bob Foster, KO by 14, 9/26/72, London. Lost European title, Rudi Schmidtke, KO by 12, 11/14/72, London. 1973: defended British, Empire titles: Roy John, won 15; John Conteh, lost 15, London. Recap: bouts 29, KO 16, decision 9, lost decision 1, KO by 3.

FINNEGAN, HONEYBOY (Richard G. Finnegan) B. 8/22/02, Boston, Mass. Irish. 5'8", 135. Atlantic Fleet champ 1920; Navy title 1922; Army-Navy title 1923. First pro, Freddie Williams, KO 5, 1924. Creditable two years to 1926–27, undefeated including top rankers: Joe Glick, KO 6; beat, Ray Miller, Red Chapman, Chick Suggs, Babe Herman, Tod Morgan; draw, Benny Bass. 1928: lost Bruce Flowers, Johnny Jadick, won returns; beat Sammy Fuller, Andre Routis. Won last 3 by KO. Last fight, Lou Sanders, KO 2, 6/7/30, Los Angeles. Recap: bouts 61, KO 14, decision 31, draw 2, lost decision 8, KO by 1, ND 5.

FIRPO, LUIS ANGEL (Wild Bull of the Pampas) B. 10/11/96, Buenos Aires, Argentina. D. 8/7/60, Buenos Aires, Argentina. Italian-Spanish. 6'3", 216. First fight, Daly Chillan, KO 6, 1919. To mid-1923: 20 KOs in 25 fights, including Jess Willard, 2; Bill Brennan, 12. Heavy title, Jack Dempsey, KO by 2, 9/14/23 in fight in which Dempsey was knocked out of ring. Historic controversy involved legality of Dempsey's being boosted back into ring. Firpo down 7 times, Jack 2 in short fight. To 1936: creditable. Last fight, Arturo Godoy, KO by 3, 7/11/36. Millionaire, autos, farm equipment. Recap: bouts 35, KO 25, decision 4, won foul 1, KO by 2, ND 3.

FITZSIMMONS, BOB (Robert L.) (Ruby Robert) B. 6/4/62, Helston, Cornwall, England. D. 10/22/17, Chicago, Ill., pneumonia. 5'11", 165. Blacksmith. 1880–81: won New Zealand amateur middleweight championships in Timaru, kayoing 4 opponents one night for first title, 5 one night next year. Turned pro. 1882–88: 13 KO. Only 1889 fight, Dick Ellis, won 3, 12/17, Sydney, Australia. Jem Hall, KO by 4, 2/10/90, Sydney. To San Francisco, Billy McCarthy, KO 9, 5/29/90; Arthur Upham, KO 5, 6/28/90. Won middleweight title, Nonpareil Jack Dempsey, KO 13, 1/14/91, New Orleans. Never lost middleweight title. Return bout, Hall, KO 4, 3/8/93, New Orleans. Light heavy and heavyweight: Joe Choynski, police stopped, draw 5, Boston; Con Riordan, exh. 2, 11/19/94, Syracuse, N.Y. (Riordan died after bout, Fitzsimmons exonerated). Tom Sharkey, lost foul, 12/2/96, San Francisco. Won world heavyweight title, Jim Corbett, KO 14, 3/17/97, Carson City, Nev. Lost title (first defense), Jim Jeffries, KO by 11, 6/9/99, Coney Island. 1899–1900: 5 KO, including Tom Sharkey 2, 8/24/1900, Coney Island. Title, Jeffries, KO by 8, 7/25/02, San Francisco. Won light heavyweight title, George Gardner, 20, 11/25/03, San Francisco. Philadelphia Jack O'Brien, ND 6, 7/23/04, Phila. Lost title, O'Brien, KO by 13, 12/20/05, San Francisco. Jack Johnson, KO by 2, 7/17/07, Philadelphia. Four last fights: Jim Paul, KO 1, 1908; Bill Lang, KO by 12, 1909; K. O. Sweeney, ND 6, 1914; Jersey Bellow, ND 6, 2/20/14, Bethlehem, Pa. (Bob's finale, 51 years old). Famed for solar-plexus punch, now outlawed. Appeared in vaudeville and on Broadway, *The Honest Blacksmith,* 1898. Hall of Fame 1954. Boxer son "Young Bob," mediocre record. In 1973, almost 53 years after Fitz was buried in Chicago's Graceland cemetery, it was discovered that the name on his headstone was misspelled, Fitzimmons instead of Fitzsimmons. With the help of the Veteran Boxers Assn. of Illinois a new stone was obtained. Fitzsimmons lies buried about 200 feet from another great champ, Jack Johnson. Recap: bouts 41, KO 23, decision 5, draw 1, lost foul 1, KO by 6, ND 5.

FLEISCHER, NAT (Mr. Boxing) B. 11/3/87, New York, N.Y. D. 6/25/72, New York, N.Y. Died at 84 in a New York hospital, the last round of 50 years of weaving, jabbing, scoring with consequential haymakers for a sport to which his working life was dedicated.

Nathaniel Stanley Fleischer was Jewish, entertaining an almost Quakerlike outlook, a compassion for fellow man, exemplary habits and disdain for vulgarity. His career came out of the corner as a sports writer for the long gone *New York Press,* later sports editor, with ensuing rounds graduating him to sports editorship of the *New York Telegram.* During that period, as a sideline, he founded *Ring* in 1922.

Transition of New York publications and personnel confronted him with a decision: Take another sports desk job? Or devote full-time to his swaddling magazine? The magazine won the decision. It was an activating whiff of smelling salts for an oft-groggy sport.

Objectively it has been observed that if it hadn't been for Nat Fleischer, boxing couldn't have pushed off the stool for the 8th round.

It was Mr. Boxing who established protection for seriously cut contestants, more conscientious physical exams; instigated ring padding; raised standards to disqualify overmatching; established monthly ratings; encouraged home and closed TV as a stimulant for interest in the sport.

And he was an idealist. He fought boxing's hoodlums with the bullets from his typewriter, despite threats on his life.

Nat Fleischer, publisher, editor, author, referee, crusader—in sum, Mr. Boxing.

FLOWERS, TIGER (Theo Flowers) (The Georgia Deacon) B. 8/5/95, Camille, Ga. D. 11/16/27, New York N.Y., following operation. Negro. 5'10", 160. First fight, Billy Hooper, KO 11, 1918. 1918–21: undefeated in 15; KO by Panama Joe Gans 5, 1921. 1922; 5 KO; won 6; KO by 4—Kid Norfolk, Sam Walcott, Lee Anderson, Jamaica Kid; 1 draw. 1923: undefeated in 12, KO by Norfolk. 1924: undefeated in 35. 1925: undefeated in 21; KO by Jack Delaney twice, 2, 4; lost Mike McTigue, 10; lost foul, Lou Bagash, 3. Won world middle title, Harry Greb, 15, 2/26/26, NYC. First Negro to win middle title. Lost title, Mickey Walker, 10, 12/3/26, Chicago, disputed verdict. 1927: undefeated in 17; lost to Leo Lomski, 10. Last fight, Leo Gates, KO 4, 11/12/27. Recap: bouts 149, KO 49, decision 61, won foul 5, draw 6, lost decision 3, lost foul 2, KO by 8, ND 14, no contest 1.

FLYNN, JIM (Andrew Chairiglione) (Fireman) B. 12/24/79, Hoboken, N.J. 5'10", 178–188. First fight, Ed Chambers, KO 4, 1901. Unpredictable trial horse for champion and challenger, fought 10 champs: Jack Root, lost; George Gardner, draw; Tommy Burns, KO by; Billy Papke, ND twice; Phila. Jack O'Brien, ND; Battling Levinsky, ND; Jack Dillon, ND twice; Jack Dempsey, KO 1; return, Dempsey, KO by 1; Tiger Flowers, lost. Heavy title, Jack Johnson, lost 9 (police stopped), 9/14/12, Las Vegas. 1904, 05, 07; undefeated in 11. Last fight, Sam Langford, KO by 3, 10/19/23, Mexico City. Recap: bouts 113, KO 39, decision 12, won foul 3, draw 15, lost decision 7, lost foul 1, KO by 15, ND 21.

FOLLEY, ZORA B. 5/27/32, Dallas, Tex. D. 7/7/72, Tucson, Ariz. 6'1½", 190. Army at 16, Korean action. First boxing, won All-Army heavy title, Inter-Service title twice. Returned to find Chandler, Ariz., home destroyed by fire. Turned to boxing. First pro, Jimmy Ingram, won 4, 9/22/53, Los Angeles. Undefeated through May 1955, then KO by Johnny Summerlin; 3 wins later, KO by Young Jack Johnson. Back in Arizona 1956: 6 wins including Roger Rischer, Nino Valdez, Wayne Bethea. To 1959: creditable if unexciting, including Bethea return, won; Pete Rademacher, KO; Eddie Machen, dull draw; Henry Cooper, lost. 1960–61: 10 wins, KO by Sonny Liston; wins including Ed Machen, Alex Miteff, Willie Besmanoff. Title shot looming until KO by Alejandro Lavorante. Another win series including Doug Jones, Cooper, Mike DeJohn. Return Jones, KO by 7, 1962, dashed title chance hopes again. 1963; won 5, lost Ernie Terrell, 10. 1964–66: undefeated, including wins over George Chuvalo, Oscar Bonavena, Bob Foster. His 14-year wait for world title chance (Folley 34)—Muhammad Ali, KO by 7, 3/22/67, NYC, Ali's last fight before long court battle. To 1970: spotty, 10 bouts, lost to Brian London, Bonavena. Last fight, Mac Foster, KO by

1, 9/21/70, Fresno, Calif. Died in swimming pool accident. Recap: bouts 146, KO 44, decision 79, draw 5, lost decision 11, KO by 7.

FORBES, HARRY B. 5/13/79, Rockford, Ill. D. 12/19/46, Chicago, Ill. Irish. 5'4", 118. First fight, Joe Sturch, lost 4, 1/16/87, Chicago. Undefeated balance of year. Terry McGovern, KO by 15, 1898: undefeated in 24. World bantam title, McGovern, KO by 2, 12/22/99, NYC. Vacant bantam title: Casper Leon, draw 20, 9/6/1900, St. Joseph, Mo. Won vacant world bantam title, Leon, 15, 4/2/01, Memphis. Defended: Dan Dougherty, KO 4, 1/23/02, St. Louis; Tommy Feltz, won 15, 2/27/02, St. Louis; Frank Neil, won 7, 12/23/02, Oakland; Andy Tokell, won 10, 2/27/03, Detroit. Lost title, Neil, KO by 2, 8/13/03, San Francisco. Title, Neil, KO by 2, 6/17/04, Chicago. Creditable record to 1912. Last 2 fights: Johnny Coulon, KO by 3; Oscar Williams, KO by 2, 7/22/12, Paducah, Ky. Took on all competition, regardless of weight. Abe Attell, great feather champ, series of 6: won 1, draw 2, loss 1, KO by 2. Recap: bouts 128, KO 30, decision 47, won foul 3, draw 23, lost decision 5, KO by 9, ND 11.

FOREMAN, GEORGE B. 1/22/48, Marshall, Tex. Negro. 6'4", 217. From poverty-stricken family, member of Peace Corps. Managed by Dick Saddler, former vaudeville performer who recognized Foreman's potential while amateur. 1968 Olympic heavy champ. First pro fight, Don Waldheim, KO 3, 6/23/69, NYC. First year undefeated: KO 11, won 2. 1970: KO 11, won 1, including George Chuvalo, KO 3; George Peralta, won 10. 1971: 8 straight KO. To heavy title, 5 straight KO. Won world title, Joe Frazier KO 2 (4 min., 35 sec.), 1/22/73 (Foreman's 25th birthday), Kingston, Jamaica. Frazier, 3–1 favorite, down six times, one of division's greatest upsets. Defended: Jose Roman, KO 1, 9/1/73, Tokyo. Predictions anticipated that while Foreman's record was impressive, his opposition unimpressive. Married, one child, lives in Minneapolis. Recap: bouts 40, KO 37, decision 3.

FOSTER, BOB B. 4/27/42, Albuquerque, N. Mex. Negro. First fight, Duke Williams, KO 2, 3/27/61, Washington DC. Nine straight to Doug Jones, KO by 8, 1962. String KO against light heavies, heavies: Ernie Terrell, KO by 7; Zora Folley, lost 10. Undefeated to light heavy title; Dick Tiger, KO 4, 5/24/68, NYC. Defended: Frank De Paula, KO 1, 1/22/69, NYC; Andy Kendall, KO 4, 5/24/69, Springfield, Mass.; Roger Rouse, KO 4, 4/4/70, Missoula, Mont.; Mark Tessman, KO 10, 6/27/70, Baltimore. Heavy title, Joe Frazier, KO by 2, 11/18/70, Detroit. Defended light heavy: Hal Carroll, KO 4, Scranton, Pa.; Ray Anderson, 15, 4/24/71, Tampa; Tommy Hicks, KO 8, 10/29/71, Scranton; Brian Kelly, KO 3, 12/16/71, Oklahoma City. Recap: bouts 51, KO 39, decision 7, lost decision 2, KO by 3.

FOURIE, PIERRE B. 1944, Johannesburg, South Africa. 160. One of South Africa's most brilliant middle prospects. After losing first fight, Dick Duffy, 10, 9/15/69, Johannesburg, undefeated three years. S.A. middle title, Coert Fourie, won 12, 4/19/60, Johannesburg. Def.: Johnny Wood, 12, 8/2/69; Wood, KO 12, 11/6/69; Willie Luduck, L 10, 2/14/70, all Johannesburg. Don Fullmer, won 10, 1972. Recap: bouts 29, KO 4, decision 24, lost 1.

FOX, TIGER JACK (John Linwood Fox) B. 4/2/07, Indianapolis, Ind. D. 4/6/54, Spokane, Wash. Negro. 5'11½", 180. Amateur, semipro 7 years. First recorded pro, George Dixon, KO 3, 1/12/32, Terre Haute. Frustrated career sometimes compared with that of Archie Moore, difficult to obtain prestige fights. Never title chance. Against ranking opposition: Maxie Rosenbloom, lost, draw, won; Joe Sekra, won; Bob Olin, KO; Lou Brouillard, KO; Jersey Joe Walcott, KO, won; John Henry Lewis, KO by. Inactive 1941–44. To 1950: mostly wins, mediocre opposition. Last fight, Jose Ochea, KO by 2, 12/12/50, Twin Falls, Idaho. Recap: bouts 147, KO 81, decision 39, draw 6, lost decision 11, lost foul 1, KO by 6, no contest 3.

FRAZIER, JOE B. 1/12/44, Laurel Bay, S.C. Negro. 6'1", 220. Youngest of 13 children. At 13, dropped school; became mule driver, then bottling plant laborer. Left home at 16; to N.Y. garment district, then Philadelphia slaughterhouse. Frequented gym where discovered by Yankee Durham, 1962. Amateur: 1964 Olympic heavy champ. First pro bout, Woody Goss, KO 1, 8/16/65, Philadelphia. To 1966, 12 successive KOs. To heavy title, Oscar Bonavena, won, 1966; George Johnson, won, 1967 (Bonavena, Johnson only non-KOs through 1967). Won N.Y. State heavy title, Buster Mathis, KO 11, 3/4/68, NYC. Defended: Manuel Ramos, KO 2, 6/24/68, NYC; Bonavena, won 15, 12/10/68, Philadelphia; Dave Zyglewicz, KO 1, 4/22/69, Houston; Jerry Quarry, KO 7, 6/23/69, NYC. Won undisputed world title, Jimmy Ellis (NBA champ), KO 5, 2/16/70, NYC. Title, Cassius Clay, won 15, 3/8/70 (largest intake in boxing history—TV, gate, $2 1/2 million personal). Lost title, George Foreman, KO by 2 (4 min., 35 sec.), 1/22/73, Kingston, Jamaica. Joe Bugner, won 12, 7/2/73, London (Bugner, European heavy champ). Bought 368-acre Brewton estate, 19 miles from his family 4-room scrap-lumber house. Musician, fair success. Recap: bouts 29, KO 23, decision 5, KO by 1.

FREEMAN, TOMMY (Thomas H. Freeman) B. 1/22/04, Hot Springs, Ark. Irish. 5'7½", 145–56. First fight, Kid Cuty, KO 3, 1921. Slow starter, 1922–23: 4 losses, 2 draws. Impressive record followed, 1923–26: undefeated. Joe Dundee, KO by 4, 1926. Undefeated to Johnny Indrisano, lost 10, 1927; Jackie Fields, KO by 5, 1930. Won world welter title, Young Jack Thompson, 15, 9/5/30. Cleveland. Defended: Pete August, won 10, 1/10/31, Detroit; Eddie Murdock, won 10, 1/26/31, Oklahoma City; Duke Trammel, KO 5, 2/5/31, Memphis; Al Kober, KO 5, 2/9/31, New Orleans; Alfred Gaona, won 10, 3/1/31, Mexico City. Lost title, Thompson, KO by 12, 4/14/31, Cleveland. Active to 1938, creditable record, no title return. Last year, 4 KO, last fight, Ralph Chong, lost 10, 5/22/38, Ft. Smith, Ark. Navy. Recap: bouts 185, KO 69, decision 75, draw 17, lost decision 13, KO by 3, ND 8.

FUGAZY, JACK (Humbert J.) B. 1889. D. 4/8/64, New York, N.Y. Son of an Italian banker, Fugazy was a boxer, banker, grand-opera impresario and travel-agency executive. He was also Tex Rickard's closest rival, although he once categoried Rickard as the "greatest promoter of all time".

His promotional career was not lengthy, but it was spectacular. First consequential challenge to Rickard's domination was an all-star, tripleheader at the Polo Grounds, July 2, 1925: Harry Greb–Mickey Walker, Greb defended middle title, 15; Harry Wills, KO 2, Charley Weinert; Dave Shade, KO 3, Jimmy Slattery.

Following year, 6/16/26, set record gate (49,186 paid $461,789) for light heavy fight, Jack Delaney won title, 15, from Paul Berlenbach, Ebbets Field. Continued successfully at Ebbets through 1931, retired from boxing.

Returned temporarily to co-promote welter title bout. Ray Robinson defended, 15, against Charley Fusari, 8/9/50, Jersey City. Active again 1961, named promoter for Feature Sports, Inc., sponsors of the third Floyd Patterson–Ingemar Johansson fight. Fugazy was relieved of promotional duties just prior to weigh-in, named a director. (Attorney Thomas A. Bolen, treasurer, was appointed promoter.) Ironic sidelight to his discharge before the Patterson-Johansson fight is that he previously promoted title contests in every division, but the heavyweight.

FUJI, PAUL TAKESHI B. 7/6/40, Honolulu, Hawaii. First fight, Bernie Magallanes, KO 3, 1/26/65, Honolulu. Creditable record through 1967: won Orient junior welter title, Rocky Alarde, KO 3, 9/28/66, Tokyo. (Established residence in Tokyo 1966.) Defended: Carl Penalosa, KO 2, 2/12/67, Tokyo. Won world junior welter title, Sandro Lopopolo, KO 2, 4/30/67, Tokyo. Defended: Willie Quatour, KO 4, 11/16/67, Tokyo. Lost title, Nicholino Loche, KO by 10, 12/12/68, Tokyo. To 1970 undefeated. Retired. Recap: bouts 32, KO 24, decision 4, draw 1, lost decision 1, KO by 2.

FULLMER, DON B. 2/21/39, West Jordan, Utah. 165. Brother of middle champ Gene. First fight, Joe Mortenson, KO 3, 8/2/57, West Jordan. Undefeated first two years. 1959: spotty, won three, lost three. 1960: undefeated, including Virgil Akins, Stefan Redl. Won WBA American middle title, Emile Griffith 12, 8/20/65, Salt Lake City. Defended: Joey Archer 12, 3/18/66, Boston. Lost title, Jose Gonzales 12, 3/18/66, NYC. Undef. to world middle title bout, Nino Benvenuti, lost 15, 12/14/68, San Remo, Italy. Spotty record to 1973, four wins, two draws, five losses. Recap: bouts 72, KO 11, decision 37, draw 5, lost 17, KO by 2.

FULLMER, GENE B. 7/21/31, West Jordan, Utah. 5'8", 145–60. Brother Don also fighter. First fight, Glen Peck, KO 1, 6/9/51, Logan, Utah. 1951–52: KO 14, win 3. 1953 Army. 1954–56: undefeated 20, lost 3. Won world middle title, Ray Robinson, 15, 1/2/57, NYC. Lost title, Robinson, KO by 5, 5/1/57, Chicago. Won vacant NBA middle title, Carmen Basilio, KO 14, 8/28/59, San Francisco. Defended: Spider Webb, won 15, 12/4/59, Logan, Utah; Joey Giardello, draw 15, 4/20/60, Bozeman, Mont.; Basilio, KO 12, 6/29/60, Salt Lake City; Robinson, draw 15, 12/3/60, Los Angeles; Robinson, won 15, 3/4/61, Las Vegas; Florentino Ferdanez, won 15, 8/5/61. Ogden, Utah; Benny Paret, KO 10, 12/9/61, Las Vegas. Lost title, Dick Tiger, 15, 10/23/62, San Francisco. Title, Tiger, draw 15, 2/23/63, Las Vegas. Title, Tiger, KO by 7, 8/28/63, Ibadan, Nigeria. Retired. Rough, clean-living, brawler type in ring. Recap: bouts 62, KO 24, decision 30, draw 3, lost decision 3, KO by 2.

FULTON, FRED B. 4/19/91, Blue Rapids, Kans. D. 7/3/73, Park Rapids, Minn. 6'4½", 215. First fight, Jack Stone, KO 2, 1913. Fought some of best, fell short at showdowns. Undefeated first year. 1914: slowed down, Carl Morris, lost foul, 6; Al Palzer, KO by 4. Undefeated 1915–16, including Jess Willard, exh. 4; Jim Flynn, KO 2. Creditable record to mid-1918, then Jack Dempsey, KO by 1. Harry Wills, KO by 3, 1920–1922 undefeated, 9 straight KO. Wins halted by Billy Miske, KO by 1, 1922, Jack Renault, KO by 9. 1923: Tony Fuente, KO by 1 (California commission banned Fulton for lack of effort). Last recorded fight, George Godfrey, KO by 5, 12/18/25, Minneapolis. Operated resort, northern Minn. Recap: bouts 100, KO 66, decision 6, won foul 2, draw 2, lost decision 1, lost foul 4, KO by 7, ND 11, no contest 1.

GALENTO, TONY (Two Ton Tony) B. 3/10/10, Orange, N.J. Italian. 5′ 9″, 200. Hard hitter, surprisingly fast, carrying an immense stomach. First fight, Babe Farmer, KO 3, 1929. To 1937 mostly creditable. 11 successive KO mid-1937 to heavy title fight, Joe Louis, KO by 4, 6/28/39, NYC. (Knocked Louis down 1st round.) Max Baer, KO by 8, 1940; Buddy Baer, KO by 7, 1941. Last 6: won by KO; last fight, Mike Ryan, KO 4, 11/5/43, Omaha. Tavern in Orange. Recap: bouts 112, KO 58, decision 22, won foul 1, draw 6, lost decision 17, lost foul 2, KO by 6.

GANS, JOE (Joseph Gaines) (Old Master) B. 11/25/74, Phila., Pa. D. 8/16/10, Baltimore, Md. Negro. 5′6¼″, 133. Worked in fishmarket. First fight, Dave Armstrong, KO 12, 1891, Baltimore. To 1899, undefeated 56, then George McFadden, KO by 23, 1899. Undefeated 11; light title Frank Erne, KO by 12 (Gans threw in towel), 3/21/1900, NYC. Impressive record to Terry McGovern, KO by 2, 12/13/1900, Chicago. Undefeated 19, won world light title, Erne, KO 1, 5/12/02, Fort Erie, Ont. Defended: Gus Gardner, KO 5, 9/17/02, Baltimore; Steve Crosby, KO 11, 3/11/03, Hot Springs, Ark; Joe Walcott, draw 20, 9/30/04, San Francisco; Battling Nelson, won foul 42, 9/3/06. Goldfield, Nev.; Jimmy Britt, KO 6, 9/9/07, San Francisco; George Memsic, won 20, 9/27/07, Los Angeles; Rusy Unholz, KO 11, 5/14/08, San Francisco. Lost title, Nelson, KO by 17, 7/4/08, San Francisco. Title, Nelson, KO by 21, 9/9/08, Colma, Calif. Last fight, Jabez White, ND 10, 3/12/09, NYC. Classed with all-time pound-for-pound greats. Hall of Fame 1954. Recap: bouts 156, KO 55, decision 60, won foul 5, draw 10, lost decision 3, KO by 5, ND 18.

GARCIA, CEFERINO B. 1912, Philippines. 5'6", 148. First fight, Ignacio Fernandez, draw 12, Feb., 1927, Manila. No record 1928-31. Slow start, KO by 3, 1932. Spotty 1933. 1934: Peter Jackson, KO by 3; Andy DiVodi, KO 1; Joe Glick, KO 2; Bep Van Klaveren, won, lost. 1935: first series with Barney Ross; lost 2. World welter title, Ross, lost 15, 9/23/37, NYC. World welter title, Henry Armstrong, lost 15, 11/25/38, NYC. 1939: undefeated 11, 9 KO. Won world middle title, Fred Apostoli, KO 7, 10/2/39, NYC. Defended: Glen Lee, KO 13, 12/23/39, Miami; Armstrong, draw 15, 3/1/40, Los Angeles. Lost title, Ken Overlin, 15, 5/23/40, NYC. Last fight, Wild Bill McDowell, lost 15, 1/15/45, Houston. Recap: bouts 116, KO 57, decision 24, draw 9, lost 20, lost foul 11, KO by 5.

GARDNER, GEORGE B. 3/17/77, Lisdoonvarna, County Clare, Ireland. D. 7/8/54, Chicago, Ill. 5'11¾", 165. First fight, J. Young, KO 3, 1897, Manchester, N.H. 1897–1902, outstanding fights: Joe Walcott, lost, won; Jack Root, KO 17; Jack Johnson, lost; Marvin Hart, won 12, 5/13/03, Louisville. Won middle title, Root, KO 12, 7/4/03, Fort Erie, Ont. Lost title, Bob Fitzsimmons, 20, 11/25/03, San Francisco. 1904–08; Marvin Hart, draw; Root, lost, draw. Last 5 fights, lost 4 by KO. Last fight, Tony Ross, KO by 7, 5/18/08, New Castle, Pa. Recap: bouts 65, KO 19, decision 20, won foul 2, draw 10, lost decision 5, lost foul 1, KO by 5, ND 2, no contest 1.

GAULT, PAPPY (Henry Gault) B. 2/9/29, Spartanburg, S.C. 118. Golden Gloves: won Southern, Eastern 112-lb. titles, 1948. First pro bout, Don Smith, won 4, 11/6/48, Lancaster, S.C. To 1950, undefeated: KO 9, won 14. First loss, Frankie Sodana. Won N. American bantam title, Fernando Gagnon, 12, 10/27/52, Quebec. Defended: Gagnon, won 12, 12/1/52, Quebec. 7 KO, 5 won, 1 loss, Robert Cohen, to title defense, Billy Peacock, lost 12, 8/17/53, Brooklyn. World bantam title, Johnny Carruther, lost 12, 11/13/53, Sydney, Australia. To 1959, spotty record including Willie Pep, lost twice; Vic Toweel and Nate Brooks, lost. Last fight, Ross Calvin, lost 10, 12/59, Memphis. Recap: bouts 81, KO 22, decision 32, draw 2, lost 21, KO by 4.

GAVILAN, KID (Gerardo Gonzalez) (The Hawk) B. 1/6/26, Camaguey, Cuba. First fight, Antonio Diaz, won 4, 6/5/43, Havana. 1943 to mid 46, undefeated 26, all Cuba or Mexico. Came to U.S. Sept., 1946, undefeated 29, lost 4. World Welter title, Ray Robinson, lost 15, 7/11/49, NYC. Peaked 1951–53, won American welter title, Johnny Bratton, 15, 5/18/51, NYC. Defended: Billy Graham, won 15, 9/29/51, NYC; Bobby Dykes, won 15, 2/4/52, Miami. (Charles Humez, France, vacated European welter title,

Gavilan universally recognized world champ.) Defended: Gil Turner, KO 11, 7/7/52, Phila.; Graham, won 15, 10/5/52, Havana; Chuck Davey, KO 10, 2/11/53, Chicago; Carmen Basilio, won 15, 9/18/53, Syracuse; Bratton, won 15, 11/13/53, Chicago. Middle title bout, Bobo Olson, lost 15, 4/2/54, Chicago. Lost welter title, Johnny Saxton, 15, 10/20/54, Phila. Mostly losing to retirement, 1958. Last fight, Yama Bahama, lost 10, 6/18/58, Miami Beach. Recap: bouts 144, KO 28, decision 79, draw 6, lost decision 30, no contest 1.

GENARO, FRANKIE (Frank DiGennara) B. 8/26/01, New York, N.Y. Italian. 5'2½", 112. Impressive amateur, won flyweight Olympic title, Antwerp, 1920. First pro, Billy Murphy, won 6, 1920. Creditable record, won USA flyweight title, Pancho Villa, 15, 3/1/23, NYC. Lost, Fidel LaBarba, 10, 8/22/25, Los Angeles. Won NBA world flyweight title, Frenchy Belanger, 10, 2/6/28, Toronto. Defended: Belanger, 10, 6/10/30, Toronto; Midget Wolgast, draw 15, 12/26/30, NYC; Victor Ferrand, draw 15, 3/25/31, Madrid, Spain; Jackie Harmon, KO 6, 7/30/31, Waterbury, Conn.; Valentin Angelman, 15, 10/3/31, Paris. Lost title, Young Perez, KO by 2, 10/27/31, Paris. To 1934, won 3, lost 2, lost foul 1, KO by 1. Last fight, Speedy Dado, KO by 3, 2/13/34, San Jose, Calif. Recap: bouts 128, KO 18, decision 59, won foul 5, draw 9, lost decision 16, lost foul 2, KO by 4, ND 15.

GIAMBRA, JOEY (William Joseph Giambra) B. 6/30/31, Buffalo, N.Y. 5'11", 155. First fight, Lee Phillips, KO 2, 6/28/49, Fort Erie, Ont. Undefeated first 2 years. 1951: won 9, lost 1. 1952: only loss Joey Giardello, won return. Undefeated 1953. Army 1954. 1955–60, won 25, including Giardello (3rd fight), Tiger Jones twice, Rocky Castellani, Gil Turner, Al Andrews twice; lost 2, Bobo Olson, Rory Calhoun; returns, Calhoun draw, won. WBA junior middle title, Denny Moyer, lost 15, 10/20/62, Portland. Last fight, Joe DeNucci, lost 10, 4/6/63, Boston. Recap: bouts 77, KO 31, decision 34, draw 3, lost decision 9.

GIARDELLO, JOEY (Carmine Orlando Tilelli) B. 7/16/30, Brooklyn, N.Y. 5'10". First fight, Johnny Noel, KO 2, 1948, Trenton. Thru 1952, impressive record. Billy Graham, 12/19/52, NYC, produced disputed decision. State Supreme Court finally ruled Giardello won 10. To 1960: won from Tiger Jones, Charlie Cotton, Bobby Boyd, Wilf Greaves, Joey Giambra, Chico Vejar, First NBA middle title chance, Dick Tiger, draw 15, 4/20/60, Bozeman, Mont. Ray Robinson won 15, 1963. Won world middle title, Tiger, 15, 12/7/63, Atlantic City. Defended: Rubin Carter, won 15, 12/14/64, Phila. Lost title, Tiger 15, 10/21/65, NYC. Last fight, Jack Rogers, won 10,

11/8/67. Recap: bouts 133, KO 32, decision 69, draw 7, lost decision 21, KO by 4.

GIBBONS, MIKE (The St. Paul Phantom) B. 7/20/87, St. Paul, Minn. D. 8/31/56, St. Paul, Minn. Irish. 5'10", 148. First fight, Roy Moore, KO 3, 1/11/08, St. Paul. Era ND fights. Undefeated to Jimmy Clabby, 1910. Ring cleverness kept him topnotcher in welters, middles. To 1921 undefeated: Clabby, ND 3 fights; Eddie McGoorty, ND 2, KO 5; Harry Greb, ND 2; Al McCoy, ND 1; Leo Houck, ND 1; Packey McFarland, ND 1; Jack Dillon, ND 2; Mike O'Dowd, ND 2, lost 1. Last fight, Danny Fagan, KO 2, 5/16/22, Winnipeg. Never title fight. Hall of Fame 1958. Successful St. Paul businessman. Recap: bouts 127, KO 38, decision 23, won foul 1, draw 4, lost decision 3, ND 58.

GIBBONS, TOMMY B. 3/22/91, St. Paul, Minn. D. 11/19/60, St. Paul, Minn. Irish. 5'9½", 172. First fight, Oscar Kelly, KO 5, 9/5/11, Minneapolis. Like brother Mike, a scientific fighter starting as a middle, graduating to a heavy. Peaked career going 15 rounds with Jack Dempsey, 7/4/23, in a fight that broke Shelby, Montana. Fighting during ND days, undefeated 12 years. Billy Miske, ND 3, won 1, lost foul 1; George Chip, ND twice, won 2; Harry Greb, ND 3, lost 1. After Dempsey, undefeated to last fight, Gene Tunney, KO by 12, 6/5/25, NYC. Hall of Fame 1963. Business, St. Paul. Cass County (Minn.) Sheriff 24 years. Recap: bouts 106, KO 47, decision 10, draw 1, lost decision 2, lost foul 1, ND 43, no contest 1.

GIBSON, WILLIAM (Billy) B. 1876. D. 7/21/47, New York, N.Y. Promoter. Famed columnist Westbrook Pegler wrote in 1930, "Uncle Will Gibson's career is book material, but I don't think it will ever be written because he turned down a good price for it years back . . . a recitation of his memories might tend to embarrass a number of his fellow citizens. . . ."

A sensitive man and one who respected others' reactions, Gibson knew boxing's brighter and darker corners, managing two great champions, Benny Leonard and Gene Tunney, and later experiencing a mental breakdown.

Leonard has been described as the "portliest lightweight to ever hold the title," but Gibson's witchcraft by weigh-in hour kept Leonard in business.

Tunney was experiencing problems when "Uncle Will" took over the fighter's affairs until Tunney's title-winning event with Jack Dempsey. But Tunney demoted Gibson after the Dempsey upset, a climax to a running personality conflict.

A prominent Midwest sports writer described Gibson as a "grand fellow personally and generous to a fault, one of the most beloved men ever associated with boxing, just about in a class by himself.

"The fights he staged first at the Pioneer Club in N.Y. and later at Madison Square Garden were among the best ever held in the big city. Gibson had an uncanny sense of knowing bouts that would appeal to the public, and he knew how to match fighters that would assure his clientele of rousing battles."

Gibson's earliest, some say his happiest, days reflect to the years when he owned the Fairmont A.C. and boxing was outlawed in N.Y. Police invaded his weekly exhibits, arresting him as club president. Attorney fees and court costs added up until the judge, regarding him as a steady customer, scaled the fines to a nominal figure.

Gibson recalled, "It got so that I could run a monthly bill, send my check regularly at the first of the month for all four fines." By that time the judge was a member of the club.

Billy's later years weren't that happy. His wife died in 1928, grief eventually driving him to a mental condition, general paresis, hospitalized for two years. He returned to associate with boxing, but his early-day enthusiasm had diminished.

GLOVER, MIKE (Michael J. Cavanaugh) B. 12/18/90, Lawrence, Mass. Irish. 5'9", 145. First fight, Red Shaw, KO 2, 1908. Undefeated to 1915, NDs, Battling Levinsky, twice; Kid Graves, twice; Jack Dillon; Harlem Tommy Murphy; Jeff Smith; won foul, Leach Cross Series: Ted Kid Lewis, won, lost twice; Jack Britton, ND twice, lost. Last fight, Lewis, lost 12, 6/13/16, Boston. Recap: bouts 91, KO 18, decision 13, won foul 1, draw 2, lost decision 4, ND 53.

GOLDMAN, CHARLEY B. 12/21/88, Russia. D. 11/15/68, New York, N.Y. 5'5", 115. Tireless campaigner, many fights unrecorded. First recorded fight, Young Gardner, KO by 42, 6/1/04, NYC. Undefeated 1905–06. 1907: Billy Allen, KO by 4; return, ND 10. 1908: undefeated, 16 fights. 1909–11: only loss, Willie Jones; ND Knockout Brown, Harry Forbes, Frankie Burns twice. 1912–14: Johnny Coulon, ND twice; undefeated 1913; only losses, 1914, Jones, 10, Al Shubert, KO by 6. Last fight, Mike Carroll, KO 2, 1914, NYC. Recap: bouts 137, KO 20, decision 16, draw 10, lost decision 4, KO by 2, ND 84.

GOLDSTEIN, ABE B. 1900, New York, N.Y. Jewish. 5'5", 118. First fight, Georgie Lewis, KO 8, 6/30/16, NYC. 1916–17: undefeated 6, 1 setback—

Patsy Finnegan, KO by 6. 1919–20: undefeated 45. Johnny Buff, KO by 2; Joe Lynch, KO by 11, 1921. Undefeated 1923. Won world bantam title, Joe Lynch, 15, 3/21/24, NYC. Defended: Charley Ledoux, won 15, 6/16/27, NYC; Tommy Ryan, won 15, 9/8/24, NYC. Lost title, Eddie Martin 15, 12/19/24, NYC. To 1927, scrambled record. Last fight, Ignacio Fernandez, KO by 7, 6/24/27, Chicago. Army. Recap: bouts 129, KO 30, decision 59, draw 5, lost decision 9, KO by 4, ND. 22.

GOLDSTEIN, RUBY (Rueben Goldstein) (Jewel of the Ghetto) B. 10/7/07, New York, N.Y. Jewish. 5'5", 130–135. Lightweight. Outstanding amateur. First pro, Al Vano, KO 2, 1/1/25, NYC. Undefeated first year, 9 KO, 8 won. Undefeated, 1926 to Ace Hudkins, KO by 4, Billy Alger, KO by 10. 1927: 5 KO; 1 win; Sid Terris, KO by 1. Undefeated 1928. 6 straight KO, 1929, to Jimmy McLarnin, KO by 2. Undefeated 1930. To 1937: 8 KO, 3 won, Jay Macedon, KO by 7, 1931 (inactive 1934–36). Last fight, Kid Bon Bon, won 6, 8/10/37, Elizabeth, N.J. Unique record: never lost decision, lost or won foul, ND, no contest. Enlisted Army 1942, licensed N.Y. referee 1943. Book, *Third Man in Ring,* 1959. Writes "Inside the Ropes" column, *Ring* magazine. Recap: bouts 56, KO 34, decision 16, KO by 6.

GOMES, HAROLD B. 8/22/33, Providence, R.I. 5'8", 118. First fight, Billy Pierre, KO 2, 9/17/51, Providence. Undefeated three years, won New England feather title, Johnny O'Brien 12, 3/15/54, Boston. Tommy Tibbs series: won three, lost one, KO by two. Won revived NBA junior light title, Paul Jorgensen, 15, 7/20/59, Providence. Lost title, Flash Elorde, KO by 7, 3/16/60, Manila. Title, Elorde, KO by 1, 8/17/60, San Francisco. Inactive 1961. Return 1962: 4 wins, 1 loss; 1963: 3 KO by. Last fight, Dave Coventry, KO by 1, 10/30/63, London. Retired. Recap: bouts 59, KO 24, decision 25, draw 3, KO by 7.

GONZALEZ, JOSE B. 5/4/40, Arroyo, Puerto Rico. Middle. First fight, Jimmy Lynn, won 4, 4/23/59, NYC. Impressive early career, including wins over Isaac Logart, Charley Scott. Series, 1959–60: Julie Jamison, won twice, KO by one. 1961–65: Joey Archer, won, lost; Joe DeNucci, won; Florentino Fernandez, KO 8, won 10; Emile Griffith, lost; Dick Tiger, KO by 6. Won WBA world middle title, Don Fullmer, 12, 3/18/66, NYC. Defended: Ferd Hernandez, draw 12, San Juan; return, nontitle, lost disq. 9, 1967. Spotty record to 1973: Benny Brisco, lost, KO by 5; Luis Rodriguez, won, lost; Pedro Miranda, KO by 9; KO 4, won 5, lost 5, KO by 2. Recap: bouts 56, KO 12, decision 27, draw 2, lost 9, lost disq. 1, KO by 5.

GONZALEZ, RODOLFO B. Long Beach, Calif. First fight, Bob Valdez, KO by 9, 5/20/66, San Bernardino, Calif. Spotty first year. 1967–69: Undefeated, 8 straight KO. To 1972 only loss, Antonio Cervantes, KO by 8, 1970. Won WBC lightweight title, Chango Carmona, KO 13, 11/10/72, Los Angeles. Recap: bouts 28, KO 17, decision 8, lost 1, KO by 2.

GOODRICH, JIMMY (James E. Moran) B. 7/30/1900, Scranton, Pa. Irish-German, 5'8", 133. First recorded, Chubby Brown, won 12, 1921. To 1925: mediocre. (Benny Leonard retired, vacated lightweight title.) Won NY elimination for light title, Stan Loayza, KO 2, 7/13/25, Long Island City, NY. Lost title, Rocky Kansas, 15, 12/7/25, Buffalo. Rocky record to 1930, retired. Lost 7 of last 9 fights, 1930. Last fight, Pete Suskey, lost 10, 9/4/30, Scranton. Recap: bouts 110, KO 6, decision 36, won foul 2, draw 15, lost decision 32, KO by 1, ND 18.

GRAHAM, BUSHY (Angelo Geraci) B. 6/18/03, Italy. 5'5", 125. First fight, Pete Harmon, KO 6, 1921. Undefeated 1923, lost Frankie Genaro. 1924: lost, Johnny Curtin. Undefeated 1925, including win, ND, Bud Taylor. Lost 1926–27 to Young Montreal, Tony Canzoneri, Charley Rosenberg; undefeated in others. Claimed vacant N.Y. bantam title after beating Cpl. Izzy Schwartz, 15, 5/23/28, NYC. Gave up title 1929, weight problem. Creditable record (retired 1932–35) to 1936. Last fight, Enrico Venturi, lost 8, 11/27/36, NYC. Recap: bouts 127, KO 37, decision 63, won foul 1, draw 6, lost decision 11, lost foul 1, KO by 2, ND 6.

GRAVES, KID (Perry Ivia Graves) B. 7/11/92, Plattsmouth, Nebr. 5'7", 142. First fight, George Williams, KO 4, 1906. Impressive record to 1921, undefeated 9 of 12 years, 62 NDs, 5 losses, decision 3, lost foul. Claimed vacant welter title after Johnny Kid Alberts, KO 2, 7/18/14, NYC, not officially recognized. Won from Joe Grim, Harry Greb 2 (Greb broke arm); draw, Johnny Coulon; NDs, Jack Britton, Mike Gibbons, Mike Glover, Young Erne, Soldier Bartfield, Ted Kid Lewis, Mike O'Dowd. Inactive 1917–19. Last fight, Young Goldie, draw 10, 12/15/21, Omaha. Returned to Plattsmouth, elected justice of peace. Recap: bouts 157, KO 35, decision 24, won foul 3, draw 28, lost decision 3, lost foul 1, KO by 1, ND 62.

GRAY, CLYDE B. 3/10/47, Toronto, Ontario. 145 lbs. Regarded as one of Canada's most promising pugilists. First fight, Mike Belski, KO 2, 3/13/68, McKeesport, Pa. Undefeated first two years—10 KO in 17 bouts. First loss, Eddie Perkins, 10, 1970, Chicago. Six KO, 1 decision to Canadian welter title, Vic Doucette, KO 2, 8/19/71, Toronto. Nontitle upset, Armando

Muntz, KO by 9, 11/19/71, Long Beach, Calif. Undefeated 1972 to mid–1973 (5 KO, 4 dec.). Recap: bouts 41, KO 24, decision 13, won disq. 1, draw 1, lost 1, KO by 1.

GRAZIANO, ROCKY (Rocco Barbella) B. 1/1/22, New York, N.Y. Italian. 5'7", 165. First fight, Curtis Hightower, KO 2, 3/31/42, Brooklyn. 5 KO, 2 draw, 1 loss. Army. 1943: 10 KO, 5 win, 2 lost, mediocre opposition. 1945: healthy year, undefeated, 6 KO, including Al Davis, Freddie Cochrane twice. 1946: Marty Servo, KO 2. World middle title, Tony Zale, KO by 6, 9/27/46, NYC. Won title, Zale, KO 6, 7/16/47, Chicago. Lost title, Zale, KO by 3, 6/10/48, Newark. (Graziano-Zale, one of boxing's classic series.) 1949–52 undefeated in 21. Title, Ray Robinson, KO by 3, 4/16/52, Chicago. Last fight, Chuck Davey, lost 10, 9/17/52, Chicago. Retired. TV, movie character actor, authored *Somebody up There Likes Me* (starring Paul Newman). Emerged from a rugged childhood. Recap: bouts 83, KO 52, decision 14, won foul 1, draw 6, lost decision 7, KO by 3.

GREB, HARRY (Edward Henry Greb) (The Human Windmill) B. 6/6/94, Pittsburgh, Pa. D. 10/22/26, New York, N.Y., eye operation. Irish-German. 5'8", 158. Started fighting 1913. Fought in middle, lightheavy, heavyweight divisions. Won world middle title, Johnny Wilson, 15, 8/31/23, NYC. Defended: Bryan Downey, won 10; Wilson, won 15; Fay Kaiser, KO 12; Ted Moore, won 15; Mickey Walker, won 15; Tony Marullo, won 15. Lost title, Tiger Flowers, decision 15, 2/26/26, New York. Title, Flowers, lost 15, 8/19/26, New York (last fight). Won American light heavyweight title, Gene Tunney, 5/23/22, NYC. Fought Tunney 5 times, losing 2, winning 1, 2 no decisions (reporters conceded fights to Tunney). Lost title to Tunney, 2/23/23. Greb, blind in one eye, one of ring's most fearless competitors. Only fighter to defeat Gene Tunney. An 8–5 underdog, conceding over 20 pounds and 5 inches, Greb painted the future heavy champ blood red. Tunney later credited Greb for rise from tyro to champ. Hall of Fame 1955. Recap: bouts 291, KO 46, decision 65, won foul 1, draw 3, lost decision 7, KO by 2, ND 166, no contest 1.

GRIFFITH, EMILE (Emile Alphonse Griffith) B. 2/3/38, Virgin Islands. Amateur: 1958, NY and Inter-City Golden Gloves welter titles. First pro, Joe Parnham, won 4, 6/2/58, NYC. Impressive to welter title, which he won from Benny Paret, KO 13, 4/1/61, Miami Beach. Defended: Gaspar Ortega, KO 12, 6/3/61, Los Angeles. Lost title, Paret, 15, 9/30/61, NYC. Regained title, Paret, KO 12, 3/24/62. NYC (Paret died, fight injuries.) Defended: Ralph Dupas, won 15, 7/13/62, Las Vegas; Jorge Fernandez, KO 9, 12/8/62, Las Vegas. Lost welter title, Luis Rodriguez, 15, 3/21/63, Los

Angeles; regained title, Rodriguez, 15, 6/8/63, NYC. Defended: Rodriguez, won 15, 6/12/64, Las Vegas; Brian Curvis, won 15, 9/22/64, London; Jose Stable, won 15, 3/30/65, NYC; Manuel Gonzales, 15, 12/10/65, NYC. Vacant WBA middle title, Don Fullmer, lost 12, 8/20/65, Salt Lake City. Won world middle title, Dick Tiger, 15, 4/25/66, NYC. Defended: Joey Archer won 15, 7/13/66, NYC. Lost middle title, Nino Benvenuti, 15, 4/17/67, NYC. Regained title, Benvenuti 15, 9/29/67, NYC. Lost title, Benvenuti, 15, 3/4/68. NYC. Lost welter title, Jose Napoles, 15, 10/18/69, Los Angeles. Undefeated to middle title fight with Carlos Monzon, KO by 14, 9/25/71, Buenos Aires. Title, Monzon, lost 15, 6/2/73, Monte Carlo. Recap: bouts 84, KO 21, decision 50, lost decision 11, KO by 2.

GRIFFO, YOUNG (Albert Griffiths) B. 3/31/71, Miller's Point, Sydney, Australia. D. 12/7/27, New York, N.Y. 5'4", 125. First fight, Bob O'Neil, won 15, bare knuckles, no recorded date. First recorded fight, Abe Willis, draw 20, 7/27/89, Sydney. Eight years undefeated except Jack McAuliffe, lost 10, 1894, never clear title chance, claimed feather title, not generally recognized. Several draws: Kid Lavigne, twice; George Dixon, twice; Joe Gans, twice; Ike Weir, won. 1896: Billy McCarthy, KO 20 (McCarthy died following day of fight injuries). 1897: injured in accident day of bout with Tom Tracey, St. Louis. Griffo insisted on fighting, but pain forced him to retire after first round. Thru 1903: Gans, KO by 8, 1900, rest undefeated. 1904: Tommy White, KO by 1. Retired 7 years. Returned, 1 fight, Mike Leonard, ND 6, 5/10/11, NYC. Recap: bouts 107, KO 5, decision 42, won foul 2, draw 37 lost decision 6, KO by 3, ND 12.

GRIM, JOE (Saverio Giannone) (The Iron Man) B. 3/14/81, Monetello, Avellino, Italy. D. 8/19/39, State Hospital, Byberry, Pa. 130–165 lbs. Un-recorded, some 300 fights. Often floored, but only 3 KO by (Sailor Burke, Sam McVey, Young Zeringer). Possibly boxing's most durable man. Color-ful. Met top-flight. 1903: Phila. Jack O'Brien, ND; Peter Maher, lost foul; Joe Walcott, Bob Fitzsimmons Joe Gans, ND. 1904: Gans, Jim Jeffords, lost; Peter Maher, ND; Zeringer, KO by 3. 1905: Dixie Kid, lost; Johnson, ND. After spotty 1908 went to Fiji Islands, vaudeville, fought Malley Jackson for Tasmania title, lost 20. To West Indies, vaudeville; Italy, London exhibitions. Sam McVey, KO by 12, Paris, 1910. To U.S., Jack Fitzgerald, lost 12, 1910. Organized Joe Grim A.C., which failed, lost 5 fights. Guard Pa. shipyard. Continued boxing. ND undated fights. Recap (recorded): bouts 134, KO 2, decision 8, draw 8, lost decision 28, lost foul 2, KO by 4, ND 82.

HALIMI, ALPHONSE B. 2/18/32, Constantine, Algeria. French-Algerian. Outstanding amateur, 189 bouts, held French title 1953–55. First pro bout, Georges Lefage, KO 1, 9/26/55, Paris. Undefeated, won world bantam title third year as pro, beating Mario D'Agata, 15, 4/1/57, Paris. (KO by 9 next fight, Jimmy Carson, London, nontitle.) Defended: Raton Marcias, won 15, 11/6/57, Los Angeles. Lost title, Joe Becerra, KO by 8, 7/8/59, Los Angeles. Return title bout, Becerra, KO by 9, 2/4/60, Los Angeles. Won European version of world title, Freddie Gilroy, 15, 10/25/60, London. Lost title, Johnny Caldwell, 15, 5/30/61, London. Return, Caldwell, lost 15, 10/31/61, London. Regained European title, Piero Rollo, 15, 6/26/62, Tel Aviv. Lost title, Rollo 15, Cagliari, Italy. Last fight, Victor Cano, 10, 11/27/64, Bogota. Recap: bouts 50, KO 21, decision 19, won foul 1, draw 1, lost decision 5, KO by 3.

HARADA, FIGHTING (Masahimo) B. 4/5/43, Japan. First fight, Mausi, KO 4, 2/21/60, Tokyo. 1 defeat to world flyweight title, which he won from Pone Kingpetch, KO 11, 10/10/62, Tokyo. Lost title, Kingpetch, 15, 1/12/63, Bangkok, Thailand. 1965, joined bantams. Won world bantam title, Eder Jofre, 15, 5/17/65, Nagoya, Japan. Defended: Alan Rudkin, won 15, 11/30/65, Tokyo; Jofre, won 15, 6/1/66, Tokyo; Joe Medel, won 15, 1/3/37, Nagoya; Bernardo Caraballo, won 15, 7/4/67, Tokyo. Lost title, Lionel Rose, 15, 2/26/68, Tokyo. Feather title bout, John Famechon, lost 15, 7/28/69, Tokyo. Feather title, Famechon, KO by 14, 1/6/70, Tokyo. Retired. Recap.: bouts 63, KO 22, decision 33, draw 1, lost decision 5, KO by 2.

HARRIS, HARRY (Human Scissors) B. 11/18/80, Chicago, Ill. D. 6/5/59, New York, N.Y. 5'7½", 115. First fight, Dennis Mahoney, won 5, 4/5/96, Chicago. To 1901, 44 fights, 2 lost. Won vacant world bantam title, Pedlar Palmer, 15, 3/18/01, London. Vacated title to fight as feather. Undefeated to 1907. Last fight, Harlem Tommy Murphy, won foul 8, 6/3/07, NYC. Recap: bouts 54, KO 15, draw 24, won foul 1, draw 7, lost decision 2, ND 5.

HART, MARVIN B. 9/16/76, Jefferson County, Ky. D. 9/17/31, Fern Creek, Ky. 5'11¼", 190. First fight, Bill Schiller, KO 7, 12/12/99, Louisville. 13 KO, won foul 1, until Billy Hanrahan, KO by 1, 12/17/01, Louisville. 1902–04: 17 fights; lost, Jack Root; draws, Gus Ruhlin, Georgie Gardner, John Willie; ND, Kid Carter, Jack O'Brien (2), Gus Ruhlin, Joe Choynski. Jack Johnson, won 20, 3/28/05, San Francisco. Root, KO 12, 7/3/05, Reno (James J. Jeffries declared winner of Hart-Root fight champion of his vacated title). Pat Callahan, KO 2, 1/15/06, Butte, Mont. Lost title, Tommy Burns, decision 20, 2/23/06, Los Angeles. Last fight, Carl Morris, KO by 3, 12/20/10, Sapulpa, Okla. Recap: bouts 48, KO 20, decision 4, won foul 5, draw 4, lost decision 3, KO by 4, ND 8.

HAWKINS, DAL B. May 1871, San Francisco, Calif. 5'6", 122. Bare knuckle 1887–88. Won feather title, Fred Bogan, 6/3/89, San Francisco. After fighting 75 rounds, fight postponed to next day, Hawkins KO 15; first feather fight, Queensberry rules, 2 oz. gloves. Outgrew division, vacated title, 1889. Mostly successful as light. To 1893, undefeated. Joe Gans, won 15, 1896. Gans, KO by twice, 1900. Last year, won 1, draw 1, KO by 3. Last fight, Jack Clifford, KO by 7, 9/18/02, Butte, Mont. Recap: bouts 54, KO 16, decision 17, won foul 1, draw 8, lost decision 3, lost foul 1, KO by 7, ND 1.

HEENEY, TOM (Hard Rock from Down Under) B. 5/18/98, Gisborne, New Zealand. 5'10½", 200. First fight, Bill Bartlett, KO 9, 1921. Seven years active in New Zealand, Australia, England, South Africa, Ireland. Creditable record. KO, won, Johnny Squires; Bartley Madden, won; Phil Scott, lost twice. To U.S. 1927, first fight, Charley Anderson, KO 9. Through 1928, fought name fighters, Paulino Uzcudun, won, lost; beat Jack DeMave, Bud Gorman, Johnny Risko, Jack Delaney; Jim Maloney, KO 1, Jack Sharkey, draw. Heavy title, Gene Tunney, KO by 11, 7/26/28, NYC. To 1933 downhill record, KOs by Vittorio Campolo, Tuffy Griffith, Max Baer, Charley Retzlaff; lost 8, draw 3, won 5, ND 1. Last fight, Stanley Poreda, KO by 10, 3/27/33, NYC. Retired, became American citizen. U.S. Navy, World War II. Operated Miami Beach tavern. Recap: bouts 70, KO 15, decision 19, won foul 5, draw 7, lost decision 15, lost foul 1, KO by 6, ND 1, NC 1.

HERMAN, PETE (Peter Gulotta) B. 2/12/96, New Orleans, La. D. 4/15/73, New Orleans, La. Italian. 5'2", 116. First recorded fight, Eddie Coulon, draw 10, 1912. First 4 years mostly successful. World bantam title, Kid Williams, draw 20, 2/7/16, New Orleans. Undefeated to 1917. Title, Williams, won 20, 1/9/17, New Orleans. Defended: Frankie Burns, won 20, 11/5/17, New Orleans. Didn't defend for 3 years. Lost title, Joe Lynch, 15, 12/22/20, NYC. Regained title, Lynch, 15, 7/25/21, Brooklyn. Lost title, Johnny Buff, 15, 9/23/21, NYC. Last fight, Roy Moore, won 10, 4/24/22, Boston. Blindness prompted retirement. Hall of Fame 1960. Recap: bouts 148, KO 19, decision 52, draw 8, lost decision 10, lost foul 1, KO by 1, ND 57.

HERNANDEZ, CARLOS B. 4/21/40, Venezuela. First fight, Felix Gil, KO 3., 1/25/59, Caracas. Undefeated 1959–60. Won Venezuela light title, Vincente Rivas, KO 8. 7/5/60, Caracas. To 1965, creditable record including Kenny Lane, draw, lost, KO 2. Won world junior welter title, Eddie Perkins, 15, 1/18/65, Caracas. Defended: Mario Rossito, KO 4, 5/15/65, Maracaibo; Percy Hayles, KO 3, 7/10/65, Kingston, Jamaica. Lost title, Sandro Lopopolo, 15, 4/29/66, Rome. Impressive comeback, 8 straight KO before title match with Nicolino Loche, lost 15, 5/4/69, Buenos Aires. Last fight, Ken Buchanan, KO by 8, 5/11/71, London. Retired 5/13/71. Recap: bouts 71, KO 39, decision 17, draw 4, lost decision 6, KO by 5.

HERRERA, AURELIO B. 6/17/76, San Jose, Calif. D. 4/12/27, San Francisco, Calif. Mexican-American. 5'5", 130. Regarded brilliant prospect. Despite outstanding record, seldom a title chance. First fight, Jack McCormack, KO 4, 6/7/98, Bakersfield, Calif. Undefeated first three years; 1899, 8 fights, 8 KO. First setback, title, Terry McGovern, KO by 5, 1901. 1902: 8 KO, 1 dec., only loss, Abe Attell, 15. 1903: 11 straight KO, including Kid Broad, 4, Jack Downey, 1; only loss, Jack Cordell. 1904, creditable: lost, Battling Nelson, 20; Louis Long, KO by 4, won return. Undefeated 1905. Young Corbett, KO 5, 1906. Inactive 1907. Returned 1908, lost Willie Fitzgerald 12. Series: Charley Neary, KO one, draw three, KO by one. Last fight, Dick Hyland, KO by 6 (broke hand), 9/23/09, Bakersfield. Recap: bouts 81, KO 47, decision 6, draw 15, lost decision 7, KO by 4, ND 2.

HERRERA, RAFAEL (Raul) B. Mexico City, Mexico. 118. First fight, Peleas Ganades, won 4, 1/64, Mexico City. Undefeated first three years: 5 KO, 8 dec., 1 draw. 1967–69 spotty. Undefeated 1970. Won North American bantam title, Chuchu Castillo, 12, 8/23/71, Los Angeles. Won WBC world bantam title, Rodolfo Martinez, KO 12, 5/73, Monterrey, Mex. Recap: bouts 47, KO 14, decision 19, draw 3, lost decision 6, KO by 5.

HOSTAK, AL B. 1/7/16, Seattle, Wash. Czechoslovakian. First fight, Jimmie Smith, KO 3, 1934. To 1938 undefeated in 55. 1937–38: 14 straight KO. Won NBA middle title, Freddie Steele, KO 1, 7/26/38, Seattle. Lost title, Solly Krieger, 15, 11/1/38, Seattle. Regained title, Krieger, KO 4, 6/27/39, Seattle. Defended: Erick Seelig, KO 3, 12/11/39, Cleveland. Lost title, Tony Zale, KO by 13, 7/19/40, Seattle. Title, Zale, KO by 2, 5/28/41, Chicago. Army 1942. Last fight, Jack Snapp, KO 9, 1/7/49, Seattle. Recap: bout 83, KO 47, decision 21, draw 6, lost 6, KO by 3.

HOUCK, LEO (Leo Florian Hauck) B. 11/4/88, Lancaster, Pa. D. 1/21/50, Lancaster, Pa. German. First fight, Carl Kreckel, draw 4, 9/30/02, Lancaster. One of most versatile, from bantam through light heavy. Jack Britton, won twice; Young Erne, ND three; Kid Broad, won three. Lost foul, Frank Perron. Outstanding to 1926, never title fight. Against heavier, Harry Greb, lost, ND twice; Frank Klaus, ND, lost; George Chip, ND; Battling Levinsky, won, ND two, Gene Tunney, ND two. Last fight, Jack Brady, KO 3, 7/4/26, Lancaster. Coached boxing at Penn State. Hall of Fame 1969. Recap: bouts 212, KO 21, decision 137, draw 11, lost decision 8, lost foul 1, KO by 1, ND 34.

HUDKINS, ACE (Nebraska Wildcat) B. 8/30/05, Valparaiso, Nebr. D. 4/17/73, Los Angeles, Calif. Scotch-Irish. 5'8", 160. First fight, Ever Hammer, KO 6, 1923. Rugged, colorful, faced all weights. Outstanding. Phil McGraw, won twice, 1926; Lew Tendler, won twice, 1927, 1928. World middle title, Mickey Walker, lost, 6/21/28, Chicago. Title, Walker, lost 10, 10/28/29, Los Angeles. 1930–32: 8 fights, Max Rosenbloom, Dave Shade, lost; King Levinsky, won; Jack McVey, no contest, Won California heavy title, Dynamite Jackson, 10, 9/15/31, Los Angeles. Last fight, Lee Ramage, lost 10, 2/23/32, Los Angeles. Army. After World War II operated ranch in Calif. that supplied horses for Western movies. Recap: bouts 76, KO 18, decision 31, won foul 1, draw 5, lost decision 10, lost foul 2, KO by 1, ND 7, no contest 1.

HUMEZ, CHARLES B. 5/19/27, Mirecourt, France. 155 lbs. In France, grouped with such greats as Georges Carpentier, Marcel Cerdan, Marcel Thil. Amateur, 300 fights, won 294, draw 3, lost 3. Pro, as European welter, later middle champ, blocked international recognition of Johnny Bratton and Kid Gavilan as world welter champs until he retired from welter class. Only 3 U.S. appearances. Amateur, 1948, defeated Dave Coleman in International Golden Gloves, Chicago, to give Europe 4–4 tie. Lost 2, 1956, Gene Fullmer, Tiger Jones. Won Jones return, same year, Paris. First pro, Hazil Henin, KO 3, 9/26/48. All 5 first-year fights, KO wins. 1949: 11 KO, 9 dec.; only loss,

Stan Raypens, 10. Won French welter title, Omar Kouidri, 15, 2/4/50, Algiers. Defended: Pierre Langlois, 15, 4/24/50, Paris. Lost title, Titi Clavel, foul 7, 5/26/50, Lens, France. Undefeated to regain title, Gilbert Lavoine, 15, 2/26/51, Paris. Won European welter title, Eddie Thomas, 15, 6/13/51, Porthcawl, Wales. Defended European title, Emile Delmine, KO 7, 9/24/51, Paris. Undefeated to European middle title, Randy Turpin, lost 15, 6/9/53, London. Won vacant French middle title, Claude Milazzo, 15, 2/24/51, Paris. Won European middle title, Tiberto Mitri, KO 3, 11/13/54, Milan. Undefeated to U.S. visit, 1956: lost, Gene Fullmer, Tiger Jones; won Jones return, Paris, 1956. Defended European middle title: Franco Festucki, 12, 10/13/56, Milan. Undefeated to last fight, lost European middle title, Gustav Scholz, KO by 12, 10/4/53, Milan. Recap: bouts 99, KO 47, decision 43, won disq. 1, lost decision 4, lost foul 1, KO by 2, ND 1.

HURLEY, JACK   B. 12/9/97, Moorhead, Minn. D. 11/16/72, Seattle, Wash. Promoter-manager. The "Old Professor" stalked through boxing's jungles for some 50 years as a loner. Hurley, who said he never counted the number of fighters he handled or the number of fights he promoted, refused to affiliate himself or his charges with any syndicate, corporation or individual ruling boxing with an iron glove. Jack and his charges survived many monopolies and threats, moving in boxing's upper crust, including championship events. His prize package, Billy Petrolle, the "Fargo Express," fought seven champions and former champions, including return bouts with Jimmy McLarnin, Tony Canzoneri and Barney Ross. There was always a stall in Hurley's stable for a heavy whom he ballyhooed to banner recognition. Charley Retzlaff, a hard-punching North Dakota farmer, remained a factor on the division's fringe for years until Joe Louis took him out in one round. That was Joe's last fight prior to his ill-fated engagement with Max Schmeling (KO by 12, 6/19/36, NYC).

Hurley had convinced some sideliners that his unbeaten Harry Matthews could derail blockbusting Rocky Marciano as the "Rock" headed for his title showdown with Jersey Joe Walcott. In his last fight prior to gaining the title, Marciano leveled the Hurley hopeful in two (7/28/52, NYC).

Boone Kirkhorn was Jack's last threat to scramble the heavy picture, and it's fair to assume that the Old Professor entertained some faith in Kirkhorn. Paired with George Foreman, who was on the verge of winning the heavy title, Boone was psyched with a deliberate push that spilled him in the first round. Hurley's fighter never regained his poise, was counted out in second (10/12/70, NYC). Hurley threw up his hands, publicly disowned Kirkhorn.

Hurley's promoting ventures included Chicago and the Dakotas, but it was Seattle that provided the site for a heavy championship event without precedent, and chances are it will never be duplicated. The spectacle featured Floyd Patterson defending his heavy championship against world Olympic champion Pete Rademacher, who had never fought a pro bout.

The announcement was accorded mixed reaction. Many old timers regarded it with disgust, claimed it shouldn't be sanctioned. Many sports experts went along with that thinking, but some were intrigued with the possibilities. A pro argument was that Rademacher had more to offer fistically than much of the opposition that was provided champions and leading contenders for warmups. One group that found it interesting was the general public, which provided a lively advance sale.

Hurley's long-time disdain for TV was evident as he banned both TV and radio from the fight. His oft-quoted remark: "Boxing is ruined by TV and 'amachoors'."

The event was a financial success, drawing $243,000, and fistically adequate, the amateur champ providing a creditable performance before being stopped in the sixth.

Hurley, plagued by ulcers for years, was 74 when he died. He was buried in Fargo, N.Dak.

HUTCHINS, LEN B. 1950, Detroit, Mich. 175. Outstanding amateur. Michigan Golden Gloves champ 1966–68. National Golden Gloves, AAU champ 1968. Regarded outstanding light heavy prospect, he signed three-year contract with Cloverlay Syndicate. First pro fight, Lee Phillips, won 6, 12/10/68, Phila. First loss, Richie Kates, 1971. Split with Cloverlay, signed with Andy (Pop) Foster; first fight, Jim Parks, KO 9, 1972. To Albuquerque, work with light heavy champ Bob Foster for Mike Quarry fight. 1972: Harold Carter, KO 4; Eddie Jones (No. 5 contender), won 10. 1973: Vincente Rondon, won 10. Recap: bouts 19, KO 4, decision 13, draw 1, lost 1.

INDRISSANO, JOHNNY B. 11/1/06, Boston, Mass. Italian. 5'9", 147. 1922: amateur, New England bantam champ. 1924: fought as Johnny Andrews, won 27 unrecorded bouts. First recorded, Walter Riley, KO 5, 1925. To 1927: creditable record. Inactive 1928–29. Undefeated to 1932, including wins over Sgt. Sammy Baker, Clyde Hull, Vince Dundee, Canada Lee, Jackie Fields. Lou Brouillard series: lost, won twice. Never sought title fight. Last fight, Jimmy Smith, won 10, 5/5/33, Boston. Became one of Hollywood's outstanding advisors on films involving boxing. Recap: bouts 53, KO 8, decision 38, won foul 1, draw 1, lost decision 3, KO by 1, ND 1.

JACK, BEAU (Sidney Walker) B. 4/1/21, Atlanta, Ga. Negro. 5'6", 134. First fight, Frankie Allen, draw 4, 5/20/40, Holyoke, Mass. Impressive KO record. 1943: Fritzie Zivic, won twice; Henry Armstrong, won. NY Commission named Jack champ on Angott's vacating light title. NY title, Bob Montgomery, lost 15, 5/21/43, NYC. Regained title, Montgomery 15, 11/19/43, NYC. Army. Lost title, Montgomery, 15, 3/3/44, NYC. World light title, Ike Williams, KO by 6, 7/12/48, Phila. Inactive 1952–54. 1955: Williams draw. Last fight, Williams, KO by 9, 8/12/55, Augusta. Frittered his money. Comeback as prosperous shoeshine boy, Miami. Hall of Fame 1973. Recap: bouts 112, KO 40, decision 43, draw 5, lost decision 20, KO by 4.

JACKSON, HURRICANE (Thomas Jackson) B. 8/9/31, Sparta, Ga. 6'6½". Heavy. First fight, Terry Halpine, KO 4, 7/14/52, Brooklyn. Undefeated first year. Erratic style established him as No. 1 heavy challenger. Ezzard Charles, won twice, 1955; Rex Layne, KO twice; Archie McBride, won twice; Bob Baker, won twice; Floyd Patterson, lost 12, 1956. World title, Patterson, KO by 10, 7/29/57, NYC. Eddie Machen, KO by 10, 1957. 1958–59, KO two, dec. two. Recap: bouts 41, KO 15, decision 18, draw 1, lost 4, KO by 3.

JACKSON, PETER B. 7/3/61, St. Croix, West Indies. D. 7/13/01, Roma, Queensland, Australia. Negro. 6'1½", 192. One of his time's most feared and popular boxers. First fight, Jack Hayes, KO 7, 1883. 1886–92: undefeated, including Peter Maher, KO 2, 1889. Jim Corbett, draw 61, 1891. Won British Empire heavy title, Frank Slavin, KO 10, 5/30/92, London. On stage five years (*Uncle Tom's Cabin* and others), exhibitions. Jim Jeffries, KO by 3, 1898. Jim Jeffords, KO by 4, 8/24/99. Last fight, Billy Warren, draw 25, 12/2/99, Melbourne, Australia. Never world title chance. When he died, admirers erected a cemetery monument. Hall of Fame 1956. Recap: bouts 38, KO 12, decisions 16, won foul 1, draw 3, lost decision 1, KO by 2, ND 1, no contest 2.

JACOBS, JOE B. 5/7/97, New York, N.Y. D. 4/24/40, New York, N.Y. Manager. In a sport replete with characters, Jacobs was a main eventer. The little man with the big cigar could have been cast for a Damon Runyon story, unintentional humor, intrigue, success and an easy touch for the some half million dollars he gleaned.

"Yussel the Muscle" managed four champs, heavy Max Schmeling, light heavy Mike McTigue and feathers Andre Routis and Johnny Dundee.

An accomplishment that established a page in boxing history was screaming Schmeling into the heavyweight championship in Max's first fight with Jack Sharkey, 6/12/30, NYC.

Sharkey, holding a margin, allegedly hit the German below the belt as the fourth round neared conclusion. Referee Johnny Crowley obviously regarded the punch as fair, started counting as the bell rang. The official walked to a neutral corner, awaiting the fifth round. Jacobs whirled into action, grabbing Crowley by the shirt, screamed that his fighter was fouled, Sharkey should be disqualified. In seconds Jacobs had 80,000 spectators yelling foul. The ring was a scene of pandemonium for 15 minutes. New York commissioner Jim Farley called Crowley aside, advised, "Make one decision immediately and stick to it!" Aware that calling a foul would be the popular decision, the referee awarded the title to Schmeling.

Background to Jacobs' successful protest was his running, well-publicized prefight commentary accusing Sharkey of being a foul fighter, hoping that the referee and commission would extend his fighter a fair deal.

A classic line was added to fistic phraselogy when Sharkey decisioned the German for the title two years later (6/21/32, Long Island). Howled Joe, "We wuz robbed!"

Another Jacobs classic was, "I should have stood in bed," made one cold forenoon when Mike Jacobs routed him out of bed to see a baseball game.

Although he was banned from Germany in 1933 as an American Jew, Jacobs continued to handle Schmeling's affairs for several years. Earlier he visited

Germany when the German persecution was beginning, traveling in his usual grand style, and was Max's manager when he upset Joe Louis with a 12th-round knockout (6/19/36, NYC).

He picked Tony Galento off the fistic scrap heap, guided him to a title fight with Louis, an uproarious event in which Tony floored the champion (Galento, KO by 4, 6/28/39, NYC).

Jacobs was 42 when he died of a heart attack in a New York doctor's office. Son of a poor tailor in "Hell's Kitchen" area in New York, he earned an estimated half-million dollars. But he left an estate of about $5000.

JACOBS, MIKE (Michael S.) B. 3/10/90, New York, N.Y. D. 1/25/53, New York, N.Y. Promoter. All that Jacobs touched turned to dividends, from selling newspapers and peddling sandwiches in Tammany Hall to forming the massive 20th Century Sporting Club.

The Jacobs financial foundation was laid by the ticket brokerage business, an occupation inspired when Mike, as a newsboy, was given two fight passes by the circulation manager. He was offered two dollars for the tickets. The amazed youngster sold promptly and thereby was born what was to become New York's largest ticket broker.

A midtown neighborhood was named "Jacobs' Beach," originally because his ticket office was located there, later because it became the unofficial headquarters for shoptalk of the boxing fraternity.

Before discovering the gold in boxing's hills, he operated a river steamboat line, built a real estate development, managed an Enrico Caruso concert tour and a speaking series for Emily Pankhurst, noted British suffragette.

His introduction to boxing was as an advisor to Tex Rickard. He showed Rickard how to "stretch an arena" for more seating capacity, came up with $100,000 for promotion of the Dempsey-Carpentier event by contacting New York ticket brokers, raising the cash in eight hours with promises of choice seats to sell. At the Dempsey-Firpo fight, his promotional efforts were climaxed sitting on a policeman's horse selling tickets to fight time.

With Rickard's death in 1929, boxing promotion faded until Jacobs emerged as promoter of Milk Fund and Christmas Fund fights in New York. Prompting the organization of the 20th Century Sporting Club was a card at Bronx Coliseum in 1934 that turned away 10,000.

As Joe Louis began to bomb his way through the ranks, Jacobs anticipated the fighter's potential, signed him for exclusive services. The Bomber was the coin that stimulated the jackpot.

Mike and Madison Square Garden continued their feud until a historic legal contest involving the signing of the Louis–Jimmy Braddock title fight in Chicago (6/22/37). Jacobs won the court battle and Madison Square Garden conceded its disadvantage, offered 20th Century the opportunity to take over Garden operations. Within four years Jacobs had control of division champions from heavy to light.

Prosperity continued for Jacobs until health and pressure took their toll and he sold his Garden holdings to Jim Norris in 1949.

Jacobs was 72 when he died of "coronary insufficiency." Born in lower New York, he was the son of a tailor who left school in 6th grade. His probated estate was $171,000.

JADICK, JOHNNY B. 6/16/08, Philadelphia, Pa. Ukrainian. 5'8½", 135. First fight, Harry Decker, KO 3, 1925. Undefeated 3 years. First loss, Eddie Anderson, 10, 1927. To 1932, up-down record. Won junior welter title, Tony Canzoneri, 10, 1/18/32, Phila. Defended: Canzoneri, 10, 7/18/32, Phila. Lost title, Battling Shaw, 10, 2/20/33, New Orleans. To 1937, never another title chance, record spotty. Last fight, Mike Piskin, lost 8, 8/27/37, Long Beach, Calif. Army. Recap: bouts 134, KO 9, decision 63, won foul 1, draw 8, lost decision 44, KO by 7, ND 2.

JEBY, BEN (Morris Jebaltowsky) B. 11/21/07, New York, N.Y. Polish. 5'8", 157. First fight. Benny Bonvita, KO 3, 1928. To 1932, mostly good record, KO by Frankie Battaglia, 1, 3/18/32, Chicago. Won vacant NY Commission middle title, Chick Devlin, 15, 11/21/32, NYC. Defended: Battaglia, KO 12, 1/13/33, NYC: Vince Dundee; draw 15, 3/17/33, NYC. Lost title, Lou Brouillard, KO by 7, 8/9/33, NYC. 1933–36 lost 5 of 11. Last fight, Jackie Aldare, won 8, 7/14/36, Brooklyn. Retired. Recap: bouts 73, KO 22, decision 32, draw 4, lost decision 12, KO by 2, no contest 1.

JEFFRA, HARRY (Ignacius Pasquale Guiffi) B. 11/30/14, Baltimore, Md. Italian. First fight, Angelo Brocato, won 4, 9/21/33. Undefeated 3 years. Won world bantam title, Sixto Escobar, 15, 9/23/37, NYC. Lost title, Escobar, 15, 2/20/38, San Juan, P.R. Feather title, Joey Archibald, lost 15, 9/28/39, Washington, D.C. Won world feather title, Archibald, 15, 5/20/40, Baltimore. Defended: Spider Armstrong, won 15, 7/29/40, Baltimore. Lost title, Archibald, 15, 5/12/41, Washington, D.C. Title, Chalky Wright, KO by 10, 6/15/42, Baltimore. Fair record to last fight, Packy McFarland, lost 10, 12/13/50, Wichita. Recap: bouts 119, KO 27, decision 65, draw 7, lost dec. 17, KO by 2, no contest 1.

JEFFRIES, JAMES J. (The Boilermaker) B. 4/15/75, Carroll, Ohio. D. 3/3/53, Burbank, Calif. Scotch-Dutch. 6'2½", 220. First fight, Hank Griffin, KO 14, 1896, Los Angeles. 4 KOs followed. Draws: Gus Ruhlin, 20, 7/17/97, San Francisco; Joe Choynski, 20, 11/30/97, San Francisco. 1898: 3 KOs, Tom Sharkey, won 20; Bob Armstrong, won 10. Won heavyweight title, Bob Fitzsimmons, KO 11, 6/9/99, Coney Island. Defended: Jim Corbett, KO 23, 5/11/1900, Coney Island; Ruhlin, KO 5, 11/15/01, San Francisco; Fitzsimmons, KO 8, 7/25/02, San Francisco; Corbett, KO 10, 8/14/03, San Francisco; Jack Munroe, KO 2, 8/26/04, San Francisco. Retired. Prompted Marvin Hart and Jack Root to contest for title. Jeffries refereed; Hart, KO 12, 7/3/05, Reno. Tommy Burns decisioned Hart for title, 20 rounds, 2/23/06, Los Angeles. Burns lost title to Jack Johnson, 14, 12/26/08, Sydney, Australia. Inspired Jeffries' comeback, but was kayoed in 15, 7/4/10, Reno (Jeffries' only loss). Last ring appearance, Jack Jeffries, exh. 3, 3/3/21, Los Angeles. One of strongest men ever to enter a ring. Quiet, good businessman, operated farm at Burbank, Calif., promoted fights in "Jeffries' Barn." Hall of Fame 1954. Recap: bouts 23, KO 16, decision 4, draw 2, KO by 1.

JENKINS, LEW (Verlin Jenks) (Sweetwater Swatter) B. 12/4/16, Milburn, Tex. Irish. 5'7", 134. First fight, Fay Koshey, won 4, 1934, N. Mex. 1934–40, bumpy career, 7 straight KO. Won light title, Lou Ambers, KO 3, 5/10/40, NYC. Nontitle Henry Armstrong, KO by 6, 1940. Defended: Pete Lello, KO 2, 11/22/40, NYC. Lost title, Sammy Angott, 15, 12/19/41, NYC. To 1950, rocky years, last fight, Beau Jack, KO by 6, 4/14/50, Washington, D.C. Army career. Recap: bouts 109, KO 47, decision 19, draw 5, lost decision 26, KO by 12.

JENNETTE, JOE (Joseph Jeanettei) B. 8/26/79, North Bergen, N.J. D. 7/2/58, Weehawken, N.J. 5'10", 190. First fight, Bill Gorman, ND, 1904. Probably more series than any top-flight fighter: Sam Langford 14 times, Jack Johnson 9, Black Bill 9. Langford: won 2, lost 4, draw 2, ND 4, KO by 1; Johnson: ND 4, won foul 1, draw 2, lost dec. 2; Black Bill: KO 5, won 1, ND 3. Fought Jim Jeffords thrice: 2 KO, 1 ND; Sam McVey thrice: KO, draw, loss. Rugged 16-year career. Last fight, Bartley Madden, won foul 4, 11/11/19, Bayonne, N.J. Referee, owned gymnasium, garage. Hall of Fame 1957. Recap: bouts 151, KO 56, decision 13, won foul 3, draw 8, lost decision 8, KO by 1, ND 62.

JOFRE, EDER B. 3/26/36, Sao Paulo, Brazil. First fight, Raul Lopez, KO 5, 3/23/57, Sao Paulo. Undefeated to 1964. Won S. American bantam title, Ernesto Miranda, 15, 2/19/60, Sao Paulo. Won NBA bantam title, Eloy

Sanchez, KO 6, 11/18/60, Los Angeles. Won vacant world bantam title, Piero Rollo, KO 10, 3/25/61, Rio de Janeiro. Defended: Ramon Arias, KO 7, 8/19/61, Caracas; Jim Caldwell, KO 10, 1/18/62, Sao Paulo; Herman Marques, KO 10, 5/4/62, San Francisco; Joe Medel, KO 6, 9/11/62, Sao Paulo; Katsutosh Aoki, KO 3, 4/4/63, Tokyo; John Jamito, KO 12, 5/18/63, Manila; Barnardo Caraballo, KO 7, 11/27/64, Bogota. (Seventeen straight KO, including title.) Lost title, Fighting Harada, 15, 5/17/65, Nagoya, Japan. Return, Harada, lost 15, 6/1/66, Nagoya. Retired. Comeback as feather. Undefeated through 1971. WBC feather title, Jose Legra, won 15, 5/5/73, Brasilia, Brazil. Recap: bouts 63, KO 41, decision 16, lost decision 4, lost foul 2.

JOHANSSON, INGEMAR B. 9/22/22, Sweden. 6'½", 195. Amateur: 1951, European team vs. American Golden Gloves, Ernest Fann, KO 2; Swedish team, 1952 Olympics, Helinski, finals, lost disq. Ed Sander, U.S.: bouts 71, lost 11. First pro: Robert Masson, KO 4, 12/5/52, Gothenburg, Sweden. Won Scandinavian heavy title, Erik Jensen, 6, 3/12/53, Copenhagen. Swedish Navy. To 1960, undefeated. Won European title, Franco Cavicchi, KO 13, 9/30/56, Milan. Defended: Henry Cooper, KO 5, 5/19/57, Stockholm; Joe Erskine, KO 13, 2/21/58, Gothenburg. Eddie Machen, KO 1, 1958. Won heavyweight title, Floyd Patterson, KO 3 (Patterson down 7 times), 6/26/59, NYC. (Visit in U.S. highlighted by playboy capers.) Lost title, Patterson, KO by 5, 6/20/60, NYC. Return, title, KO by 6, 3/13/61, Miami Beach. (First time same 2 heavies fought 3 times for title.) Returned Sweden, 3 KO, 1 win, including European title, Dick Richardson, KO 8, 6/17/62, Gothenburg. Last fight, Brian London, won 12, 5/21/63, Stockholm. Part time, operated successful construction business; retired to manage full time. Recap.: bouts 28, KO 17, decision 8, won foul 1, KO by 2.

JOHNSON, HAROLD B. 8/9/28, Manayunk, Pa. Negro. 5'10", 175. First fight Joe Riley, KO 2, 1946, 4 straight KO first year. Undefeated until lost to Archie Moore, 10, 4/26/49, Phila. Won four, then Joe Walcott, KO by 3, 1950. Moore, 3 successive fights 1951–52, lost 2, won 1. World light heavy title, Moore, KO by 14, 8/11/54, NYC. KO by Billy Smith, 2, 1954, KO by Julio Mederos, 2, 1955. 1955–60, 12 straight wins. Won vacant NBA title, Jesse Bowdry, KO 9, 2/7/61, Miami Beach. Defended: Von Clay, KO 2, 4/24/61, Phila; Eddie Cotton, won 15, 8/29/61, Seattle. Non-title, Eddie Machen, won 10, 7/1/61, Atlantic City. Total recognition as champ, Doug Jones, won 15, 5/12/62, Phila. Lost title, Willie Pastrano, 15, 6/1/63, Las Vegas. Inactive 1965. 1966–68, won 5, lost 1. Retired. Returned, last fight, Herschel Jacobs, KO by 3, 3/30/71. Recap: bouts 88, KO 33, decision 44, lost decision 6, KO by 5.

JOHNSON, JACK (John Arthur Johnson) (Little Artha) B. 3/31/78, Galveston, Tex. D. 6/10/46, car accident, Raleigh, N.C. Negro. 6'¼", 200. Janitor, cotton picker, stable boy. Spotty early career, battles royal, impromptu fights, no records. First recorded fights 1897: Jim Rocks, KO 4; Sam Smith, won 10. Through 1908, approximately 70 fights, including "Klondike," KO by 5 (1899), and Joe Choynski, KO by 3 (1901). Won heavyweight title, Tommy Burns, 14, 12/26/08, Sydney, Australia. Nontitle, Victor McLaglen, ND 6, 3/10/09, Vancouver (same McLaglen who became noted movie star; was better-than-average heavy before Hollywood beckoned). Defended: Stanley Ketchel, KO 12, 10/16/09, Colma, Calif.; James J. Jeffries, KO 15, 7/4/10, Reno; Jim Flynn, won 9 (police stopped), 7/4/12, Las Vegas, N. Mex.; Andre Sprool, KO 2, 11/28/13, Paris; Jim Johnson, draw 10, 12/19/13, Paris; Frank Moran, won 20, 6/27/14, Paris. Lost title, Jess Willard, KO by 26, 4/5/15, Havana, Cuba. Jack wanted for violation of Mann Act, prompting his overseas fights. Returned to U.S. 1928, KO by Bearcat Wright, Bill Hartwell. Fought exhibitions to 1945. Was first Negro to win heavyweight title. Many acclaim him the greatest of all the heavyweights. Hall of Fame 1954. Recap: bouts 113, KO 44, decision 30, won foul 4, draw 14, lost decision 1, lost foul 1, KO by 5, ND 14.

JOHNSTON, JAMES J. B. 1876. D. 5/7/46, New York, N.Y. Promoter-manager. Probably no other man of his trade splashed more color on the fistic picture than James Joy Johnston, knighted by Damon Runyon as the "Boy Bandit."

Weight to his leverage on boxing during the late 1920s, early 30s was provided by his four world champions, three British titleholders and what Runyon described as " several hundred gladiators in his active stable."

Johnston guided world champs Ted (Kid) Lewis, welter; Harry Greb, middle; Mike McTigue, light heavy; Johnny Dundee, feather, British champs Phil Scott, heavy; Len Harvey, middle; Jem Driscoll, feather. As promoter he fought Madison Square Garden millions, eventually named Garden matchmaker in a partnership with millionaire William F. Carey.

His influence in the promotional field was often attributed to his association with James A. Farley, N.Y. boxing commission head and high on the political ladder. It embraced rulings on such as the Carnera-Schmeling-Sharkey showdown technicalities, and Johnston's control of Ebbets Field as a fistic site.

Meanwhile, the Boy Bandit's fingers were peeling bills from the paydays of other fighters. George Barton, respected *Minneapolis Tribune* sports columnist, NBA president, referee (once ordered Jimmy Braddock–Maxie Rosenbloom from ring for stalling), reported in 1931 that Johnston was "One of Gotham's leading 'chislers,' an expression meaning an individual who cuts himself in on other persons' business. It is a well known fact that Johnston has a piece of most of the fighters appearing in N.Y. rings. . . . able to obtain a 'cut' of the boxer's earnings by using his influence to get him matches. . . . Even Jack Sharkey and his managers were forced to give Johnston 10 per cent when Sharkey fought Jimmy Maloney, Mike McTigue, Jack Delaney, Harry Wills in NY. . . ."

Johnston's association with his own fighters was often close and personal. His favorite was Lewis, Runyon writing, ". . . Johnston secretly thinks that the greatest fighter he ever handled was Ted-Kid Lewis, always advertised by him as "The Slashing, Dashing, Bashing, Crushing, Ted-Kid. . . ." The "Ted-Kid" hyphen was Johnston's pet reference to his favorite.

Lewis was an English Jew with mismatched feet, unhealthy complexion, aggressive "cut 'em up style," always a crowd-pleaser. Despite mutual admiration, they argued constantly, Lewis broke contract, returned to England, won European welter, middle titles.

When Carey resigned as Madison Square Garden head, the Johnston bulb flickered out.

Johnston was 70 when he died of a heart attack. At time he was working on project to promote outdoor boxing in Brooklyn's Ebbets Field. He left a modest estate.

JONES, GORILLA (William Jones) B. 5/12/06, Memphis, Tenn. Negro. 5'6", 158. First fight, Jim Williams, lost 4, 1924. Return, Williams KO 3, 1928. To mid-1931 (inactive 1925–27) creditable record, including Sammy Baker, ND; Tommy Freeman, ND, draw; Izzy Grove, KO 6; Jack McVey, won 10; Bobby Brown, lost 10 (return Brown, KO 3); Bucky Lawless, lost 3, won, 2; Jackie Fields, lost 1, NC 1; lost to Tiger Williams, Harry Smith, Jackie Brady; lost foul, Nick Testo. Mickey Walker vacated title to enter light heavies. NBA, N.Y. Commission staged separate elimination tournaments. Jones, winner of NBA (Tiger Thomas, won 10, 8/25/31, Milwaukee); Ben Jeby, N.Y. champ (Chick Devlin, won 15, 10/21/32, NYC). Jones defended: Oddone Piazzo, KO 6, 1/25/32, Milwaukee; Young Terry, won 12, 4/26/32, Trenton, N.J. (Nontitle, Frankie O'Brien, Jones disqualified for lack of effort, 4, 3/14/32, Holyoke, Mass). Lost title, Marcel Thil, foul 11, 6/11/32, Paris. Jones still claimed title, NBA recognized Thil. Varied success to 1940. Last fight, Vern Earling, lost 10, 5/29/40, Kellogg, Idaho. Recap: bouts 141, KO 53, decision 44, draw 13, lost decision 21, lost foul 2, ND 5, no contest 3.

JONES, TIGER (Ralph Jones) B. 3/14/28, Brooklyn, N.Y. 5'8", 155. First fight, Jimmy Garcia, won 4, 5/27/50, Brooklyn. Undefeated first year. Rugged campaigner, trial horse, TV favorite. Impressive 1951–53: upset Johnny Bratton, 1952; KO 7, won 22, draw 3, lost 6, including Kid Gavilan, 10; only KO by, Harry Burroughs, 1, 1951. 1954 spotty. 1955, Ray Robinson, won 10, Chicago. Series: Gavilan, won, lost twice; Joey Giardello, won, lost twice. Spotty 1960–62. Last fight, Lazlo Papp, lost 10, 3/21/62, Vienna. Recap: bouts 88, KO 13, decision 38, draw 5, lost decision 31, KO by 1.

KANE, PETER B. 2/28/18, Golborne, Lancaster, England. First fight, Joe Jacobs, KO 5, 12/13/34, Liverpool. First two years, 13 straight KO. Undefeated to flyweight title fight, Benny Lynch, KO by 13, 10/13/37, Glasgow. Title, Lynch, draw 15, 3/24/38, Liverpool. Claimed vacant fly title, Jackie Jurich, 15, 9/22/38, Liverpool. British army 1941. Lost title, Jackie Paterson, KO by 1, 6/19/43, Glasgow. Inactive 1944–'45. Undefeated thru 1947, won European bantam, Theo Medina, 15, 9/26/47, Manchester. Defended: Joe Cornelis won 15, 12/15/47, Manchester. Lost title, Guido Farracin, 15, 2/20/48, Manchester. Last fight, Stan Rowan, lost 12, 11/19/48, Manchester. Recap: bouts 95, KO 51, decision 33, won foul 1, draw 2, lost decision 3, KO by 4, no contest 1.

KANSAS, ROCKY (Rocco Tozze) B. 4/21/95, Buffalo, N.Y. D. 1/10/54, Buffalo, N.Y. Italian. 5'2", 130. First fight, Young Thomas, KO 3, 1911. Long trail to light title, mostly ND, Lew Tendler, won 15, 1921; title, Benny Leonard, lost 15, 2/10/22, NYC; title, Leonard, KO by 8, 7/4/22, Michigan City. Won title, Jimmy Goodrich, 15, 12/7/25, Buffalo. Lost title, Sammy Mandell, 10, 7/3/26, Chicago. Last fight, Joe Trippe, lost 6. Recap: bouts 165, KO 32, decision 32, draw 7, lost decision 8, lost foul 2, KO by 3, ND 81.

KAPLAN, LOUIS (Kid) B. 1902, Russia. Jewish. 5'4", 120–35. Settled in Meriden, Conn., 1907. Amateur, starting at 13. First pro, Romeo Roach, won 10, NYC. To 1925, popular, creditable record, won over Eddie (Kid)

Wagner, Kid Sullivan, Jimmy Goodrich. Babe Herman, draw three fights, lost 1. Won vacant world feather title, Danny Kraemer, KO 9, 1/2/25, NYC. Defended: Herman, draw 15, 8/27/25, Waterbury, Conn.; Herman, won 15, 12/18/25, NYC. 1926, outgrew division. Lightweight record mostly impressive, beat Billy Petrolle, Wagner, Al Foreman, Jackie Fields, Bruce Flowers, Johnny Jadick, Phil McGraw, Joey Glick, Bat Battalino, Sammy Mandell. Jimmy McLarnin, KO by 8; Billy Wallace, KO by 5, won return, 10. Last fight, Cocoa Kid, lost 10, 2/20/33, New Haven, Conn. Recap: bouts 131, KO 17, decision 84, draw 10, lost decision 9, lost foul 1, KO by 3, ND 7.

KEARNS, JACK (John Leo McKernan) B. 7/17/83, Waterloo, Mich. D. 6/17/63, Miami Beach, Fla. Manager. One of boxing's most colorful and successful managers, Jack Kearns is identified with the Golden Age of Boxing, providing part of the Dempsey-Rickard-Kearns unbeatable trio.

One story backgrounding the Dempsey-Kearns affiliation has it that a rowdy attacked Kearns in an Oakland saloon and Dempsey provided the rescue act. At the time, 1916, Dempsey entertained the notion of quitting boxing. He was nursing two broken ribs received in a fight with John Lester Johnson.

The pair arrived at a manager-fighter agreement, Kearns altering the Manassa Mauler's style and within three years Dempsey was world heavyweight champion. Through the Luis Firpo fight in 1923, the pair split nearly $2 million. At about that time they split partnership. Speculation was that Dempsey's marriage to movie actress Estelle Taylor prompted the parting, but Dempsey claimed it involved financial matters. The New York Supreme Court sustained the fighter's charges, declaring him a free agent. The bitterness diluted during ensuing years, and Dempsey was a pallbearer at his former manager's funeral.

After Dempsey, Kearns continued down his money-making path. He took over Mickey Walker after the Toy Bulldog won the welter title, made a fortune pairing Walker with middles, light heavies and heavies. Other top shelf fighters he managed included Jackie Fields, Archie Moore, Joey Maxim, Ace Hudkins, Eddie McGoorty, Frankie Neil, Battling Nelson, Jimmy Clabby, and in the later years of their careers, Benny Leonard, Abe Attell, George Godfrey, Harry Wills.

His early career was also splashed with color, fighting as a lightweight and prospecting in Alaska where he associated with Jack London, Rex Beach, Robert Service, Tex Rickard and a young engineer named Herbert Hoover. He experienced little luck, returned to the U.S. as a manager.

Kearns' last hopeful was a young Utah heavy, Jeff Davis, whom he planned to introduce in a preliminary to the second Sonny Liston–Floyd Patterson affair, but died five weeks before the fight, almost broke.

KELLY, HUGO (Ugo Mitchell) B. 2/10/83, Florence, Italy. 5'8", 158. First fight, Jack Falvey, won 6, 9/29/99, Chicago. Creditable early record: Rube Ferns, won; Joe Grim, won; Phila. Jack O'Brien, draw. Returns O'-Brien, lost, won. Series: Jack (Twin) Sullivan, 1 won, 3 draw, 1 lost. Tommy Burns, 2 draw. Others he fought: Billy Papke, Frank Klaus, Tommy Ryan, Eddie McGoorty, Stanley Ketchel (KO by 3, 1908). Last fight, Jack Dillon, KO by 3, 5/28/12. Owned movie house chain, Illinois. Recap: bouts 76, KO 17, decision 18, draw 24, lost decision 7, KO by 4, ND 6.

KELLY, TOMMY (Spider; the Harlem Spider) B. 9/6/67, New York, N.Y. Irish. 5'4", 105. Claimed world bantam title, 1887. Lost claim, Hughey Boyle, KO by 8, 10/24/87, Glouster, N.Y. George Dixon, draw 9, 5/10/88, Boston. (Boyle retired undefeated, Kelly and Dixon claiming.) American title (105 lbs.), Cal McCarthy, draw 8, 10/24/88, Harlem. British champ Chappie Moran, won 4, 6/5/88, Hoboken, N.J. Many recognized as world title bout. Return title, lost 10, 6/5/89, Brooklyn. Rewon title, Moran, KO 10, 1/31/90, Brooklyn. Defended: Benny Murphy, KO 3, 3/5/90, NYC. Lost title (110 lbs.), Billy Plimmer, 10, 5/9/92, Coney Island. Lost American title, Tim Murphy, KO by 4, 9/24/92, NYC. Losing record to last fight, Kid Abel, draw 6, May, 1900. Recap: bouts 44, KO 11, decision 19, draw 4, lost decision 5, KO by 4, ND 1.

KENDALL, ANDY B. 9/30/39, Portland, Oreg. Light heavy. First fight, Ernie Gipson, won 4, 8/3/62, Yakima, Wash. Impressive early career; undefeated 1963–64. World light heavy title, Bob Foster, KO by 4, 5/24/69, West Springfield, Mass. Regarded as No. 2 light heavy, stumbling block for title aspirants. 1972, undefeated, including KO, Pat O'Connor, Billy Marsh; dec., Henry Hank. Recap: bouts 59, KO 20, decision 23, draw 8, lost 6, KO by 2.

KETCHEL, STANLEY (Stanislaus Kiecal) (Michigan Assassin) B. 9/14/87, Grand Rapids, Mich. D. 10/15/10, New York, N.Y. (shot and killed by Walter A. Display in Conway, Mo.). Polish. 5'9", 154. First fight, Kid Tracy, KO 1, 5/2/03, Butte, Mont. 1904: 11 KO, Maurice Thompson, lost 2, 1 draw. 1905–07: 23 KO; Joe Thomas, draw, KO, won. Vacant world middle title, Mike (Twin) Sullivan, KO 1, 2/22/08, Colma, Calif. Defended: Billy Papke, won 10, 6/4/08, Milwaukee; Hugo Kelly, KO 3, 7/31/08, San Francisco; Thomas, KO 3, 8/18/08, San Francisco. Lost title, Papke, KO by 12, 9/7/08, Los Angeles. Regained title, Papke, KO 11, 11/26/08, San Francisco. 1909, Phila. Jack O'Brien, ND 10 (bell saved O'Brien from KO), O'Brien, KO 3, 1909. Title, Papke, won 20, 7/5/09, Colma. Heavy title, Jack Johnson, KO by 12, 10/16/09, Colma. 1910: 2 ND, 3 KO. Last fight, Jim Smith, KO 5, 6/10/10, NYC. Recap: bouts 61, KO 46, decision 3, draw 4, lost decision 2, KO by 2, ND 4.

KID, DIXIE (Aaron L. Brown) B. 12/23/83, Fulton, Mo. D. 10/3/35, Los Angeles, Calif. Negro. 5'5", 145. First fight, Tony Rivers, KO 1, 1899. Undefeated 8 yrs. including Joe Grim, won, won foul, Philadelphia Jack O'Brien, ND. 1899–1903: 24 KO, 27 fights. First loss: Sam Langford, KO by 5, 1909, also KO by 3, 1910. NDs; Willie Lewis, twice; Jimmy Clabby; Mike (Twin) Sullivan. Georges Carpentier, KO 5, 1911. Lost ref's decision, Lewis, reversed by sportsman's jury, Paris, 1911. Fought three more years, creditable. Last fight, Bill Bristowe, KO 2, 3/30/14, England. Recap: bouts 122, KO 63, decision 12, won foul 2, draw 6, lost decision 11, lost foul 2, KO by 3, ND 23, no contest 1.

KID, YOUNG ZULU (Giuseppe Dimelfi) B. 4/22/97, Potenza, Italy. 4'11", 110. First fight, Kid Dennis, ND 4, 1912. To 1915 undefeated, including NDs, Joe Rossner three, Jackie Sharkey; Pete Herman, draw. 1916: Sharkey, KO 5; vacant world fly title, Jimmy Wilde, KO by 11, 12/18/16, London. Creditable record to 1921 including NDs, Herman twice, Wilde; lost, Johnny Buff. Series: Rosner, ND three, KO by; Mason ND three. Inactive 1922–23. Last fight, Willie Darcy, lost 10, Yonkers, N.Y. Recap: bouts 101, KO 9, decision 4, won foul 1, draw 10, lost decision 11, lost foul 1, KO by 3, ND 62.

KILBANE, JOHNNY (John Patrick Kilbane) B. 4/18/89, Cleveland, Ohio. D. 5/31/57, Cleveland, Ohio. Irish. 5'5", 122–126. First fight, Kid Campbell, KO 6, 1907. Undefeated to Abe Attell, lost 10, 1910; Attell, KO 4, 1911. Won world feather title, Attell, 20, 2/22/12, Vernon, Calif. Defended: Jimmy Walsh, draw 12, 5/21/12, Boston; Johnny Dundee, draw 20, 4/29/13, Los Angeles; George Chaney, KO 3, 9/4/16, Cedar Point, Mo. Light title, Benny Leonard, KO by 3, 7/25/17, Phila. 1918, army boxing instructor. To 1922 undefeated in 18. Defended: Alvie Miller, KO 7, 4/21/20, Lorain, Ohio. Danny Frush, KO 7, 9/17/21, Cleveland. Lost title, Eugene Criqui, KO by 6, 6/2/23, NYC. Retired, boxing instructor, referee. Hall of Fame 1960. Recap: bouts 140, KO 22, decision 23, won foul 1, draw 8, lost decision 2, KO by 2, ND 81, no contest 1.

KINGPETCH, PONE B. 2/12/36, Hui Hui Province, Thailand. 5'6½". First recorded fight, G. Noknid, KO 2, 1955, Tor Sor. Thailand. Creditable early record. Won Thailand fly title, Kunio Vitichai, 10, 11/6/56, Bangkok. Won Orient fly title, Danny Kid, 12, 1/6/57, Bangkok; Defended Orient title: Hitoshi Misako, 12, 9/14/57, Bangkok. Won world fly title, Pascual Perez, 15, 4/16/60, Bangkok. Defended: Perez, KO 8, 9/22/60, Los Angeles; Mitsunori Seki, won 15, 6/27/61, Tokyo; Kyo Noguchi, won 15, 5/30/62, Tokyo. Lost title, Fighting Harada, KO by 11, 10/10/62, Tokyo. Regained title, Harada, 15, 1/12/63, Bangkok. First to regain fly title. Lost title, Hiroyuki Ebihara, KO by 1, 9/18/63, Tokyo. Regained title, Ebihara, 15, 1/23/64, Bangkok. Lost title, Salvatore Burruni, 15, 4/23/65, Rome. Last fight, Kumantong Yontrakit, KO 4, 4/13/66, Bangkok. Retired 5/30/66. Recap: bouts 40, KO 10, decision 21, won foul 1, lost decision 5, KO by 3.

KLAUS, FRANK B. 12/30/87, Pittsburgh, Pa. D. 2/8/48, Pittsburgh, Pa. German. 5'7½", 158–160. First fight, Joe Morgan, KO 2, 1904. 1904–09 undefeated. First loss, Jimmy Gardner, 12, 11/29/10, Boston—last fight that year. Had undefeated skein of 58. Jack (Twin) Sullivan, won 12, 1910; Frank Mantell, KO 9, 1910; Mantell, ND, 1910; Jack Dillon, ND, 1911; Dillon, won, ND, 1912. Middle title, Billy Papke, won foul 15, 3/5/13, Paris. Dillon, ND, 1913. Lost title, George Chip, KO by 6, 10/11/13, Pittsburgh. Title, Chip, KO by 5, 12/23/13, Pittsburgh. Last fight, Harry Greb, ND 6, 2/7/18. Recap: bouts 89, KO 25, decisions 20, won foul 4, draw 2, lost decision 2, KO by 2, no decision 34.

KLICK, FRANKIE B. 5/5/09, San Francisco, Calif. Polish-Irish. 5'6", 130. From 1925 not recorded. First recorded, Bobby Herman, won 6, 1928. Mediocre 5 years, 1933, fair record to upset, won junior light title Kid Chocolate, disqual. KO 7, 12/26/33, Phila. Defended: Barney Ross, draw, 10, 3/5/34, San Francisco. Title faded from recognition until 1959 when Harold Gomes was paired with Paul Jorgensen, winning NBA-sanctioned crown, 7/20/59, Providence, R.I. Active to 1943, mostly losses. Last fight, Al Citrins, lost 8, 4/16/43, San Francisco. Recap: bouts 61, KO 6, decision 22, won foul 1, draw 6, lost decision 24, KO by 2.

KOBAYASHI, HIROSHI B. 8/23/44, Isezaki City, Japan. First fight, Hisatsugu Kyoya, won 4, 7/2/62, Tokyo. Undefeated first year. Creditable to Japanese feather title, Soo Bok Kwan, KO 7, 3/1/65, Tokyo. Defended: Sigeo Sioyama, won 10, 5/9/65, Tokyo; Sumio Nobata, won 10, 11/10/66, Nagoya; Takao Mihashi, won 10, 5/8/67, tokyo. Won WBA junior light title, Song Ki Chin, KO 8, 10/16/67, Tokyo. Won world junior light title, Yosiaki Numata, KO 12, 12/14/67, Tokyo. Defended: Rene Barrientes, draw, won 15, 3/30/68, Tokyo; Jaime Valladares, won 15, 10/6/68, Tokyo; Antonio Amaya, won 15, 8/24/70, Tokyo; Carlos Canete, won 15, 11/9/69; Ricardo Arredondo, won 15, 3/4/71, Tokyo. Lost title, Alfredo Marcano, KO by 10, 2/29/71, Aomori, Japan. Recap: bouts 72, KO 10, decision 49, draw 4, lost decision 6, KO by 3.

KRIEGER, SOLLY B. 3/28/09, New York, N.Y. Jewish. 5'8", 165–175. First fight, Duffy Moore, KO 3, 1928. To 1938, mostly up, sometimes down. Won NBA middle title, Al Hostak, 15, 11/1/38, Seattle. Lost title, Hostak, KO by 4, 6/27/39, Seattle. Billy Conn, won 12, 1937, lost 12, 1939. Last fight, Lee Savold lost 10, /22/41, Brooklyn. Recap: bouts 111, KO 53, decision 27, draw 7, lost 21, KO by 3.

LABARBA, FIDEL B. 9/29/05, New York, N.Y. 5'3", 108. Outstanding amateur. U.S. champ 1924; world champ, Olympic Games 1924, Paris. First pro fight, Frankie Grandetta, won 4, 10/14/24, Vernon, Calif. Won American flyweight title, Frankie Genaro, 10, 8/22/25, Los Angeles. Won world vacated fly title, Elky Clark, 12, 1/21/27, NYC. Retired from title, 1927, entered Stanford U., journalism major. Returned boxing 1928 as bantam, feather, mostly success. Feather title, Bat Battalino, lost 15, 5/22/31, NYC; feather title, Kid Chocolate, lost 15, 12/9/32, NYC. Last fight, Mose Butch, won 10, 2/13/33, Pittsburgh. Army. Hall of Fame 1973. Recap: bouts 97, KO 15, decision 57, draw 8, lost decision 15, ND 2.

LABLANCHE, GEORGE B. 12/17/56, Point Levi, Que. D. 5/10/18, Lawrence, Mass. 5'8½", 140–158. Early Canadian record indefinite. First recorded U.S. fight, Witzell Brown, lost foul 4, 9/18/83, Lewiston, Me. Enlisted U.S. Marines 1883. 1884: won 3, lost 1. Discharged from marines June 1884. Creditable record to middle title fight, Jack (Nonpareil) Dempsey, KO by 13, 1886. Title, Dempsey scored KO 32, but disqualified for illegal punch, claimed title 8/27/89, San Francisco, claim generally disregarded. Spotty record to 1898: name fighters, Joe Dundee, lost 5; Kid McCoy, KO by 2. Last fight, Bert Woods, KO by 4, 4/10/98, Toledo. Recap: bouts 69, KO 17, decision 18, draw 6, lost decision 10, lost foul 2, KO by 14, ND 1, NC 1.

LAGUNA, ISMAEL B. 6/28/43, Colon, Panama. First fight, Al Morgan, KO 2, 1/8/61, Colon. Undefeated to mid-1963; lost, Antonio Herrera, 10; return, KO 7, 1963. Won world light title, Carlos Oriz, 15, 4/10/65, Panama

City. Lost title, Ortiz, 15, 11/13/65, San Juan. Title return, Ortiz, lost 15, 8/16/67, NYC. Undefeated to Eugenio Espinoza, lost 10, 1968; won return, 10. Regained title, Mando Ramos, KO 9, 3/3/70, Los Angeles. Defended: Ishimatsu Suzuki, KO 13, 6/7/70, Panama City. Lost title, Ken Buchanan, 15, 9/26/70, San Juan. Title return, Buchanan, lost 15, 9/13/71, NYC. Recap: bouts 74, KO 36, decision 28, draw 1, lost decision 9.

LAMOTTA, JAKE (Jacob LaMotta) (Bronx Bull) B. 7/10/21, New York, N.Y. Italian. 5'8", 168. First fight, Charley Mackley, won 4, 3/3/41, NYC. Rugged competitor of Rocky Graziano school. Won middle title, Marcel Cerdan, KO 10, 6/16/49, Detroit. Defended: Tiberio Mitri, won 10, 7/12/50, NYC; Laurent Dauthuille, KO 15, 9/13/50, Detroit. Lost title, Ray Robinson, KO by 13, 2/13/51. Next fight, Bob Murphy, KO by 7, 1951. Danny Nardleo, KO by 8, 1952. Inactive, 1953. Robinson series, 6, 1942–51, won 1, lost 5 including title. Fritzie Zivic series, 4, 1943–44, won 3, lost 1. Last fight, Billy Kilgore, lost 10, 4/14/54, Miami Beach. Recap: bouts 106, KO 30, decision 53, draw 4, lost decision 15, KO by 4.

LANE, KENNY B. 4/9/32, Big Rapids, Mich. 5'7", 135. For 12 years, troublesome opposition for top rankers. First fight, Clinton McDade won 4, 4/9/53, Grand Rapids. First year, 14 straight wins to Ron Stribling, KO by 2 (won return). 1954, John Barnes, KO by 1, lost dec., won return; balance of year wins, including Orlando Zulueta. From 1955 to title match, impressive; undefeated 1956–57. World light title, Joe Brown, lost 15, 7/23/58, Houston. To vacant jr. welter: Carlos Ortiz, won; Johnny Busso, KO 6; title, Ortiz, KO by 2, 6/12/59, NYC. 1959–64 record impressive, including Virgil Akins, won twice; won, Tommy Tibbs; draw, Curtis Cokes; Len Matthews, KO by 3, won return. Mich. version of world light title, Paul Armstead, won 15, 8/19/63, Saginaw. World light title, Ortiz, lost 15, 4/11/64, San Juan. Lost three straight. Last fight, Eddie Perkins, lost 10, 10/25/65, New Orleans. Recap: bouts 94, KO 16, decision 61, draw 2, lost decision 10, KO by 5.

LANGFORD, SAM (Boston Tar Baby) B. 3/4/86, Weymouth, Nova Scotia. D. 1/12/56, Cambridge, Mass. Negro. Fought lights to heavies. First fight, Jack McVicker, won 3. One of greatest and most tragic of all eras. Fought almost 300, several not recorded, never world title fight. Jack McVey, KO 1, won 3, draw 2, ND 3; Jack Johnson, lost; Stanley Ketchel, ND; Joe Jennette, won 3, ND 6, lost 5; Young Peter Jackson, KO 2, won 3, draw 1, lost 1; Joe Walcott, lost, draw; Jack Blackburn, draw 4, ND 1. Lost Negro heavy title, Harry Wills, 15, 11/5/19, Tulsa. Unrecorded records estimate 22 with Wills. Records indicate 16, KO 2, ND 8, lost decision 3, KO by 2, plus

112

losing Negro title. Al Laney, sports writer *N.Y. Herald Tribune,* found Langford destitute, blind in Harlem tenement 1944, wrote story prompting $11,000 for Langford. Hall of Fame 1955. Recap: bouts 252, KO 99, decision 37, won foul 1, draw 31, lost decision 19, KO by 4, ND 59, no contest 2.

LARKIN, TIPPY (Tony Pilleteri) B. 11/11/17, Garfield, N.J. Italian. 5'7", 140. First fight, Johnny Priore, KO 2, 1935. Undefeated four years, except Mickey Duca, lost 8. Winning streak to Al Davis, KO by 5, 12/15/39, and Lew Jenkins, KO by 1, 3/8/40. Undefeated to Beau Jack, KO by 3, 12/18/42. Henry Armstrong, KO by 2, 3/8/43. Won vacated junior welter title, Willie Joyce, 12, 4/29/46, Boston. Defended: Joyce, 12, 9/13/46, NYC. Lack of interest paled division until 1959 when Carlos Ortiz was officially named champ, KO 2, Kenny Lane, 6/12/59, NYC. Active to 1952, spotty record. Last fight, Steve Marcello, KO by 4, 12/29/52, Providence. Recap: bouts 151, KO 57, decision 79, draw 1, lost decision 3, KO by 10, no contest 1.

LASTARZA, ROLAND B. 5/12/27, Bronx, N.Y. 5'10½". Heavy. Regarded as potential champ. First fight, Dave Glanton, won 6, 7/7/47, NYC. Undefeated first three years, including 17 KO. First loss, Rocky Marciano, 10, 1950. 1951–52: lost, Dan Bucceroni, Rocky Jones; won both returns. World title, Marciano, KO by 11, 9/24/53, NYC. Never fully recovered: 1954–55, Julio Mederos KO by 5, lost Don Cockrell, Charley Norkus. Inactive 1956. Comeback 1957, KO one, dec. one. Last fight Larry Zernitz, lost 10, 12/1/58, NYC. Recap: bouts 63, KO 25, decision 30, lost 6, KO by 2.

LATZO, PETE B. 8/1/02, Coloraine, Pa. Slav. 5'8", 140–168. Started career under name Young Clancy. First fight, Red Ferguson, KO 3, 1919. First loss, Frankie Schoell, 12, 1922. 1919–22: undefeated in 55. Won world welter title, Mickey Walker, 10, 5/20/26, Scranton. Defended: Willie Harmon, KO 5, 6/29/26, Newark; George Levine, won foul 4, 7/9/26, NYC. Lost title, Joe Dundee, 15, 6/3/27, NYC. Light heavy title, Tommy Loughran, lost 10, 6/1/28, Brooklyn; title, Loughran, lost 10, 7/16/28, Wilkes Barre. 1930–34, fights 19, lost 15. Last fight, Teddy Yarosz, KO by 4, 6/5/34, Pittsburgh. Recap: bouts 150, KO 25, decision 36, won foul 4, draw 3, lost 29, KO by 2, ND 50, no contest 1.

LAVIGNE, GEORGE KID (Saginaw Kid) B. 12/6/69, Saginaw, Mich. D. 4/6/36, Detroit, Mich. French. 5'3½", 133. First fight, Morris McNally, KO 1, 9/7/85, Saginaw. Undefeated through 1896, Young Griffo, draw twice; Joe Walcott, won; Jack McAuliffe, ND, draw. Won undisputed lightweight title claim, Dick Burge, KO 17, 6/1/96, London. Defended: Jack Everhardt, KO 24, 10/27/96, NYC; Kid McPartland, won 25, 2/8/97, NYC; Eddie Connolly, KO 11, 4/28/97, NYC; Walcott, won 12, 10/29/97, San Francisco; Jack Daly, draw 20, 3/17/98, Cleveland; Frank Erne, draw 20, 9/28/98, Coney Island; Tom Tracey, won 20, 11/25/98, San Francisco. Lost title, Erne, 20, 7/3/99, Buffalo. High living overtook man whom many historians regard as greatest lightweight. KO 19 by George McFadden, KO by 8, Jimmy Britt. Last appearance, Ad Wolgast, exh. 2, 1910, Detroit. Hall of Fame 1959. Recap: bouts 55, KO 16, decision 19, draw 8, lost decision 3, KO by 2, ND 7.

LEDOUX, CHARLES B. 10/27/92, Nievre, France. 5'½", 116. First fight, Charley Meyer, KO 1, 1909, Paris. First year, 17 KO; 1 win; lost, Georges Carpentier, 15. Impressive to 1911. 1912: Joe Bowker, KO 10; only loss, Digger Stanley, 20; return, KO 7. Undefeated 1914, 5 straight KO, Eugene Criqui, won 12. World War I, 1914–19. Undefeated 1919, including Jem Driscoll, 16. 1920, Johnny Coulon, KO 6; KO 4; won 1; draw 1; ND 3; lost, Jackie Sharkey, 15; Kid Williams, 12. Won European bantam title, Tommy Harrison, KO 18, 10/9/22, Hanley, Eng. French bantam title, Andre Routis, lost 20, 1/22/24, Paris. French feather title, Edward Mascart, won 20, 2/19/24, Paris. World bantam title, Abe Goldstein, lost 15, 7/16/24, NYC. Lost French feather title, Mascart, 20, 11/18/24, Paris. Last fight, Durocher, KO 2, 4/8/26, Strasbourg. Recap: bouts 110, KO 57, decision 23, won foul 3, draw 3, lost decision 15, KO by 2, ND 7.

LEGRA, JOSE B. 4/19/43, Cuba. Early detailed record unavailable, KO 4, decision 20, draw 2, lost decision 4, KO by 1. Undefeated: 1963 to mid-1965. First loss, Howard Winstone, 10, 1965. To 1969 undefeated. Won European vacant feather title, Yves Desmerets, KO 3, 12/22/67, Madrid. Vacated title 1968. Vacant world feather title, Johnny Famechon, lost 15, 1/21/69, London. Re-won European feather title, Tommasso Galli, 15, 6/26/70, Madrid. Defended: Jimmy Evie, won 15, 1/25/71, London. Nontitle, Ben Hassan, KO by 4, 1971, Madrid. Defended: Giovanni Girgenti, KO 9, 8/14/71, Alicante; Evan Armstrong, won 15, 2/15/72, London; Dan Vermandere, won 15, 10/6/72, Madrid. Awarded WBC feather title, Clemente Sanchez, KO 10, 12/16/72, Monterrey (Sanchez couldn't make weight). Lost WBC feather title, Eder Jofre, 15, 5/5/73, Brasilia, Brazil. Recap: bouts 146, KO 48, decision 84, draw 4, lost decision 8, KO by 2.

LEMOS, RICHIE B. 2/6/20, Los Angeles, Calif. Mexican. 5'5", 126. First fight, Tony Navarro, won 4, 7/2/37, Hollywood. Thru 1940, mostly winning, Petey Scalzo, KO by 7, 1940. Won NBA feather title, Scalzo, KO 5, 7/1/41,

Los Angeles. Lost title, Jackie Wilson, 12, 11/18/41, Los Angeles. Title return, Wilson, lost 12, 12/16/41, Los Angeles. Chalky Wright, KO by 6, 1942. Lackluster record to last fight, Tyree White, won 10, 8/27/43, Hollywood. Recap: bouts 79, KO 26, decision 25, draw 3 lost decision 20, lost foul 3, KO by 2.

LEON, CASPER (Gasper Leoni) B. 12/8/72, Palermo, Sicily. D. 5/6/26, New York, N.Y. 5'3½", 118. First fight, Jim Burns, KO 1, 1891. Impressive to American bantam and claimed world title, Jimmy Barry, KO by 28, 9/15/94, Lemont, Ill. Return title, Barry, draw 14, 3/30/95, Chicago; Barry, draw 20, 5/30/98, Davenport, Iowa. Barry (nontitle), draw 6, 1898. Terry McGovern, KO by 12, 1899; Harry Forbes, draw, 1900; lost, 1901. Last 3 years, spotty. Last fight, Morris Rauch, draw 20, 12/12/01. Hot Springs. Recap: bouts 99, KO 29, decision 33, won foul 1, draw 22, lost decision 8, lost foul 2, KO by 3, ND 1.

LEONARD, BENNY (Benjamin Leiner) (The Ghetto Wizard) B. 4/7/96, New York, N.Y. D. 4/18/47, New York, N.Y. Jewish. 5'5", 130– 133. Knocked out in first fight, Mickey Finnegan, 2, 1911, and in his last, Jimmy McLarnin, 6, 1932. Won world lightweight title, Freddie Welsh, KO 9, 5/28/17, New York. Defended: Johnny Kilbane, KO 3; Charley White, KO 9; Joe Welling, KO 14; Richie Mitchell, KO 6; Rocky Kansas, won 15; Kansas, KO 8; Lew Tendler, won 15. Retired 1925. Comeback as welterweight 1931: 20 bouts, 11 decisions, 7 KOs, 1 draw, 1 loss (McLarnin). Title, Jimmy McLarnin, KO by 6, 10/7/32. Retired. Regarded as one of the great scientific boxers. Lieutenant, Merchant Marine; referee. In Broadway show *Yip-Yip-Yak, Yank* 1918. Hall of Fame 1955. Recap: bouts 209, KO 68, decision 20, draw 1, lost foul 1, KO by 4, ND 115.

LESNEVICH, GUS B. 2/22/15, Cliffside, N.J. D. 2/28/64, Cliffside Park, N.J. Russian. 5'9", 175. Golden Glover, subnovice, intercity champ 1933, 1934. First pro, Justin Hoffman, KO 2, 5/5/34, Brooklyn. 1934–1936: 30, KO 8, win 18, draw 3, lost 1 to Jackie Aldare, defeated him on return. Freddie Steele, KO by 2, 1936. Young Corbett, KO by 5, 1937. Lost Ron Richards 1938. Winning streak victims included Lou Brouillard, Bob Olin. Light heavy title, Billy Conn, lost 15, 11/17/39, NYC. Title return, Conn, lost 15, 6/5/40. Detroit. Vacant NBA light heavy title, Anton Christoforidis, won 15, 5/22/41, NYC. Defended: Tami Mauriello, won 15, 8/26/41, NYC; Mauriello, won 15, 11/14/41, NYC. 1942: lost Bob Pastor and Jimmy Bivins, nontitle. Joined Coast Guard. Nontitle, Lee Oma, KO by 4, 1946. Title, Freddie Mills, KO 10, 5/14/46. Nontitle, Bruce Woodcock, KO by 8, 9/17/46, London. Title, Billy Fox, KO 10, 2/28/47, NYC. Title, Billy Fox,

KO 1, 3/5/48, NYC; Lost title, Mills, 15, 7/26/48, London. Vacant American title, Joey Maxim, lost 15, 5/23/49, Cincinnati. Last fight, NBA heavy title, Ezzard Charles, KO by 1, 8/10/49, NYC. Referee in N.Y., N.J. Remembered for his checkerboard of title bouts. Recap: bouts 76, KO 21, decision 36, draw 5, lost decision 9, KO by 5.

LEVINSKY, BATTLING (Barney Lebrowitz) B. 6/10/91, Philadelphia, Pa. D. 2/12/49, Philadelphia, Pa. Jewish. 5'11", 175. Started 1906 as Barney Williams, changed name 1913. First recorded fights 1910, several KOs, decisions, NDs and 3 losses through 1915—Leo Houck, Jack Dillon, Gunboat Smith. Return Dillion, light heavy title, lost 15, 4/25/16, Kansas City. Title return, Dillon, won 12, 10/24/16, Boston. Jack (Nonpareil) Dempsey, KO by 6, 11/6/18, Phila. Lost title, Georges Carpentier, KO by 4, 10/12/20, Jersey City. Lost American light heavy title, Gene Tunney, 12, 1/13/22, NYC. Last two fights 1929, KOs by Otto Von Porat, 5; Herman Weiner, 1. Hall of Fame 1966. Recap: bouts 272, KO 25, decision 40, won foul 1, draw 13, lost decision 13, lost foul 2, KO by 4, ND 174.

LEWIS, HARRY (Henry Besterman) B. 9/16/88, New York, N.Y. D. 2/22/56, Philadelphia, Pa. Jewish. 5'7", 142. First fight, Mexican Jim, KO 4, 1904, Phila. Impressive early career, all early fights in Pa. Prior to welter title claim, Joe Gans, ND; Young Erne, draw, ND; Mike (Twin) Sullivan, won; Jack Blackburn, ND; Frank Mantell, KO. Honey Mellody, KO 4, 4/20/08, Boston. Claimed vacant world welter title, not officially recognized. To 1913, creditable record, Frank Klaus, lost foul, ND; Georges Carpentier, lost; Leo Houck, ND, lost twice; Dixie Kid, KO 8. 1910–13: highly popular Paris, London. Returned to U.S. last fight, Joe Borrell, KO by 5, 10/13/13, Phila. (Collapsed in ring, retired.) Recap: bouts 163, KO 42, decision 37, won foul 1, draw 11, lost decision 12, lost foul 3, KO by 1, ND 56.

LEWIS, HEDGEMON B. Detroit, Mich. 145. First fight, Arnold Bush, KO 3, 5/13/66, Cincinnati; undefeated first two years. 1968–70, undefeated except Ernie Lopez series, won 1, KO by twice. World welter title, Jose Napoles, lost 15, 12/14/71, Los Angeles. N.Y. Commission version of world welter title, Billy Backus, won 15, 6/16/72, Syracuse. (N.Y. dethroned Napoles because of failure to acknowledge contract.) Defended title: Backus, won 15, 12/8/72, Syracuse. Recap: bouts 50, KO 24, decision 22, lost decision 2, KO by 2.

LEWIS, JOHN HENRY B. 5/1/14, Los Angeles, Calif. Negro. 5'11", 175. First fight, Tommy Cadena, KO 1, 1931. First year 10 successive KO, tragedy of Kid Terrain, KO 4, died after fight. In 1932 fought top rankers:

Yale Okun, won 10; Jim Braddock, won 10; Fred Lenhart, KO 4; Lou Scozza, won 10; Maxie Rosenbloom, lost 10. In 1933 beat Rosenbloom twice. (Rosenbloom won 2, 1935). Bob Olin, won 10 (nontitle), 1935. Won light heavy title, Olin, 15, 10/31/35, St. Louis. Lost two nontitle before defending, Rosenbloom and Emilio Martinez. Two returns, Martinez, 1937, 1938, won 10, KO 4. Defended: Jock McAvoy, won 15, 3/13/36, NYC; Len Harvey, won 15, 11/9/36, London, England; Olin, KO 8, 6/3/37, St. Louis; Martinez, KO 4, 4/25/38, Minneapolis; Al Gainer, won 15, 10/28/38. Between title defenses, fought heavies, beating Max Marek, Red Burman (KO), Al Ettore, Salvadore Ruggierello (KO), Isadore Gastanaga (KO), Johnny Risko, Marty Gallagher (KO), Elmer Ray (KO), Jimmy Adamick. Joe Louis signed for heavy title defense reluctantly, knowing his long-time friend wouldn't have chance, but fight would provide payday for John Henry. Mercifully, KO by 1, 1/25/39, NYC. Retired, relinquishing light heavy title. Recap: bouts 104, KO 54, decision 37, draw 5, lost decision 7, KO by 1.

LEWIS, NATHAN (Nate) B. (date uncertain). D. 11/18/52, Chicago, Ill. Manager-promoter. The career of the "Old Bald Eagle" spanned 46 years. His fighters left an imprint on almost every division. He even played a consequential role in the early days of Joe Louis.

A native of Wishtinetz, Poland, Lewis came to Chicago as a boy, was attracted to the boxing gyms, intrigued by the managing aspect. In the early years he guided Pete Herman, Joe Burman, Memphis Pal Moore, Charley White, later Leo Rodak, NBA feather champ, and Harry Thomas, who provided Nate's boxing heartbreak.

In 1929, vacated the manager's corner to become matchmaker for the newly built Chicago Stadium, an impressive site that enhanced Chicago's claim as one of the world's great boxing centers.

During his matchmaking period he played what he described as a "small part" in Joe Louis' career. Nate is credited with providing the Brown Bomber financial encouragement. During his first 8 bouts, Joe's biggest payday was less than $500. Lewis explained, "I underwrote a $1000 purse for him against Charley Massera when Joe thought that was all the money in the world.

"Next I gave him $2500 against Lee Ramage. Louis thought I was a miracle man, but the truth was that he was well worth it. All I did was recognize and gamble on a great fighter. I knew I couldn't miss while other promoters were sitting on their wallets."

His heartbreak was prompted by Thomas, a lumbering Minnesota heavy whom Nate had maneuvered into prosperous pairings with top-flight gate attractions. Thomas implicated Lewis in testimony that he had cooperated in KOs by Max Schmeling, 12/13/37, NYC, and Tony Galento, 11/14/38, Phila.

Nate's statement: "I have been connected with boxing since 1900, and in all those years the shadow of suspicion never has crossed my path. My record is clear. Thomas' story hurts me deeply." The boxing fraternity agreed with Old Bald Eagle.

When he died, after five years of illness, in a Chicago nursing home, available records indicated he was 71, but intimates suggested 77 was closer.

LEWIS, TED (Gershon Mendeloff) (Kid) B. 10/24/94, St. George's-in-the-East, London, England. D. 10/14/70, London, England. 5'5½, 126–170. First fight, Johnny Sharp, lost 6, 9/13/09, London. Impressive English record. Won English feather title, Alec Lambert, KO 17, 10/6/13, London. Won European feather title, Paul Til, foul 12, 2/2/14, London. To U.S. 1914: Phil Bloom, ND 10, NYC. Outstanding U.S. record. Jack Britton 1915–21, longest series between top-ranked boxers in history, 20: 1915, won 2, ND 1; 1916, lost 3, ND 2; 1917, ND 4, won world welter title, 20, 6/25/17, Dayton, Ohio; 1918, ND 4; 1919, lost title, KO by 9, 3/17, Canton, Ohio and ND; 1921, lost 15, 2/7, NYC. Defended: John Griffith, ND 15, 7/4/17, Akron, Ohio; Albert Badoud, KO 1, 8/31/17, NYC; Johnny Tillman, won 20, 5/17/18, Denver; Griffiths, ND 20, 7/4/18. Akron. European middle title, Frankie Burns, won 10, 10/4/23, London. Lost Britain and European welter titles, Tommy Milligan, 20, 11/26/24, Edinburgh. 1925–29, creditable record including seven straight KO 1927. Last fight, Johnny Basham, KO 3, 12/13/29, Hoxton, England. Settled in Vienna, boxing instructor. Hall of Fame 1964. Recap: bouts 253, KO 68, decision 85, won foul 2, draw 9, lost decision 13, lost foul 7, KO by 4, ND 65.

LEWIS, WILLIE B. 5/21/84, New York, N.Y. D. 5/17/49, New York, N.Y. Irish. 5'8", 158. First fight, Tom Lockwood, KO 2, 1900. Started at 15, fought to light heavies. Became favorite in France, responsible for much of boxing popularity there from 1908. Mostly impressive early years in U.S. Setbacks: Sam Langford, KO by 2; Joe Tipman, KO by 2; Honey Mellody, KO by twice, return, won KO 4, 1909, Paris. To Paris 1908, undefeated to Billy Papke, KO by 3, 1910. Stanley Ketchel, KO by 2, 1910; Georges Carpentier, lost 20, 1920. Returned U.S., 1911–12: KO 3, won 1, ND 7, draw 1; lost 1, KO by Mike Gibbons, 2. 1913–14 in France: KO 2, won 4, draw 2, lost 2. Last fight, Ercole Balzac, won 20, 1/31/14, Paris. Tavern operator, boxing manager. Recap: bouts 155, KO 57, decision 24, draw 14, lost decision 7, KO by 9, ND 44.

LIM, KI-SOO B. 9/17/39, Buk-Chong, Korea. Middle. Among greatest Orient fighters. Unrecorded 19 fights. Undefeated 1962–65, 12 KO, 5 dec., 2 draw. 1966, won Orient middle title, Fumio Katzu, KO 7, 1/4/66, Seoul, Korea. Defended: Nakao Saszaki, KO 6, 9/7/27, Tokyo. Won world WBA jr. middle title, Nino Benvenuti, 15, 6/25/66, Seoul. Defended: Stan Harrington, 15, 12/15/66, Seoul; Freddie Little, 15, 10/3/67, Seoul. Lost title, Sandro Mazzinghi, 15, 5/25/68, Milan. Lost Orient title, Hiseo Minami, 12, 11/20/68, Osaka; regained title, 15, 3/1/69, Seoul. Retired. Recap: bouts 34, KO 17, decision 13, draw 2, lost 2.

LISTON, SONNY (Charles Liston) (The Bear) B. 5/8/32 (some set age at 44 when died), Forest City, Ark. D. 12/30/70, Las Vegas, Nev. 6′1″, 220. First fight, Don Smith, KO 1, 9/2/53, St. Louis. Only defeat 10 years, Marty Marshall, 1954, won return 1956. Inactive 1957. 1958–62, 16 KO, 19 fights. (Floyd Patterson advised to avoid showdown because of Sonny's criminal background, hoodlum attachments. N.Y. Boxing Commission wouldn't grant license.) Won world heavy title, Patterson, KO 1, 9/25/62, Chicago. Defended: Patterson, KO 1, 7/22/63, Las Vegas. Lost title, Cassius Clay, KO by 7 in upset, 2/25/64, Miami Beach (quit after 7th). Return title, Clay, KO by 1, 5/25/65, Lewiston, Maine. 1966–68: 11 successive KOs followed. Leotis Martin, KO by 9, 12/6/69, Las Vegas. Last fight, Chuck Wepner, KO 10, 7/29/70, Jersey City. Found by wife week later, Liston died of undetermined circumstances. Recap: bouts 54, KO 39, decision 11, lost decision 1, KO by 3.

LOCHE, NICOLINO B. 9/2/39, Mendoza, Argentina. First fight, Luis Garcia, KO 2, 12/11/58, Mendoza. Impressive 14-year record confined to Argentina, two defeats, both reversed, in 121 fights. Won Argentine light title, Jaime Gine, 12, 11/4/61, Buenos Aires. Defended: Manuel Alvarez, won 12, 10/20/62, Buenos Aires. Won S. American light title, Sebastino Nascimento, 15, 6/29/63, Buenos Aires. Lost Argentine title, Abel Laudonio, 12, 11/14/64, Buenos Aires. Regained S. American title, Abel Laudonio, 12, 4/10/65, Buenos Aires. Regained Argentine title, Hugo Rambaldi, 12, 12/18/65, Buenos Aires. Won world junior welterweight title, Paul Fuji, KO 10, 12/12/68, Tokyo. Defended: Carlos Hernandez, won 15, 5/4/69, Buenos Aires; Joao Henrique, won 15, 10/12/69, Buenos Aires; Adolph Pruitt, won 15, 5/16/70, Buenos Aires; Domingo Barrera, won 15, 4/3/71, Buenos Aires; Antonio Cervantes, won 15, 12/12/71, Buenos Aires. Recap: bouts 115, KO 13, decision 86, draw 14, lost decision 2.

LOGART, ISAAC B. 4/11/33, Camaguey, Cuba. 5'7", 145. First fight, Ramon Varona, KO 3, 11/12/49, Camaguey. Impressive early record to Cuban light title, Rafael Lastre, KO by 8, 10/5/52, Havana. First U.S. fight, Kid Chocolate, won 6, 1954, Miami. Successful U.S. campaign to Virgil Akins loss, won return; won, Gil Turner. 1956–57: Gaspar Ortega series, won twice, lost twice; undefeated other bouts, including Joe Micelli (won twice), Yama Bahama, Turner, Ramon Fuentes. To 1966, spotty, including, 1958, Rudell Stich, won, lost; Don Jordan, lost; Akins, KO by 6. Lost all 4, 1959. 1966, Andy Heilman, KO by 5. Last fight, Blair Richardson, draw 10, 7/17/66, Halifax. Recap: bouts 108, KO 25, decision 44, draw 8, lost 24, KO by 7.

LOI, DUILIO B. 4/4/29, Trieste. First fight, Frangioni, won 6, 11/1/48, Genoa. To mid-1952 undefeated. Italian light title, Luigi Male, draw 12, 11/8/50, Milan. Won vacant Italian light title, Gianluigi Uboldi, 12, 7/18/51, Milan. Defended: Emilio Marconi, 12, 4/2/52, Cagliari European light title, Jorgen Johansen, lost 15, 8/18/52, Copenhagen. Defended: (Italian title): Ernesto Formento, KO 9, 1/29/53, Milan; Marconi, draw 12, 9/13/53, Grosseto. Won Europeon light title, Johansen, 15, 2/6/54, Milan. Defended: European (and Italian), Bruno Visintin, 15, 5/13/54, Milan; Jacques Herbillon, 15, 7/16/54, Milan; (and Italian) Giancarlo Garbelli, 15, 7/2/55, Milan; Seraphin Ferrer, 15, 11/26/55, Milan; Jose Hernandez, draw 15, 5/12/56, Milan; Hernandez, won 15, 12/28/56, Milan; Felix Chiocca, won 15, 12/26/57, Milan; Mario Vecchaiato, draw 15, 9/5/58, Milan; Marconi, won 15, 4/19/59, Milan. Vacated European light title. Won European welter title, Visintin, 15, 2/13/60, Milan. Defended: Chris Christensen, won 15, 8/5/61, St. Vincent; Fortunato Mancain, won 15, 7/15/62, Cagliari World junior welter, Carlos Ortiz, lost 15, 6/15/60, Milan. Won junior welterweight title, Ortiz, 15, 9/1/60, Milan. Defended: Ortiz, won 15, 5/10/61, Milan; Eddie Perkins, draw 15, 10/21/61, Milan. Lost title, Perkins, 15, 9/14/62, Milan. Regained title, Perkins, 15, 12/15/62, Milan. Retired 1/23/63. Recap: bouts 125, KO 25, decision 89, won foul 1, draw 7, lost decision 3.

LONDON, BRIAN B. 6/19/34, Blackpool, England. Amateur, fought as Jack Harper, won British Empire Games heavy title 1954, ABA title 1955. First pro fight, Dennis Lockton, KO 1, 3/22/55, London. Undefeated first year: 9 KO, 1 dec. 1956: 5 KO; Henry Cooper, KO by 1. Impressive record to Joe Erskine, won British and Empire titles, KO 8, 6/3/58, London. Willie Pastrano, lost 10, KO 5, 1958. Lost title, Cooper, 15, 1/12/59, London. World heavy title, Floyd Patterson, KO by 11, 5/1/59, Indianapolis. European heavy title, Dick Richardson, KO by 8, 8/29/60, London. British,

Empire and European heavy titles, Cooper lost, 15, 2/24/64, Manchester. Undefeated 1965. World title, Muhammad Ali, KO by 3, 8/6/66, London. 1968–69, 5 bouts, KO by 4 times. Last fight, Jerry Quarry, KO by 2, 9/3/69, Oakland. Recap: bouts 57, KO 26, decision 10, won disq. 1, draw 1, lost decision 9, KO by 10.

LOPOPOLO, SANDRO B. 12/18/39, Milan, Italy. Olympic lightweight finals 1960. First pro, Fernando Favia, KO 1, 3/4/61, Milan. Undefeated 3½ years, won vacant Italian light welter title, Antonio DeJesus, 10, 6/19/63, Verona. Defended: Giordano Campari, won 12, 6/28/64, St. Vincent; Massimo Consolati, won 12, 7/25/64, Senigallia. Lost title, Piero Brandhi, 12, 9/24/64, Treviso. Regained, Brandhi, KO 8, 3/12/65, Genoa. European light welter, Juan Sombrita, lost 15, 7/17/65, Santa Cruz. Defended: Italian title: Romano Bianchi, won 12, 12/14/65, Ascoli Piceno. Won world junior welter title, Carlos Hernandez, 15, 4/30/66, Rome. Defended: Vincente Rivas, KO 7, 10/21/66, Rome. Lost world title, Paul Fuji, KO by 2, 4/30/67, Tokyo. European junior welter title, Rene Roque, lost 15, 4/22/70, Montecatini. Creditable record thru 1971. Recap: bouts 72, KO 20, decision 35, won foul 1, draw 7, lost decision 8, KO by 1.

LOUGHRAN, TOMMY B. 11/29/02, Philadelphia, Pa. Irish. 5'11", 175. First fight, Eddie Carter, KO 2, 1919. Undefeated until Harry Greb, 15, 1/30/23, N.Y. Return, Greb, won, lost; lost Jack Delaney, Young Stribling twice, Ad Stone. Winning streak started 1926, won vacant light heavy title, Mike McTigue, 15, 10/7/27, NY. Defended: Jimmy Slattery, won 15, 12/12/27; Leo Lomski, won 15, 1/6/28, NYC; Pete Latzo, won 15, 6/1/28, Brooklyn; Mickey Walker, won 10, 3/25/29, Chicago; Jimmy Braddock, won 15, 7/18/29, NYC. Vacated title, campaigned as heavy. Jack Sharkey, KO by 3, 9/26/29, NYC. 1930–33, fair success as heavy, Max Baer, won; Sharkey return, win. Avenged losses to Ernie Schaaf, King Levinsky, Steve Hama. Title, Primo Carnera, lost 15, 3/1/34, Miami (outweighed 86 lbs., 270–184, greatest difference ever in championship bout). To 1937, spotty. Last fight, Sonny Walker, won 10, 3/18/37, Phila. Enlisted U.S. Marines 1942. Hall of Fame 1956. Recap: bouts 171, KO 18, decision 76, won foul 1, draw 8, lost decision 21, KO by 2, ND 45.

LOUIS, JOE (Joseph Louis Barrow) (Brown Bomber) B. 5/13/14, Lafayette, Ala. Negro. 6'1½", 200. Poverty. Large family. Father, state institution, died two years later. Mother remarried. Moved to Detroit. Worked ice wagon after school, cabinetmaker. First amateur, 16, floored by Johnny Miller 7 times, 2 rounds. Amateur: won 50 of 54, 41 KO. 1933: AAU light heavy finals, lost, Max Marek. Pro, 1934: John Roxborough manager, Jack

Blackburn trainer. First bout, Jack Kracken, KO 1, 7/4/34, Chicago ($50 purse). 1934–35: KO 22, 4 wins. Upset, KO by 12, Max Schmeling, 6/19/36, NYC. Followed by 11 KOs, 1 decision (Bob Pastor). Heavyweight title, Jim Braddock, KO 8, 6/22/37, Chicago. Defended most times of any heavy, 25 (22 KOs, 2 decisions, 1 disqualification win). Highlights defending: Schmeling, KO 1, 6/22/38, NYC (probably most gratifying of Louis's career; also, earned $349,228 for 1 round); John Henry Lewis, KO 1, 1/25/39, NYC., close friend; Jack Roper, KO 1, 4/17/39, Los Angeles; Tony Galento (floored Louis 1st round), KO 4, 6/28/39, NYC; Bob Pastor (had earlier, 1937, lost decision, 10, to Joe), KO 11, 9/20/39, Detroit; Arturo Godoy, won close dec., 15, 2/9/40, NYC; return, KO 8, 6/20/40, NYC. KO string prompted phrase, "Bum of the Month Club." Buddy Baer knocked Louis out of ring, 5/23/41, disqualified 7, Wash., D.C.; Billy Conn, KO 13, 6/18/41, NYC (overconfident Conn held edge at KO). Buddy Baer return, KO 1, 1/9/42, NYC. Army service 1942. (Donated Baer, other purses to Army Relief Fund.) Exhs. Defended: Conn, KO 8, 6/19/46, NYC; Tami Mauriello, KO 1, 9/18/46, NYC; Joe Walcott, won 15, split dec., 12/5/47, NYC. Walcott, KO 11, 6/25/48, NYC. Announced retirement 3/1/49 after holding title 11 years, 8 months, longer than any other heavy; defended 25 times. Exhs. Comeback, Ezzard Charles, lost 15, 9/27/50, NYC. Rocky Marciano, KO by 8, 10/26/51, NYC. Exhs. through 1951. Retired. Movie of Bomber's life, *The Joe Louis Story,* with Coley Wallace, heavy turned actor. Referee, promoter, business ventures. Hospitalized, nervous problem, recovered. Beset with income tax problems. Ring earnings $4,626,781, include purses, radio, TV, exhibitions, etc. Regarded as one of greatest, most popular fighters. Credit to boxing. Hall of Fame 1954. Recap: bouts 71, KO 54, decision 13, won foul 1, lost decision 1, KO by 2.

LYLE, RON B. 1943, Denver, Colo. Negro. 6'3", 215. From family of 19 children. Fighter background without precedent, served 7½ years of 15–20-year term, Canon City, Colo., state prison, charged second-degree murder in gang fight. Outstanding prison athlete, basketball captain, baseball .400 hitter, football quarterback; learned boxing from Lt. Cliff Mattax, athletic director. Wounded in prison knife fight, twice pronounced dead, required 35 pints blood to keep alive. Recovering, saw Mattax at bedside, changed his life's outlook: "To see a white man really worrying about me, changed my whole life." Outstanding amateur: 25–4 record, 17 KO, won National AAU title, member U.S. boxing team touring Europe, only loss, Ivan Alexi, Romania, Olympic bronze medalist. Won N. American title, International Boxing League. First pro bout, A.J. Staples, KO 2, 4/23/71, Denver. First year undefeated, 8 KO, 2 won. 1972: 7 straight KO, including Buster Mathis, 2; Luis Pires, 3. 1973: Larry Middleton, KO 3; Jerry Quarry, lost 12; Gregorio

Peralta, won 10, Denver. Recap: bouts 21, KO 17, decision 3, lost decision 1.

LYNCH, BENNY B. 4/2/13, Glasgow, Scotland. D. 8/6/46, Glasgow, Scotland. 5'5", 112. First fight, Young McColl, KO 3, 6/11/31, Glasgow. From 1932 undefeated thru 1935, won world, European, British fly title, Jackie Brown, KO 2, 9/8/35, Manchester. Defended world title: Small Montana, won 15, 1/19/37, London; Peter Kane, KO 13, 10/13/37, Glasgow. To bantams, 1938, vacated titles. Fair success. Last fight, Aurel Toma, KO by 3, 10/3/38, London. Recap: bouts 72, KO 27, decision 29, won foul 1, draw 9, lost decision 4, lost foul 1, KO by 1.

LYNCH, JOE B. 11/30/98, New York, N.Y. D. 8/1/65, Brooklyn, N.Y. Irish. 5'8", 118. First fight, Terry Martin, ND 10. Impressive first 5 years. From early 1919 thru 1920, undefeated. Won World bantam title, Pete Herman, 15, 12/22/20, NYC. Lost title, Herman, 15, 7/25/21, Brooklyn. Regained title, Johnny Buff, KO 14, 7/10/22, NYC. Defended: Midget Smith, won 15, 12/22/22, NYC. Lost title, Abe Goldstein, 15, 3/21/24, NYC. Last fight, Pal Moore, draw 10, 3/4/26, Miami. Postmaster New City, N.Y. Drowned in Sheepshead Bay. Recap: bouts 134, KO 29, decision 13, draw 15, lost decision 13, ND 64.

McAULIFFE, JACK B. 3/24/66, Cork, Ireland. D. 11/5/37, Forest Hills, N.Y. Irish. 5'6", 133. Regarded by some historians as first lightweight champ, but technically never held world light title; one of last bare-knuckle champs. Dispute reverts to America champion Abe Hickson, holding title 1868–72, retired. Elimination tourney surfaced Artie Chambers, who won championship, retired 1873. Nonpareil Jack Dempsey recognized as champ until outgrowing class. McAuliffe claimed American title, Jim Carney, draw 74, 1887 (loosely to settle world title dispute). First fight, Bob Mace, won 3, 7/1/84, NYC. Won disputed title bout, Billy Frazier, KO 21, 10/28/86, Boston. Won forfeit, Frazier, 12/15/86, Boston. 1887–96, undefeated in 26. Last appearance, title claimant Dick Burge, exh. 3, 1/15/14, London. First champ to retire undefeated. On Broadway and English stage, *King of the Turf,* 1893. Hall of Fame 1954. Recap: bouts 52, KO 9, decision 32, draw 9, ND 2.

McCARTY, LUTHER B. 3/20/92, Hitchcock County, Nebr. D. 5/24/13, Calgary, Alberta. Scotch-Irish. 6'4", 205. First fight, Watt Adams, KO 2, 1/7/11, Culbertson, Mont. Early in career regarded as "white hope" to dethrone Jack Johnson. First year undefeated including 7 straight KO. 1912: 8 KO including Carl Morris, Jim Flynn. Jess Willard, ND 10. Won "white heavy title," Al Palzer, KO 18, 1/1/13, Vernon, Calif. ND: Flynn, Frank Moran. Lost title, Arthur Pelkey, KO by 1, 5/24/13, Calgary, Alberta. McCarty died immediately after bout. Coroner's jury determined cause was a brain hemorrhage, result of a previous injury. (Pelkey's blow was called light during a clinch.) Regarded as one of great heavy prospects, favored to win title of troubled Jack Johnson whose legal woes had him fighting in exile. Recap: bouts 25, KO 16, KO by 1, ND 8.

McCOY, AL (Al Rudolph) B. 10/23/94, Rosenhayn, N.J. D. 8/22/66, Los Angeles, Calif. German. 5'8", 158–60. First fight unrecorded, 1908. 1908–14, undefeated in 95. Won world middle title, George Chip, KO 1, 4/6/14, Brooklyn. 1914–17: undefeated until O'Dowd. Lost title, Mike O'Dowd, KO by 6, 11/14/17, Brooklyn. 1918–19: lost 3, 2 ND. Last fight, title, O'Dowd, KO by 3, 7/17/19, St. Paul. Retired. Recap: bouts 146, KO 28, decision 22, draw 8, lost decision 3, KO by 2, ND 83.

McCOY, CHARLES (Norman Selby) (Kid; the Corkscrew Kid) B. 10/13/73, Rush County, Ind. D. 4/18/40, Detroit, Mich. (suicide). 5'11", 160. First fight, Pete Jenkins, won 4, 6/2/91, St. Paul. Undefeated in 19. Billy Steffers, KO by 1, 1894, won return, 10. May, 1894–Dec., 1898, undefeated 45, lost 1. Won welter title, Tommy Ryan, KO 15, 3/2/96, Maspeth, L.I. Outgrew welters. Tom Sharkey, KO by 10, Jack McCormick, KO by 1, undefeated 10. Jim Corbett, KO by 5, 1900. Light heavy title, Jack Root, lost 10, 5/22/03, Detroit. 1904–16 undefeated. Last fight, Artie Sheridan, won 4, 8/4/16. Became a successful movie actor (made over million dollars in Hollywood) and continued to box exhibitions. Legend is that expression "The real McCoy" originated here. Character was making the bars, passing himself as Kid McCoy. McCoy happened by as the man was boasting his prowess, and incidentally cadging a few drinks. He stiffened him with a right hand. "That," announced The Kid, "is the real McCoy." Hall of Fame 1957. Recap: bouts 105, KO 35, decisions 45, won foul 1, draw 9, lost decision 2, KO by 4, ND 9.

McFARLAND, PACKEY (Patrick McFarland) B. 11/1/88, Chicago, Ill. D. 9/23/38, Joliet, Ill. Irish. 5'8", 130. First fight, Pete West, KO 2, 1904. One of boxing's most paradoxical records: Only 1 loss in 104, KO by Dusty Miller, 5, first year, 1904. To 1915 undefeated. Top-drawer opposition: Freddie Welsh, won twice, draw 1; Leach Cross, 3 ND; Jack Britton, 3 ND; Tommy Murphy, 2 ND, 1 won; Cyclone Thompson, won; Dick Hyland, ND 2; Owen Moran, ND; Last fight Mike Gibbons, ND 10, 9/11/16, NYC. Never title shot. Hall of Fame 1957. Recap: bouts 104, KO 47, decision 17, draw 5, KO by 1, ND 34.

McGOORTY, EDDIE (Eddie Van Dusart) B. 7/31/89, Eureka, Wis. D. 11/2/29, Milwaukee, Wis. (Soldiers Home). Irish. 5'10", 158. Outstanding amateur 1904. First pro, Young Schumacher, KO 2, 8/6/05, Green Bay,

Wis. Recognized as a "fighter's fighter," never clear shot at title. Only loss to late 1913, Tom Lancaster, 20, 1909, Dublin (won return 20, 1910, Dublin). Jimmy Clabby, lost 12, 1913. Jack Dillon, won 1, ND 1, 1911. 1915: Mike Gibbons, ND; Les Darcy, KO by 15, 7/31/15, Sydney, Australia (recognized as world middle title in Australia). Return, Darcy, KO by 8, 1915, Sydney. Return U.S., 1918, George Chip, Harry Greb, ND. Joe Beckett, Frank Goddard, Bombardier Wells, all KO by, 1919–20, London. Last fight, Bud Gorman, ND 10, 3/9/22, Oshkosh, Wis. Recap: bouts 128, KO 41, decision 24, draw 10, lost decision 7, lost foul 2, KO by 6, ND 38.

McGOVERN, TERRY (John Terrence McGovern) (Terrible Terry) B. 3/9/80, Johnstown, Pa. D. 2/26/18, Brooklyn, N.Y. Irish, 5'4", 128. First fight, Frank Barnes, won 10, 4/24/87, Brooklyn. To 1901 undefeated (except Tim Callahan, lost foul; return bouts, draw 20, KO 10, 1898.) Won vacated world bantam title, Pedler Palmer, KO 1, 9/12/99, Tuckahoe, N.Y. Overweight, vacated bantam title. Won feather title, George Dixon, KO 8, 1/9/1900, NYC. Dixon, won 6; Joe Gans, KO 2, 1900. Lost title, Young Corbett, KO by 2, 11/28/01, Hartford, Conn. Corbett (nontitle), KO by 11, 1903. To retirement 1908, 1 defeat (George Barton, 1904, later Mpls. sports writer, dean of Midwest referees). Last fight, Spike Robson, ND 6, 5/26/08, NYC. Also acted on Broadway, *The Bowery After Dark, Terry on the Spot, The Road to Ruin,* 1900–01. Hall of Fame 1955. Recap: bouts 77, KO 34, decision 24, won foul 1, draw 4, lost decision 1, lost foul 1, KO by 2, ND 10.

McGOWAN, WALTER B. 10/13/42, Burnbank, Lanarkshire, Scotland. Outstanding amateur, won 122 of 124. British ABA champ 1961. First pro fight, George McDade, KO 3, 8/9/61, Glasgow. Impressive first three years. Won British and Empire fly titles, Jackie Brown, KO 12, 5/2/63, Paisley, Scotland. Defended: King Solomon, KO 9, 9/12/63, Paisley. European title, Salvatore Burruni, lost, 15, 4/24/64, Rome. European bantam title, Tommasso Gallo, draw 15, 12/3/65, Rome. Won world fly title, Burruni, 15, 6/14/66, London. Won British, Empire bantam titles, Alan Rudkin, 15, 9/6/66, London. Lost world title, Chartchai Chionoi, KO by 9, 12/30/66, Bangkok. Title return, Chionoi, KO by 7, 9/19/67, London. Lost British, Empire titles, Rudkin, 15, 5/13/68, Manchester. Last fight, Antonio Chiloiro, won 8, 11/11/69, London. Recap: bouts 40, KO 14, decision 18, draw 1, lost decision 3, KO by 4.

MACIAS, RAUL (Raton) B. 7/28/34, Mexico City, Mex. 5'3½", 118. Lost in second series 1952 Olympics. First pro bout, Manuel Armenteros, won 10, 4/15/53, Mex. City. Undefeated 1953–54, won Mexican bantam title, Beto Couary, 12, 10/17/53, Mex. City. North American title, Nate Brooks, 12,

9/26/54, Mex. City. Defended Mexican title: Fili Nava, 12, 4/10/54, Mex. City. Won vacated world NBA title, Chamrern Songkitrat, KO 11, 3/9/55, San Francisco. Nontitle, Billy Peacock, KO by 3, 6/15/55, Los Angeles. Defended: Leo Espinosa, KO 10, 3/25/56, Mex. City; Dommy Ursa, KO 11, 6/15/57, San Francisco. Lost NBA title, Alphonse Halimi, 15, 11/6/57, Los Angeles. Undefeated to retirement and last fight, Chocolate Zambrano, KO 5, 10/13/62, Guadalajara. Recap: bouts 38, KO 22, decision 14, lost decision 1, KO by 1.

McLARNIN, JIMMY (Baby Face) B. 12/17/05, Belfast, Ireland. Irish. 5'5½", 145. To U.S. early age. First fight, George Ainsworth, won 4, 1923. Undefeated in 19. 1925: Bud Taylor, lost 10, won foul 2; Jackie Fields, KO 2. 1926: 3 lost, Taylor, Johnny Farr, Doc Snell. 1927: undefeated. World lightweight title, Sammy Mandell, lost 15, 5/21/28, NYC. Ray Miller, KO by 7. Bounced back, 9 straight including return Miller, won 10, Mandell, Joey Glick twice, KO Sgt. Sammy Baker, Ruby Goldstein, Al Singer. Lost 10, Billy Petrolle, 1930. Won two returns, 1931. Lost Lou Brouillard; KO Benny Leonard, 6; Sammy Fuller, 8, 1932. Won world welter title, Young Corbett III, KO 1, 5/29/33, Los Angeles. Lost title, Barney Ross, 15, 5/28/34, NYC. Regained title, Ross, 15, 9/17/34, NYC. Lost title, Ross, 15, 5/28/35, NYC. Last 3, Tony Canzoneri, lost 10, won 10; Lou Ambers, won 10, 11/20/36. Retired. Protege Pop Foster, guided him through success, left him fortune. Great box office fighter. Hall of Fame 1966. Recap: bouts 77, KO 20, decision 42, won foul 1, draw 3, lost decision 10, KO by 1.

McTIGUE, MIKE (Michael Francis McTigue) B. 11/26/92, County Clare, Ireland. Irish. 5'9", 175. Started 1909. First recorded fight, Happy Howard, lost foul, 1914. Impressive 1915–23, setbacks, Jim Healy, KO by 1; losses, Jeff Smith, Young Fisher (returns reversed Smith, Fisher). Won light heavy title, Battling Siki, 20, 3/17/23, Dublin (St. Pat's Day). Lost title, Paul Berlenbach, 15, 5/30/25, NYC. Tommy Loughran, lost 15, 9/7/27, NYC (for light heavy title vacated by Jack Delaney). 1927–30: spotty, KOs by Mickey Walker, Tuffy Griffiths, George Hoffman, Jack Gagnon, Isidoro Gastanaga. Last fight, Garfield Johnson, KO by 4, 9/22/30, Utica, N.Y. Recap: bouts 144, KO 57, decision 24, draw 6, lost decision 10, lost foul 2, KO by 9, ND 36.

McVEY, SAM (Samuel McVea) B. 5/17/85, Oxnard, Calif. D. 12/21/21, New York, N.Y. 5'10½", 205. First recorded fight, Jack Johnson, lost 20, 2/27/03, Los Angeles. Returns, lost 20, 1903; KO by 20, 1904, exh. 1915. Good share of 79 bouts against Sam Langford: won, 2; draw, 5; ND, 4; KO by twice, last ND, 10, 1920. 1907–09: 10 string KO. Claimed avoidance by title aspirants, name opponents mostly Negro. Last fight, Harry Wills, no contest 6, 9/8/20, Phila. Recap: bouts 79, KO 33, decision 13, won foul 1, draw 8, lost decision 5, KO by 7, ND 11, no contest 1.

MAHER, PETER B. 3/16/69, Galway, Ireland. D. 7/22/40, Baltimore, Md. 5'11¾", 190. First fight, Martin O'Hara, KO 2, 1888, Dublin. Won middle title Ireland, John Seenan, KO 5, 8/27/88, Dublin. John L. Sullivan Competition, beat Jack Wallis, Tom Water, Larry Drew, each 3-round fights. 1899–90: exhs., Al Bowman, KO 6. 1891: Gus Lambert, KO 1; arrived U.S. 10/7/91, won five straight. Bob Fitzsimmons, KO by 12, 3/2/92, New Orleans. 1893–95 undefeated, including 10 KO. Fitzsimmons, KO by 1, 2/21/96, Langtry, Tex. To 1898, undefeated, including Joe Choynski, KO 6. 1898: Joe Goddard, KO by 1, won return. Kid McCoy, KO by 5, Choynski, lost 6, only defeats to 1902. Jeff Smith series: won KO four times, one ND. Tom Sharkey, Phila. Jack O'Brien, Joe Grim, NDs. Record spotty to last fight, Marvin Hart, KO by 2, 4/1/07, Hot Springs. Recap: bouts 76, KO 31, decision 13, won foul 3, draw 5, KO by 14, ND 10.

MANDELL, SAMMY (Samuel R. Mandella) B. 2/5/04, Rockford, Ill. D. 4/20/61, Oak Park, Ill. Italian-Albanian. 5'5½", 135. First fight, John Hagerman, KO 3, 1920. Undefeated to 1923. Joey Sangor, KO by 7, 1923. To 1926, undefeated except lost Phil Salvadore, 4, 1924; Jimmy Goodrich, lost foul, 6, 1925. Won world light title, Rocky Kansas, 10, 7/3/26, Chicago. Defended: Jimmy McLarnin, won 15, 5/21/28, NYC. (Nontitle, Goodrich, KO by 2, 9/25/28, Flint, Mich.) Tony Canzoneri, won 10, 8/2/29, Chicago. (McLarnin, lost 10, 1929 and 30, nontitles.) Lost title, Al Singer, KO by 1, 7/17/30, NYC. To 1934, losing record. Last fight Joe Bernai, KO by 6, 6/27/34, Oakland, Calif. Operated tavern, Rockford. Recap: Bouts 168, KO 28, decision 53, won foul 1, draw 8, lost decision 11, lost foul 1, KO by 5, ND 60, NC 1.

MANDOT, JOE (Baker Boy) B. 7/3/91, New Orleans, La. D. 7/29/56, New Orleans, La. French. 5'6", 133. First fight, Charley Donnelly, KO 3, 12/12/08, New Orleans. Impressive first 5 years, including Charley White, won, draw; Owen Moran, won; Matty Baldwin, draw; Willie Ritchie, Ad Wolgast NDs; Joe Rivers, won, lost. First major setback, Leach Cross, KO by 10, 1913. Undefeated 1914 including Freddie Welsh, Wolgast, NDs; Johnny Kilbane, draw; Rivers, won. 1915: Johnny Dundee, draw, ND; Rocky Kansas, ND two; Benny Leonard, KO by 7. Next fight, Dundee, won. Undefeated 1917. KO 1, won 5, ND 1, draw 2, lost 2, KO by 3, to last fight, Eddie Smith, won 4, 9/1/22, Los Angeles. Operated Louisiana fishing and farm camps, worked New Orleans fairgrounds during racing season. Recap:

bouts 98, KO 15, decision 35, won foul 1, draw 11, lost decision 8, KO by 6, ND 22.

MANTELL, FRANK (Frank Otto Mintell) B. 6/25/86, Brandenburg, Germany. D. 10/9/51, Phoenix, Ariz. 5'9½", 154–158. First fight, George Perry, KO 2, 2/22/06, Providence, R.I. Undefeated in 17. Rube Smith, lost 20, 1907. Harry Lewis, KO by 3, 1908; Billy Papke, KO by 1, 1908. Undefeated in 13. Frank Klaus, KO by 9, 1910. Billy Papke, won 20, 2/22/12, Sacramento, claimed title. Jack Herrick, won 20, 3/30/12, advertised title. No other record of title bouts, last 2 fights, KO by Harry Greb, 1917, KO by Mike Gibbons, 10/12/17, St. Paul. Recap: bouts 101, KO 23, decision 14, won foul 1, draw 18, lost decision 13, lost foul 1, KO by 5, no decision 25, no contest 1.

MARCANO, ALFREDO B. 1/17/47, Sucre, Venezuela. First fight, Pedro Chirinos, won 4, 3/4/66, Caracas. Impressive early record, including 1968 undefeated, 9 KO, 1 win. Won world junior light title, Hiroshi Kobayashi, KO 10, 7/29/71, Aomori, Japan. Defended: Kenji Iwata, KO 4, 11/7/71, Caracas. Recap: bouts 43, KO 20, decision 12, draw 4, lost decision 5, KO by 2.

MARCEL, ERNESTO B. 5/23/48, Colon, Panama. First fight, Valentin Worrell, KO 1, 4/12/66, Panama. Undefeated first year. Impressive early record. Series: Augustin Ceden, won, KO 9, lost, 1967–68. Undefeated 1969, 8 KO, 2 decision. Only loss to 1972, Roberto Duran, KO by 10, 1970. World feather title, Kuniaki Shibata, draw 15, 11/10/71, Matsuyama. Won WBA feather title, Antonio Gomez, 15, 8/19/72, Marcay. Defended: Enrique Garcia, KO 6, 12/3/72, Panama City. Recap: bouts 40, KO 22, decision 13, draw 2, lost decision 2, KO by 1.

MARCIANO, ROCKY (Rocco Marchegiano) (Brockton Blockbuster) B. 9/1/23, Brockton, Mass. D. 8/31/69, Newton, Iowa, plane crash. Italian. 5'11", 184. All-round athlete, baseball catcher, tryout with Cubs. Amateur, KO 4 in two nights. First pro fight, Les Epperson, KO 3, 3/17/47, Holyoke, Mass. 1948–52: 37 KO, 5 dec. Won heavyweight title, Joe Walcott, KO 13, 9/23/52, Phila. Defended: Walcott, KO 1, 5/15/53, Chicago; Roland LaStarza, KO 11, 9/24/53, NYC; Ezzard Charles, won 15, 6/17/54, NYC; Charles, KO 8, 9/17/54, NYC; Don Cockell, KO 9, 5/16/55, San Francisco; Archie Moore, KO 9, 9/21/55. Retired 4/27/56, only heavy champ without career defeat. Regarded by some as the unheralded greatest. Family man.

Disregarded many urgings to return when Floyd Patterson champion. Hall of Fame 1959. In a computer-matched series of bouts to choose all-time champion, won over Muhammad Ali in U.S. version. In English version Ali won. Recap: bouts 49, KO 43, decision 6—record not matched by any other champion.

MARINO, DADO (Salvador Marino) B. 8/26/16, Honolulu, Hawaii. First fight, Paul Francis, KO 2, 6/20/41, Honolulu. Undefeated first two years. Won Hawaiian fly title, Alfred Chavez, 10, 4/29/44, Honolulu. To 1947 lost only Al Chavez, 6, all fights Honolulu. Rinty Monaghan, lost foul 9, Glasgow, Scotland. NBA fly title, Monaghan, lost 15, 10/20/47, London. World bantam title, Manual Ortiz, lost 15, 3/1/49, Honolulu. Won world flyweight title, Terry Allen, 15, 8/1/50, Honolulu. Defended: Allen, 15, 11/1/51, Honolulu. Lost title, Yoshio Shirai, 15, 6/19/52, Tokyo. Return title bout, Shirai, lost 12, 11/15/52, Tokyo. Recap: bouts 74, KO 21, decision 35, won foul 1, draw 3, lost decision 11, KO by 3.

MARINO, TONY B. 1912, Pittsburgh, Pa. D. 2/1/37, New York, N.Y. Italian. 5'3", 118. First fight, Young Ketchel, won 6, 1931. To 1936, so-so record. Won world bantam title, Baltazar Sangchilli, KO 14, 6/29/36, NYC. Lost title, Sixto Escobar, KO by 13, 8/31/36, NYC. To 1937, lost to Sangchilli 10; won 4. Last fight, Indian Quintana, lost 8, 1/30/37, Brooklyn (brain hemorrhage, died next day). Recap: bouts 40, KO 7, decision 19, draw 2, lost decision 10, KO by 2.

MARTIN, BOB (Fighting Bob) B. 11/11/98, Terra Alta, W. Va. Scotch-Irish. 6'2", 216. 1918–19: champion American Expeditionary Forces; only loss, Gene Tunney, 4. First pro bout, Bob Scanlon, KO 11, 7/11/19, Paris. 1919: 8 straight KO. 1920: 15 KO, lost foul 1, Bob Roper lost. 1921: 6 KO including Martin Burke, Gunboat Smith; Roper ND; lost 2, Bill Brennan, Fay Keiser. 1922: 3 KO, Brennan ND, Floyd Johnson, KO by 10. Seriously injured, auto accident. Returned 1923: 3 fights, KO 1, lost 1, Burke, KO by 7. Last fight, Ray Vaulliermet, KO 4. Recap: bouts 101, KO 87, draw 1, lost decision 5, lost foul 1, KO by 2, ND 5.

MARTIN, EDDIE (Edward Vittorio Martino) (Cannonball Martin) B. 3/3/03, Brooklyn, N.Y. Italian. 5'4", 118. First fight, Sam Jackson, KO 2, 1922. 1923–24: undefeated in 38. Won world bantam title, Abe Goldstein, 15, 12/19/24, NYC. Lost title, Charlie Rosenberg, 15, 3/20/25, NYC. Junior light title, Tod Morgan, lost 15, 7/18/28, Brooklyn. Rocky record to last fight, Al Dunbar, lost 10, 7/18/32, Brooklyn. Recap: bouts 90,

KO 27, decision 45, draw 3, lost decision 8, KO by 3, ND 3, no contest 1.

MARTINEZ, VINCE B. 5/5/29, Mt. Kisco, N.Y. Italian. 5'9", 130. First fight, Joe Lucarelli, won 4, 3/9/49, Jersey City. Undefeated first year, 13 bouts. Undefeated 1951–52. 1953–55 impressive, including Chico Vejar, lost, won return; Chuck Davey, KO 7; Art Aragon, won 10; Al Andrews, won 10; undefeated 1955. 1957: Kid Gavilan, won twice; Ralph Dupas, only loss. Vacant welter title, Virgil Akins, KO by 4, 6/6/58, St. Louis. Creditable record to 1961, including four straight KO, 1960. Last fight, Miguel Aguero, lost 10, 5/8/61, NYC. Recap: bouts 75, KO 35, decision 32, lost decision 6, KO by 2.

MASON, FRANKIE (Frank McCan) B. 1896, Fort Wayne, Ind. 5'4½", 108–115. First fight, George Dale, KO 8, 1910. Undefeated 5½ yrs. First loss, Frankie Conley, KO by 3, 1915. Undefeated to 1917. NDs Johnny Coulon, Young Zulu Kid twice, KO by Pete Herman, 3, 1917. Undefeated to Carl Tremaine, lost 8, mid-1919, KO by 1, 1920. Johnny Ertle, won twice; NDs Tremaine, Jackie Sharkey, Ray Moore, Johnny Rosner two, Johnny Buff. American fly title, Buff, lost 15, 2/11/21, New Orleans. 1922 undefeated. 1923: Pancho Villa, KO by 5. Inactive to last fight, Willie LaMorte, KO by 2, 1926. Recap: bouts 213, KO 45, decision 19, draw 11, lost decision 4, KO by 5, ND 128, no contest 1.

MATTHEWS, MATTY (William R. Matthews) B. 7/13/73, New York, N.Y. D. 12/6/48, Brooklyn, N.Y. Irish. 5'7½", 138. First fight, Johnny Bennis, KO 12, 1891, NYC. Undefeated in 15, losing to Jack Daly, 1897. World Welter title, Billy Smith, lost 25, 8/26/98, NYC. Tom Ryan, won twice; Billy Smith, KO 19. Won world welter title, Jim Ferns, 15, 10/16/1900, Detroit. (Had lost nontitle to Ferns previous month.) Defended: Tom Couhig, won 20, 4/29/01, Louisville. Lost title, Ferns, KO by 10, 5/24/01, Toronto. Thru 1904, indifferent success. Last fight, Ed Kennedy, draw, 10/26/04, Carnegie, Pa. Recap: bouts 83, KO 14, decision 30, won foul 2, draw 17, lost decision 12, KO by 1, ND 7.

MAXIM, JOEY (Guiseppe Antonio Berardinelli) B. 3/28/22, Cleveland, Ohio. Italian. 6'1", 175. First fight, Bob Perry, won 4, 1/13/41, Cleveland. Top-shelf competition first year: decisioned Lee Oma, Nate Bolden, Red Burman, lost to Orlando Trotter. Ezzard Charles slowed down career, two straight losses, 1942. Curtis Sheppard, KO by 1, 1943, return Sheppard, won 10. In army, 1943. 1944: 4 straight wins, losses to Lloyd Marshall,

Johnny Flynn. Jersey Joe Walcott, won 1946; lost 2, 1947. Vacant American light heavy title, Gus Lesnevich, won 15, 5/23/49, Cincinnati. Won world light heavy title, Freddie Mills, KO 10, 1/24/50, London. Heavy title, Charles, lost 15, 5/30/51, Chicago. Return (Charles had lost title), lost 12. Defended light heavy: Bob Murphy, won 15, 8/22/51, NYC; Ray Robinson, KO 14, 6/25/52, NYC (Robinson, leading on points, overcome by heat exhaustion). Lost title, Archie Moore, 15, 12/17/52, St. Louis. Return, Moore, lost 15, 6/24/53, Ogden, Utah; Moore, 1/27/54, Miami. Floyd Patterson, won 8, 1954. Lost 2, 1955, Bobo Olson, Willie Pastrano. 1957: Eddie Machen lost 2. Last fight, Ulli Ritter, lost 10, 5/17/58, Mannheim, Germany. Recap: bouts 115, KO 21, decision 61, draw 4, lost decision 27, lost foul 1, KO by 1.

MAZZINGHI, SANDRO B. 10/3/38, Pontedera, Italy. Jr. middle. First fight, Severino Gagliardi, KO 2, 9/15/61, Florence. Undefeated first year, four KO, one dec. Undefeated 1963, including Don Fullmer, KO 8, Wilfie Greaves, KO 5. Won WBA jr. middle title, Ralph Dupas, KO 9, 9/7/63, Milan. Defended: Dupas, KO 13, 12/2/63, Sydney; Tony Montano, KO 12, 10/3/64, Genoa; Fortunato Manca, 15, 12/11/64, Rome. Nontitle, Gaspar Ortega, KO 7, 1964. Isaac Logart, KO 5, won, 1965. Lost WBA jr. middle title, Nino Benvenuti, KO by 6, 6/18/65, Milan; return title, lost 15, 12/17/65, Rome. Undefeated 1966–69. Won European jr. middle title, Yoland Leveque, KO 12, 6/17/66, Rome. Defended: Bo Hoberg, KO 14, 11/11/66, Stockholm; Jean Roland, KO 10, 2/3/67, Milan; Joe Gonzales, KO 4, 12/1/67, Rome. Won WBA jr. middle title, Ki-Soo Lim, 15, 5/25/68, Milan. Defended: Freddie Little, NC 8, 10/25/68, Rome. 1969–70, KO three, dec. one, no contest one. Recap: bouts 66, KO 42, decision 18, won foul 1, lost 2, KO by 1, no contest 2.

MELLODY, BILLY (Honey) B. 1/15/84, Charlestown, Mass. D. 3/15/19, Charlestown, Mass. Irish. 5'7", 145. First fight, Jack Kearns, KO 2, 3/20/01, Boston. Impressive start: first year, 7 straight KO. 1902–03: undefeated in 21; first loss, Jim Stone, KO by 13, 1903, 2 returns, draws. Won world welter title, Joe Walcott, 15, 10/16/06, Chelsea, Mass. Return, nontitle, Walcott won 12. Lost title, Mike (Twin) Sullivan, 20, 4/23/07, Los Angeles. Active to 1913, never regained stature to challenge for title. Last fight, Dave Powers, won 10, 1/30/13, Lawrence, Mass. Recap: bouts 95, KO 36, decision 20, draw 13, lost decision 6, lost foul 1, KO by 6, ND 13.

MENETREY, ROGER B. 6/16/45, Annemasse, France. 145. 1967–68, won 14, lost 1. 1969, undefeated, 13 KO, 2 dec. 1 draw; won French welter title, Jean Josselin, KO 6, 11/17/69, Paris. Defended: Robert Gallois, KO 5,

1/26/70, Paris: Yvon Mariolle, KO 3, 6/13/70, Grenoble; Guy Vercoutter, KO 4, 10/20/70, Paris. European welter title, Ralph Charles, KO 7, 6/4/71, Geneva. Defended European title: Silvano Bertini, KO 13, 11/26/71, Geneva; Joe Hansen, KO 10, 6/22/72, Copenhagen; Sandro Lopopolo, KO 13, 12/9/72, Grenoble. 1973, Art Kettles, won 10. Recap: bouts 37, KO 27, decision 6, draw 1, lost decision 2, KO by 1.

MILDENBERGER, KARL B. 11/23/37, Kaiserslautern, Germany. One of West Germany's great amateur, pro heavies. First fight, M. Striemer, KO 1, 10/15/58, Stuttgart. Undefeated first year. 1959, only setback Helmut Ball, KO by 7, return won 8. Undefeated 1960–61. 1962, Pete Rademacher, won. European heavy title, Dick Richardson, KO by 1, 2/24/64, Dortmund, West Germany. Undefeated to 1966, including Billy Daniels, KO 3; won, Eddie Machen, Wayne Bethea, Archie McBride, Alonzo Johnson; draw, Zora Folley. Won vacant European heavy title, Sante Amonti, KO 1, 10/17/64, Berlin. Defended: Piero Tomasoni, 15, 5/14/65, Frankfurt; Gerhard Zech, 15, 11/26/65, Frankfurt; Yvan Prebeg, 5, 6/15/66, Frankfurt. World heavy title, Muhammad Ali, KO by 12, 9/10/66, Frankfurt. Defended European title: Tomasoni, 15, 2/1/67, Frankfurt; Billy Walker, KO 8, 3/21/67, London; Zech, 15, 12/31/67, Berlin. 1967, Oscar Bonavena, lost 12. 1968, Leotis Martin, KO by 7. Last fight, lost title, Henry Cooper, disq. 8, 9/18/68, London. Never fought in U.S. Recap: bouts 62, KO 19, decision 34, draw 3, lost disq. 1, lost decision 1, KO by 4.

MILLER, FREDDIE B. 4/3/11, Cincinnati, Ohio. D. 5/8/62, Cincinnati, Ohio. German. 5'5", 126. First fight, Billy Barnes, KO 2. Impressive early years: 1927–28, 1 loss; 1929, undefeated; 1930, 1 loss. World feather title, Battling Battalino, lost 10, 7/23/31. Won NBA feather title, Tommy Paul, 15, 1/13/33, Chicago. Defended: Baby Arizmendi, won 10, 2/24/33, Los Angeles; Speedy Dado, won 10, 3/21/33, Los Angeles; Jackie Sharkey, won 10, 1/1/34, Cincinnati: Nel Tarleton, won 15, 9/21/34, Liverpool, England; Jose Girones, KO 1, 2/17/35, Barcelona; Tarleton, won 15, 6/12/35, London; Vernon Cormier, won 15, 10/22/35, Boston; John Pena, won 15, 2/18/36, Seattle; Petey Sarron, won 15, 3/2/36, Coral Gables, Fla. Lost title, Sarron, 15, 5/11/36, Washington, D.C. Nontitle, Sarron, won 10, 1937. Title, Sarron, lost 12, 9/4/37, Johannesburg, So. Africa. To 1940, spotty. Last fight, Herschel Joiner, KO by 8, 4/1/40. Recap: bouts 237, KO 43, decision 156, won foul 2, draw 5, lost decision 23, lost foul 2, KO by 1, ND 4, no contest 1.

MILLER, RAY B. 10/5/08, Chicago, Ill. Jewish. 5'5", 135. First fight, Sailor Frankline, KO 2, 1924. Undefeated in 25 first year. 1925–26: creditable, Joey Sangor, won, ND; Joe Glick, won, lost; Billy Petrolle, ND. 1927: upset Eddie

Shea, 10; Pete Nebo, 10. 1928: Sid Terris, KO 1; Jimmy McLarnin, KO 8. Unpredictable career including, 1929–33, Tommy Grogan, KO 4, won 10; McLarnin, lost 10; Johnny Jacick, KO 1; Johnny Datto, won twice; Petrolle, won, lost; Barney Ross, lost. Last fight, Joe Helmer, won 8, 4/24/33, Louisville. Never KO',d, never title chance. Recap: bouts 111, KO 31, decision 43, won foul 1, draw 4, lost decision 23, lost foul 2, ND 7.

MILLS, FREDDIE B. 6/26/19, Parkstone, Dorset, England. D. 7/25/65, London, England. 5'10", 175. First fight, Reg Davis, KO 3, 3/25/36, Bournemouth. Entire career centered in England. 1936–42: 73 wins, losses 8, including KO by 8. Only familiar name to U.S. fans, Jock McAvoy, won 10, KO 1. Won British Empire light heavy title, Len Harvey, KO 2, 6/20/42, London. Empire heavy title, Jack London, lost 15, 9/15/44, Manchester. World light heavy title, Gus Lesnevich, KO by 10, 5/14/46, London. Won vacant European light heavy title, Pol Goffaux, KO 4, 9/8/47, Haringey. Won world title, Lesnevich, 15, 7/26/48, London. 1948: Bruce Woodcock, KO by 14. Lost title, Joey Maxim, KO by 10, 1/24/50, London. Retired. Operated nightclub. TV commentator. Writer. Promoter. Died of gunshot wound. Recap: bouts 96, KO 52, decision 21, draw 6, lost decision 11, KO by 6.

MIMS, HOLLY B. 2/10/29, Washington, D.C. 155 lbs. Typical journeyman fighter; more successful than most. Record studded with champions and mediocre, occasions on verge of title fights, never title chance. First fight, Angelo Marino, draw 4, 6/1/48, Washington, D.C. Slow start, first year: lost 2, draw 2, dec. 3. Impressive 1949–52, including decision, Johnny Bratton, twice; Leslie Felton; lost, Ray Robinson. Undefeated 1953–54, including Willie Troy, Eddie Green, Sammy Walker, Moses Ward, Bobby Dykes (draw). 1955–57, up, down: KO 1, dec. 4, lost 5. 1958, undefeated including Spider Webb, won 10; Bobby Boyd, draw 10. 1959, down again: lost, Boyd, Joey Giardello, Rudell Stitch, Dick Tiger; won disq., Henry Hank. Up again in 1960–62, undefeated, including Jimmy Ellis, won 10; lost return, 1962. To 1965, spotty. Last fight, Joe Adair, KO by 6, 5/13/64, Elizabeth, N.J. Recap: bouts 109, KO 23, decision 48, draw 16, lost decision 16, KO by 6.

MISKE, BILLY B. 4/12/94, St. Paul, Minn. D. 1/1/24, St. Paul, Minn. (Bright's disease). German. 6', 165–180. First fight, Soldier Gregory, KO 4, 1913. Tireless campaigner. To 1919: ND, Tommy Gibbons, Al McCoy, Harry Greb, Jack Dillon, Battling Levinsky, Carl Morris, Fred Fulton, Jack Dempsey, Jim Flynn, Bill Brennan, Mike O'Dowd. Only loss, Kid Norfolk, 12, 1917. Illness 1919, refused retirement. Heavy title, Dempsey, KO by 3, 9/6/20, Benton Harbor (a "charity" fight, to help Miske out with the medical bills). Undefeated to last fight; Brennan, Bob Roper, Martin Burke, Gibbons,

Fulton. Last fight, Brennan, KO 4, 11/7/23, Omaha. Recap: bouts 103, KO 34, decision 9, won foul 2, draw 2, lost decision 1, KO by 1, ND 54.

MITCHELL, CHARLEY (Charles Watson Mitchell) B. 3/24/61, Birmingham, England. D. 4/3/18, Brighton, England. Irish. 5'9", 165–175. Originally a bare-knuckle fighter, became a factor in modern-day boxing. First fight, Bob Cunnigham (bare knucks) won 50 minutes, 1/11/78, Birmingham. Bill Kennedy, draw 30 m., 1879, London. Success thru 1882. To U.S., 1883. First, Mike Cleary, won 3, 4/9/83, NYC. John L. Sullivan, lost 3 (Mitchell decked John L. 1st round). Record spotted with draws, 1 loss, Dominick McCaffery, 4, 1884. Returned England, 1886. John L. Sullivan, draw 20, 3/10/88, Chantilly, France. England heavy title, Jem Mace, won 3, 2/7/90, Glasgow. To U.S., Arthur Upham, won 6, 1892. Jim Corbett, KO by 3, 1/25/94, Jacksonville, Fla., $5000 side bet, regarded by some as world championship. Hall of Fame 1957. Recap: bouts 27, KO 0 (KOs often regarded as decisions), decisions 13, draw 11, lost decision 2, KO by 1.

MITCHELL, PINKEY (Myron Mitchell) B. 1899, Milwaukee, Wis. Irish. 5'11", 135. First fight, Joe Homeland, KO 3, 1917. To mid-1921, undefeated, mostly ND in Midwest. Proclaimed first junior welter champ, 1922, result of popularity poll sponsored by *Boxing Blade* magazine. Spotty nontitle, Benny Leonard, KO by 10; lost to Tommy Freeman, Jimmy Duffy, Joe Anderson, Joe Dundee, Tommy White. Lost title, Mushy Callahan, 10, 2/21/26, Vernon, Calif. Last fight, Dundee, NC 6, 8/11/27, Milwaukee. Recap: bouts 79, KO 9, decision 2, won foul 1, draw 4, lost decision 7, lost foul 1, KO by 4, ND 50, NC 1.

MONAGHAN, RINTY (John Joseph Monaghan) B. 8/21/20, Belfast, Ireland. First fight, Vic Large, KO 4, 2/17/35, Belfast. Undefeated to mid-1938, Jackie Paterson, KO by 5. Won NBA fly title, Dado Marino, 15, 10/20/47, London. Won world fly title, Paterson, KO 7, 3/23/48, Belfast. Defended: Maurice Sandeyron, won 15, 4/5/49, Belfast; Terry Allen, draw 15, 9/30/49, Belfast, last fight. Announced retirement 4/25/50. Recap: bouts 51, KO 19, decision 22, won foul 1, draw 1, lost decision 6, lost foul 1, KO by 1.

MONTANEZ, PEDRO B. 4/24/14, Cayey, Puerto Rico. Spanish-Jewish. 5'5", 135. First fight, Jesus Rodil, won 8, 1931. Won Puerto Rican light title, Emilio Moris, 10, 1933, San Juan. 1934–35: 13 straight KO. Undefeated to light title, Lou Ambers, lost 15, 9/23/37, NYC. Undefeated to mid-1939, Davey Day, KO by 8. Welter title, Henry Armstrong, KO by 9, 1/24/40.

Last fight, George Martin, lost 8, 10/29/42, Brooklyn. Recap: bouts 100, KO 51, decision 37, draw 5, lost decision 5, KO by 2.

MONTGOMERY, BOB B. 2/10/19, Sumter, S.C. Negro. 5'8", 132. Amateur; won 22, lost 2, 1937. First pro unrecorded: 8 KO, 2 win, 1938. First recorded, Johnny Buff, KO 2, 10/23/38, Atlantic City. First two years: 16 KO, 8 wins, 1 draw, 1 loss. 1940: fought division top, Lew Jenkins, Davey Day, Bobby Ruffin, Morrie Shapiro. Won N.Y. light title, Beau Jack, 15, 5/21/43, NYC. Lost title, Jack, 15, 11/19/43, NYC. Re-won, Jack, 15, 3/3/44, NYC. Army. Defended: Allie Stolz, KO 13, 6/28/46, NYC; Wesley Mouzon, KO 8, 11/26/46, Phila. Lost title, Ike Williams, KO by 6, 8/4/47, Phila. Lost last 7 fights; last, Eddie Giosa, lost 10, 3/27/50, Phila. Recap: bouts: 97, KO 37, decision 38, draw 3, lost decision 16, KO by 3.

MONTREAL, YOUNG (Morris Billingkoff) B. 1898, Russia. Jewish. 5'3", 115. First fight, Shamus O'Brien, KO 1, 1916. To 1921 undefeated, Johnny Rosner, won 12, 4/10/19, Providence, claimed American fly title, relinquished to enter bantams. Undefeated 1922 to Pancho Villa, lost 10, return ND. Fought top-rankers, Tony Canzoneri; Kid Williams; Bud Taylor KO by 3, won return; Bushy Graham, won, lost three. Popular in New England states, never world title chance. Last fight, Graham, lost 10, 12/4/29, Providence. Recap: bouts 106, KO 11, decision 46, draw 6, lost decision 20, KO by 1, ND 21, no contest 1.

MONZON, CARLOS B. 8/7/42, Santa Fe, Argentina. First fight, Ramon Montenegro, KO 2, 2/6/63, Rafaela, Argentina. To 1966, impressive record, only three defeats. Won Argentine middle title, Jorge Fernandez, 12, 9/3/66, Buenos Aires. 1966 through 1971 undefeated. Won world middle title, Nino Benvenuti, KO 12, 11/7/70, Rome. Defended: Benvenuti, KO 3, 5/8/71, Monte Carlo; Emile Griffith, KO 14, 9/25/71, Buenos Aires. Nontitle, Roy Dale, KO 5, 5/5/73, Rome. Title defense, Griffith, won 15, 6/2/73, Monte Carlo. Recap: bouts 90, KO 53, decision 24, draw 9, lost decision 3, ND 1.

MOORE, ARCHIE (Archibald Lee Wright) (Ol' Man River) B. 12/13/16 (year questioned by some; mother says 1913), Benoit, Miss. Negro. 5'11", 170–190. First fight, Poco Kid, KO 2, 1/31/36, Hot Springs, Ark. 1936: 16 KO, 2 win, 1 draw, 3 lost. 1937: 10 KO, 2 win. 1938–41: 17 KO, 5 win, 1 draw, 5 lost. Lost three times to Shorty Hogue 1939–41. Retired 1941 because of illness. 1942–52: Hogue, KO 2, string of KO, wins; lost, Ezzard Charles twice; KO by Eddie Booker, 8, 1944; KO by Jimmy Bivins, 6, 1945; Leonard Morrow, KO by 1, 1948. Harold Johnson, won 10, lost 10, 1951.

Johnson, won 10, 1952. Won light heavy title, Joey Maxim, 15, 12/17/52, St. Louis. Defended: Maxim, won 15, 6/24/53, Ogden, Utah; Maxim, won 15, 1/27/54, Miami; Johnson, KO 14, 8/11/54, NYC; Bobo Olson, KO 3, 6/22/55, NYC; Yolande Pompey, KO 10, 6/5/56, London; Tony Anthony, KO 7, 9/20/57, Los Angeles; Yvon Durelle, KO 11, 12/10/58, Montreal; Durelle, KO 3, 8/12/59, Montreal. Oct. 1960, NBA withdrew recognition as light heavy champ, N.Y. and EBU withdrew Feb. 1962. Heavy title, Rocky Marciano, KO by 9, 9/21/55, NYC. Floyd Patterson, heavy title, KO by 5, 11/30/56, Chicago. Last real fight, Mike Di Biase, KO 3, 3/16/63, Phoenix. Movies and TV. Last fight, Nap Mitchel, exh. KO 3, 8/27/65, Los Angeles. Recap: bouts 228, KO 140, decision 53, draw 8, lost decision 17, lost foul 2, KO by 7, no contest 1.

MOORE, DAVEY B. 11/1/33, Lexington, Ky. D. 3/23/63, Los Angeles, Calif., after bout. 5'2½". Amateur: 1952 bantam champ, Olympic Games 1952, Helsinki, eliminated third round. First pro, William Reece, won 6, 5/11/53 Portsmouth, N.H. Brought along slowly, creditable record. Undefeated 1957–58. Won feather title, Kid Bassey, KO 13, 3/18/59, Los Angeles. Title return, Bassey, KO 11, 8/19/59, Los Angeles. Defended: Kazuo Takayama, won 15, 9/29/60, Tokyo; Donald Valdez, KO 1, 4/8/61, Los Angeles; Takayama, won 15, 11/13/61, Tokyo; Olli Maki, KO 2, 6/7/52, Helsinki. Lost title, Sugar Ramos, KO by 10, 3/21/63, Los Angeles. (Moore died two days later, brain damage received during fight.) Recap: bouts 67, KO 30, decisions 28, won foul 1, draw 1, lost decision 5, KO by 2.

MOORE, MEMPHIS PAL (Thomas Wilson Moore) B. 7/28/94, Kenton, Tenn. D. 3/15/53, Memphis, Tenn. 5'6", 118. Called "Memphis" to avoid confusion with Pal Moore, ranking Phila. lightweight. First fight, Young Hymas, KO 2, 1913. Recorded 208 bouts including 11 champs: Sammy Mandell, Bud Taylor, Frankie Genaro, Fidel LaBarba, Kid Williams, Pete Herman, Joe Lynch, Johnny Ertle, Johnny Buff, Jimmy Wilde, Eugene Criqui. Never title chance. Navy 1918, won bantam title King's Trophy Tournament, International Games. To 1930, continued success. Last recorded fight, Bobby Allen, won 10, 3/31/30, Chicago. Successful Memphis real estate. Recap: bouts 208, KO 10, decision 77, draw 22, lost decision 15, lost foul 3, ND 81.

MORAN, CHAPPIE B. 1869, Manchester, England. Amateur, U.S. bantam title 1886. Won British title 1888, came to U.S. 1889, Frank Donovan, KO 14. Vacant world bantam title, Spider Kelly, lost 10, 6/5/89. Brooklyn. Return won title, Kelly, 10, 6/5/89, Brooklyn. Lost title, Kelly, KO by 10,

1/31/90, Brooklyn. Recorded recap: bouts 9, KO 1, decision 5, lost decision 2, KO by 1.

MORAN, FRANK B. 3/18/87, Pittsburgh, Pa. 6'1½", 198. First fight, Fred Broad, won 6, 1910, Greensburg, Pa. Creditable record to world heavy title, Jack Johnson, lost 20, 6/27/14, Paris. Comeback, undefeated 3 years to Fred Fulton, KO by 3, 1919. Undefeated to 1920. 1921: KO by 2 boxers, Bob Martin 7, Bob Roper 6. 1922: Joe Beckett, KO by 7. Last fight, Marcel Nilles, lost 15, 12/30/22, Paris. Retired. Hollywood extra. Recap: bouts 60, KO 24, decision 8, won foul 2, draw 2, lost decision 6, KO by 5, ND 13.

MORAN, OWEN (The Fearless) B. 10/4/84, Birmingham, England. D. 3/17/49, Birmingham, England. 5'4", 118–135. First fight, Bill Lovesey, KO 2, 1900. Tough, rough competitor, never title chance. Abe Attell, ND 3, draw 2; Tommy Murphy, won 1, ND 3, lost 1; Pal Moore draw 2, ND 1; Joe Bowker, ND 1, lost 1; George Dixon won. Undefeated 1905–09. Popular in U.S. KO by Young Shugrue, 7, 1914, NYC, returned England. Last fight, Billy Marchant, lost foul 2, 8/21/16, Manchester. Hall of Fame 1965. Recap: bouts 106, KO 25, decision 37, draw 6, lost decision 10, lost foul 5, KO by 2, ND 21.

MORGAN, TOD (Bert Pilkington) B. 12/25/02, Sequim, Wash. D. 8/3/53, Seattle, Wash. Scottish. 5'7½", 130. First fight, George Green, won 4, 1920. Undefeated 6 years. Won junior lightweight title, Mike Ballerino, KO 10, 12/2/25, Los Angeles. Defended: Carl Duane, won 15, 11/19/26, NYC; Eddie Martin, won 15, 7/18/28, NYC; Santiago Zorrilla, won 10, 4/5/29, Los Angeles, Baby Sal Sorio, won 10, 5/20/29, Los Angeles. Lost title, Benny Bass, KO by 2, 12/19/29, NYC. Undefeated 1930, spotty to temporary retirement 1935. Returned 1938, Australia. To 1942: 22 fights, lost 7. Last fight, Lew Edwards, won 12, 7/18/42, Melbourne. Recap: bouts 189, KO 22, decision 91, won foul 4, draw 29, lost decision 32, lost foul 1, KO by 3, ND 6, no contest 1.

MORRIS, CARL B. 2/23/87, Fulton, Ky. D. 7/11/51, Pasadena, Calif. Irish-Cherokee. 6'4", 235. First fight, Tim Hurley, KO 2, 9/23/10, Muskego, Okla. Size, ability labeled him "great white hope" to dethrone Jack Johnson. Undefeated to Luther McCarty, KO by 6, 1912. Continued undefeated except losses to Al Kubiak, Gunboat Smith, beat both in returns. Jack Dempsey: lost, lost foul, KO by 1. Inactive 1919–20. Return erratic. 1921–22: KO by 3. Last fight, Fred Fulton, KO by 4, 12/18/22, Tulsa. Never did face

Jack Johnson. Recap: bouts 72, KO 35, decision 8, won foul 4, draw 1, lost decision 2, lost foul 4, KO by 5, ND 13.

MOYER, DENNY B. 8/8/39, Portland, Oreg. 5'8½", 150. National AAU welter champ 1957. First pro bout, Jimmy McCoy, won 4, 8/17/57, Portland. Undefeated to welter title, Don Jordan, lost 15, 7/10/59, Portland. To WBA junior middle title, wins including Paddy DeMarco, Virgil Akins, Emile Griffith. Title established by WBA,* Moyer won from Joey Giambra, 15, 10/20/62, Portland, to win recognition. Defended: Stan Harrington, won 15, 2/19/63, Honolulu. Lost title, Ralph Dupas, 15, 4/29/63, New Orleans. Return title, Dupas, lost 15, 6/17/63, Baltimore. Undefeated to 1971. Won North American middle title, Art Hernandez, 12, 2/10/71, Las Vegas. Defended: Jimmy Lester, won 12, 3/30/71, Stateline, Calif.; David Oropeza, KO 6, 4/21/71, Las Vegas; Jose Chirino, 12, 6/22/71, Stateline. Recap: bouts 103, KO 22, decision 56, draw 4, lost decision 15, KO by 6.
*Jr. middle division was established in 1962 at a session of the WBA, formerly NBA, at Tacoma, Wash. A 15-round bout was approved between Moyer and Giambra. WBA is the only boxing association to recognize the division.

MUNDINE, TONY B. 6/10/51, Australia. 160. One of Australia's greater middles. First fight, Frank Graham, won 4, 3/5/69, Cammeray, Austral. First year, 8 KO, 4 dec.; only loss, Kahu Mahanga, KO by 9. 1970: 9 straight KO, including Austral. middle title, Billy Choules, KO 4, 4/23/70, Redfern, New South Wales. 1971–72, 15 KO, including Denny Moyer, 7. Won Austral. heavy title, Foster Bibron, KO 11, 2/25/72, Brisbane (outweighed by 46 lbs.). Won British Empire title, Bunny Sterling, KO 15, 4/14/72, Milton, N.S.W. Defended: Matt Donovon, KO 3, 3/73, Sydney. Recap: bouts 42, KO 35, decision 4, draw 1, KO by 2.

MURPHY, BILLY (Thomas W. Murphy) (Torpedo Murphy) B. 1863, Auckland, New Zealand. D. 7/26/39, Auckland, New Zealand. 5'6½", 117. Mostly successful early overseas career, 1887–88. To San Francisco, 1889. Johnny Griffith, KO 3. Frank Murphy, draw 27. Won world feather title, Ike Weir, KO 14, 1/13/90, San Francisco. (Confusion over world title claim, American reporters claimed neither Weir nor Murphy had right to title, only British Empire crown.) Australia feather title, Young Griffo, lost 15, 9/3/90, Sydney. To 1906, fair record. Weir, KO by 6; George Dixon, KO by, lost: Griffo, lost twice. Returned to Australia, last fight, Jim Ross, draw 4, 1906, Auckland. Recap: bouts 90, KO 17, decision 32, draw 14, lost decision 15, KO by 9, ND 1, no contest 2.

MURPHY, HARLEM TOMMY B. 4/13/85, New York, N.Y. D. 11/26/58, New York, N.Y. Irish. 5'5½", 130. First fight, Tony Bender, draw 8, 2/23/03, Elizabeth, N.J. Undefeated to Terry McGovern, KO by 1, 1905. Top opponents (never title chance): Abe Attell draw, ND three; Ad Wolgast won, draw, ND; Packey McFarland ND three, lost 1; Owen Moran won, lost, ND two; Leach Cross ND twice. 1907–13: only losses, Harry Harris, foul, Moran, McFarland. 1914: Willie Ritchie, lost. Last fight, Frankie Callahan, ND 10, 9/22/14, Brooklyn. Recap: bouts 130, KO 23, decision 15, draw 12, lost decision 4, lost foul 1, KO by 2, ND 73.

NAPOLES, JOSE (Angel Martequilla) B. 4/13/40, Santiago de Cuba, Cuba. First fight, Julio Rojas, KO 1, 8/2/56, Havana. To 1963, impressive record, 1 defeat; undefeated 1958, '60, '61, '62. Won world welter title, Curtis Cokes, KO 13, 4/18/69, Los Angeles. Defended: Cokes, KO 10, 6/29/69. Mexico City; Emile Griffith, won 15, 10/12/69, Los Angeles; Ernie Lopez, KO 15, 2/15/70, Los Angeles. Lost title, Billy Backus, KO by 4, 12/3/70, Syracuse, N.Y. Regained title, Backus, KO 4, 6/4/71, Los Angeles. Defended: Hedgemon Lewis, 15, 12/14/71, Los Angeles. Recap: bouts 70, KO 46, decision 19, lost decision 3, KO by 2.

NEIL, FRANKIE (Francis James Neil) B. 7/25/83, San Francisco, Calif. Irish. 5'5½", 115–118. First fight, Charles Anderson, KO 1, 11/8/1900, San Francisco. Impressive first 4 years, 15 KO. World bantam title, Harry Forbes, lost 7, 12/23/02, Oakland, Calif. Return title bout, Forbes, won KO 2, 8/13/03, San Francisco. Defended: Billy DeCoursey, KO 15, 9/4/03, Los Angeles; Johnny Reagan, draw 20, 10/16/03, Los Angeles. Forbes, KO 3, 6/17/04, Chicago. Lost title, Joe Bowker, 20, 10/17/04, London. 1905–09: fair record. Last fight, Willie Jones, KO by 13, 2/26/10, Baltimore. Recap: bouts 56, KO 24, decision 1, won foul 1, draw 4, lost decision 9, KO by 4, ND 13.

NELSON, BATTLING (Oscar Nielson) (Durable Dane) B. 6/5/82, Copenhagen, Denmark. D. 2/7/54, Chicago, Ill. Danish. 5'7½", 133. First fight, Wallace's Kid, KO 1, 9/3/96, Hammond, Ind. To 1906, erratic record.

143

Lightweight title, Joe Gans, lost foul 42, 9/3/06, Goldfield, Nev. Won title, Gans, KO 17, 7/4/08, San Francisco. Defended: Gans, KO 21, 9/9/08, Colma, Calif.; Dick Hyland, KO 23, 5/29/09, Colma; Jack Clifford, KO 5, 6/22/09, Oklahoma City. Lost title, Ad Wolgast, KO by 40, 2/22/10, Point Richmond, Va. Creditable record through 1917, never title return. Inactive 1918–23. Last appearance, Phil Salvatore exh. 3, 6/10/23, Los Angeles. Rough, tireless, box-office attraction. Hall of Fame, 1957. Recap: bouts 132, KO 38, decision 20, won foul 1, draw 19, lost decision 15, lost foul 2, KO by 2, ND 35.

NORFOLK, KID (William Ward) B. 7/10/93, Panama. 5'8", 170. First fight, Jack Livingston, won 10, 1914. 3½ years fights Panama area. Impressive early record including Gunboat Smith, KO 2; Arthur Pelkey, KO 13. Claimed disputed light heavy title, Billy Miske, won 12, 10/16/17, Boston. (Not seriously recognized, Battling Levinsky, having defeated overweight champ Jack Dillon 1916, generally regarded as titleholder.) Sam Langford, KO by 2, 1917. Only defeats 1921: Clay Turner, lost 12, returns, KO 4, ND; Lee Anderson, KO by 9, returns won twice; NDs, Joe Jennette twice, Miske. Harry Wills, KO by 2, 1922. Upset 3 champs: Tiger Flowers, KO 1; Battling Siki, won 15, 1923; Harry Greb, won 10, 1924. Failing vision slowed career late 1924; Tommy Gibbons, KO by 6. 1925: Bob Lawson, KO by 1; Frank Moody, KO by 4. Last fight, Ted Moore, KO by 4, 3/19/26, San Francisco. Series: Smith KO 2, ND twice; Turner KO twice, ND, KO by; Anderson won three, KO by. Blind right eye, retired. Purchased apt. house. Worked, part-time porter, Yankee Stadium. Recap: bouts 106, KO 40, decision 29, won foul 1, draw 2, lost decision 3, lost foul 3, KO by 6, ND 21, no contest 1.

NORRIS, JIM (James D.) B. 11/6/06, Chicago, Ill. D. 2/25/66, Chicago, Ill. Promoter. Norris, found guilty by two courts of operating a boxing monopoly, accused of consorting with hoodlums and delivering a knockout to the smaller boxing clubs, was judged by one boxing authority as "more Santa Claus than sinner."

The son of a multimillionaire, young Jim experienced success in promotional ventures of ice shows, hockey and horses. With his father's partner, Arthur Wirtz, Norris took a bold step into the boxing ring, establishing the International Boxing Corp. in 1949, buying the Madison Square Garden interests of ailing Mike Jacobs and establishing financial footholds at the Chicago Stadium, Detroit Olympia and sports arenas in St. Louis, Indianapolis and Omaha.

IBC promoted some 40 world title fights and exercised control over champions in almost all divisions. Norris was strong on home TV, at one time featuring twice-weekly shows from New York and Chicago, a serious blow to the smaller boxing clubs. Called "Octopus Inc." by some critics, IBC sparked a successful and exciting era of boxing.

Meanwhile, Norris came under fire for associating with hoodlums Frankie Carbo and Blinkey Palmero, both charged with "fixing" fights. And the courts were taking a close look at IBC operations.

In 1957, Norris and Wirtz were found guilty of monopolistic charges by the New York Federal Court, ordered to sell $2½ million Garden stock, dissolve the New York and Chicago division of the IBC. An appeal to the U.S. Supreme Court somewhat softened the ruling, but limited IBC to two championship fights a year, upholding the antitrust decision. The forced breakup prompted Norris' resignation from IBC, retirement from boxing.

However, Norris continued active in sports and business. He obtained interest in the Chicago Black Hawks hockey team and stadiums in Chicago and St. Louis. A member of the New York Stock Exchange, he had shares of Norris Grain Co., a fleet of Great Lake freighters, Rock Island Railroad and Norris Cattle Co.

Jim inherited his fortune and interest in sports from his father, James D. Sr. (d. 1952), a husky Canadian who played championship squash and tennis, inspired the Norris control of the Detroit and Chicago hockey teams.

Jim Jr. was 59 when he died, after a 10-day confinement in the hospital for a heart attack. His personal holdings were estimated at a quarter-billion dollars.

NORTON, KEN B. 1945, Jacksonville, Ill. Marine Corps 4½ years; won 3 All-Marine titles. Won Pan-American Games Trials. Runner-up, 1967 National AAU, San Diego. Sparring partner for Joe Frazier. First pro fight, Grady Brazell, KO 5, 11/14/67, San Diego (Brazell 1967 Golden Gloves champ). One dec., 14 straight KO to Jose Luis Garcia, KO by 8, 1970. Undefeated to Muhammad Ali, won 12, 3/31/73, San Diego (Ali's jaw broken); return, lost 12, 9/10/73, Inglewood, Calif. Recap: bouts 32, KO 22, decision 8, lost decision 1, KO by 1.

NOVA, LOU B. 3/16/15, Los Angeles, Calif. German-Irish. 6'1", 201. Amateur, AAU champ, International title 1935, Paris. Attended Calif. Col. of Agriculture. First pro bout, Ralph Barbara, 6, 1/23/36, NYC. Undefeated first 20, including Abe Simon, won; Lee Ramage, won, draw; Bob Pastor, draw. Lost, Maxie Rosenbloom 1938. Tommy Farr, won 15, 1938. Max Baer, KO 11, 1939, NYC (1st fight TV in U.S). Tony Galento, KO by 14, 1939.

Heavyweight title, Joe Louis, KO by 6, 9/29/41, NYC. KO by Lee Savold, 8, 1942; KO by 2, 1943. Three years creditable success, no top fights. Last, Tami Mauriello, KO by 1, 6/21/45, Boston. Studious, handsome, sports writer; later actor in Broadway show *The Hippies Millionaire,* 1957. Devoted to Yoga. Recap: bouts 63, KO 31, decision 18, draw 5, lost decision 3, KO by 6.

NUMATA, YOSIAKI B. 4/19/45, Japan. First fight, Kenzo Shimamura, KO 4, 9/12/63, Tokyo. Undefeated first year. Won Orient junior light title, Lim Chong-Tae, KO 2, 3/24/66, Oita. Won Orient light title, Flash Elorde, 12, 6/9/66, Tokyo. (Relinquished junior title.) Defended Orient light: Kid Rosario, won 12, 10/10/66, Tokyo. Won world junior light title, Elorde, 15, 6/18/67, Tokyo. Lost world title, Hiroshi Kobayashi, KO by 12, 12/14/67, Tokyo. Rewon Orient junior light, Kang Suhii, KO 7, 6/13/68, Tokyo. Relinquished title to campaign as lightweight. To U.S. 1969. World light title, Mando Ramos, KO by 6, 10/4/69, Los Angeles. Won WBC junior light title, Rene Barrientos, 15, 4/5/70, Tokyo. Defended: Paul Rojas, KO 5, 9/27/70, Tokyo; Barrientos, won 15, 1/3/71, Shizuoka; Lionel Rose, won 15, 5/30/71, Hiroshima. Lost title, Ricardo Arredondo, KO by 10, 10/10/71, Sendai. Recap: bouts 41, KO 8, decision 23, draw 3, lost decision 2, KO by 5.

O'BRIEN, JACK (Joseph F. Hagen) (Philadelphia Jack) B. 1/17/78, Philadelphia, Pa. D. 11/12/42, New York, N.Y. Irish. 5'10½", 158. His many Philadelphia fights gained nickname. First fight, Isador Strauss, draw 6, 12/12/96, Phila. 1901: popular in England. Major fights through 1905, Joe Choynski, won 6, ND 6; Marvin Hart, ND 6 (2); Joe Walcott, draw 10; Kid McCoy, ND 6; Tommy Ryan, ND 6; Tommy Burns, won 6. Won light heavy title, Bob Fitzsimmons, KO 13, 12/20/05, San Francisco. Heavyweight title, Burns, draw 20, 11/28/06, lost 20, 5/8/07, both Los Angeles. Stanley Ketchel, ND 10, 2/26/09, NYC (O'Brien saved by bell); Ketchel, KO by 3, 6/9/09, both Phila. Jack Johnson, ND 6. Sam Langford, KO by 5, 8/15/11, NYC. Last fight, Ben Koch, ND, 6/17/12, NYC. Never defended title. Hall of Fame 1968. Recap: bouts 181, KO 36, decision 59, won foul 6, draw 16, lost decision 3, KO by 4, ND 57.

O'DOWD, MIKE (St. Paul Cyclone) B. 4/5/95, St. Paul, Minn. D. 7/28/57, St. Paul, Minn. Irish. 5'9", 154. First fight, Henry Olson, KO 1, 1913, Undefeated in 33, 1913–16, Jack Britton, lost 12, 1916. Won world middle title, Al McCoy, KO 6, 11/14/17, Brooklyn. Harry Greb, ND 10, 1918. Enlisted army, AEF, Europe, 1918. Defended: McCoy, KO 3, 7/17/19, St. Paul. 1917–20: from title, undefeated. Lost title, Johnny Wilson, 12, 5/6/20, Boston. Undefeated in 11. Title, Wilson, lost 15, 3/17/21. Won N.Y. middle title, Dave Rosenberg, won foul, 8, 11/30/22, NYC. Last fight, Jock Malone, KO by 1, 3/16/23, St. Paul. Retired. Recap: bouts 115, KO 35, decision 16, won foul 1, decision 3, lost decision 7, KO by 1, ND 52.

O'GATTY, PACKEY (Pasuale Agati) (Speed Demon) B. 6/4/1900, Cannitello, Italy. D. 1966, New York, N.Y. 5'4½", 118. First fight, Frankie Jerome, ND 4, 9/25/15, NYC. Only loss in six years, Scotty Welsh 4, 1916; several NDs, including Frankie Burns, Benny Coster, Joe (Kid) Wagner. KO by Kid Williams, 9, Pete Herman, 1, 1921. Undefeated 1927–28, 5 straight KO, 1928. Last public appearance, Jimmy McLarnin exh., 3, 6/27/28, Detroit. Involved in first fight ever broadcast, with Frankie Burns, a prelim of Dempsey-Carpentier 7/2/21. Appeared in countless exhs. for World War I servicemen, donating time. Popular personality, physical instructor, wrote chat column for *Ring* magazine. Recap: bouts 132, KO 49, decision 7, won foul 2, draw 5, lost decision 5, KO by 3, ND 61.

OHBA, MASAO B. 11/7/49, Tokyo, Japan. D. 2/73, Tokyo, Japan. One of Japan's great ones; combined savvy and spunk. Early detailed record unavailable. Started pro 1966; bouts 21, decision 18, draw 1, lost 2. First recorded fight, Speedy Hayes, won 10, 3/3/69, Tokyo. Won WBA fly title, Berkreuk Chartvanchai, KO 13, 10/22/70, Tokyo. Defended: Betulio Gonzalez, won 10, 4/1/71, Tokyo; Fernando Cabanela, won 15, 10/23/71, Tokyo; Susumu Hanagata, won 15, 3/3/72, Tokyo; Orlando Amores, KO 5, 6/20/72, Tokyo; Chartchai Chionoi, KO 12, 1/73, Tokyo. Died three weeks after Chionoi defense, from skull fracture in auto crash. Recap: bouts 38, KO 6, decision 29, draw 1, lost decision 2.

OLIN, BOB B. 7/4/08, New York, N.Y. D. 12/16/56, New York, N.Y. 6", 175. First, Frank Morris, draw, 1929; 17 wins, then lost, 10, to Joe Banovic. 1930: won 7; lost 10, Joe Sekyra; draw 10, Banovic. Spotty record through 1934, 11 lost, KO by Martin Levandowski. Won light heavy title, upset Maxie Rosenbloom, 15, 11/16/34, NYC. 1935: nontitle, lost Dutch Weimer, John Henry Lewis. Lost title, Lewis, 15, 10/31/35, St. Louis. Title return, Lewis, KO by 8, 6/3/37, St. Louis. 1938: lost 3 of 4. To Australia, 1939. Last two fights, Gus Lesnevich, lost 12, 2/2/39, Sydney. Young Campbell, KO 4, 2/22/42, Newcastle, Australia. Retired. Coast Guard 1942. Regarded mediocre champ. Recap: bouts 85, KO 25, decision 27, won foul 1, draw 5, lost decision 23, KO by 4.

OLIVARES, RUBEN B. 1/14/44, Mexico City, Mexico. No early record. First reported fight, Isidro Sotelo, KO 1, Mexico City. 23 successive KO to Frankie Gonzales, won 10, 1967. Won world bantam title, Lionel Rose, KO 5, 8/22/69, Los Angeles. Defended: Alan Rudkin, KO 2, 12/12/69, Los Angeles; Chucho Castillo, won 15, 4/18/70, Inglewood, Calif. Lost title, Castillo, KO by 14, 10/17/70, Los Angeles. Regained title, Castillo, 15, 4/3/71, Los Angeles. Defended: Kazuyoshi Kanazawa, KO 14, 10/25/71,

Nagoya; Jesus Pimentel, KO 11, 12/14/71, Los Angeles, Recap: bouts 69, KO 63, decision 4, draw 1, KO by 1.

ORTEGA, GASPAR (Gaspar Benitez) (Indian) B. 10/21/35, Mexico. 5′ 10½″, 145. Mexican Golden Glove champ 1952. First pro, Miguel Ocana, KO 1, 1/1/53, San Luis, Mex. Undefeated first year, 10 KO, 10 dec. 7 straight KO to California welter title, David Cervantes, lost 12, 6/12/55, Mexicali. 1957, Kid Gavilan, lost, won return. World welter title, Emile Griffith, KO by 12, 6/3/61, Los Angeles, followed by six straight KO. 1963: 11 KO, 8 dec., 2 draw; only loss, Nino Benvenuti, 10. 1964: 29 fights, 14 KO; Sandro Mazzinghi, KO by 7. 1965: draw one, lost six straight. Last fight, Charlie Shipes, lost 10, 9/25/65, Modesto, Calif. Series: Paddy DeMarco, won two, lost one; Isaac Logart, won two, lost two. Recap: bouts 174, KO 69, decision 62, draw 5, lost decision 37, KO by 1.

ORTIZ, CARLOS B. 9/9/36, Ponce, Puerto Rico, 5′7″. First fight, Harry Bell, KO 1, 2/14/55, NYC. Undefeated to 1958, lost Johnny Busso, won return. Won junior welter title, Kenny Lane, KO 2, 6/12/59, NYC. Defended: Battling Torres, KO 10, 2/4/60, Los Angeles; Duilio Loi, won 15, 6/15/60, San Francisco. Lost title, Loi, 15, 9/1/60, Milan. Won world light title, Joe Brown, 15, 4/21/62, Las Vegas. Defended: Teryo Kosaki, KO 5, 12/3/62, Tokyo; Doug Vaillant, KO 13, 4/7/63, San Juan; Flash Elorde, KO 14, 2/16/64, Mexico City; Lane, won 15, 4/11/64, San Juan. Lost title, Ismael Laguna, 15, 4/10/65, Panama City. Regained title, Laguna, 15, 11/13/65, San Juan. Defended: Johnny Bizzarro, KO 12, 6/20/66, Pittsburgh; Sugar Ramos, KO 5, 10/22/66, Mexico City; Elorde, KO 14, 11/22/66, NYC; Ramos, KO 4, 7/1/67, San Juan. Laguna, 15, 8/16/67, NYC. Lost title, Carlos Cruz, 15, 6/29/68, Santo Domingo. 1971, Jimmy Legon, KO 3, Las Vegas. Recap: bouts 61, KO 22, decision 31, draw 1, lost decision 6, ND 1.

ORTIZ, MANUEL B. 7/2/16, El Centro, Calif. D. 6/70, San Diego, Calif. Mexican. 5′4″. Outstanding amateur, Calif., AAU title 1937. First pro, General Padila, won 4, 1938. First 2 years mediocre . 1940–42, 17 wins, 2 lost (Pancho Layvas, Tony Olivera, defeated Olivera return). Won world bantam title, Lou Salica, 12, 8/7/42, Hollywood. Defended 20 times (including both times held title): Kenny Lindsay, won 10, 1/1/43, Portland, Oreg.; George Frietas, KO 10, 1/27/43, Oakland, Calif.; Salica, KO 11, 3/10/43, Oakland; Lupe Cardoza, KO 6, 4/28/43, Fort Worth, Tex.; Joe Robleto, KO 7, 5/26/43, Long Beach, Calif.; Leonardo Lopez, KO 4, 10/1/43, Hollywood; Benny Goldberg, won 15, 11/23/43, Los Angeles; Ernesto Aguilar, won 15, 3/14/44, Los Angeles; Olivera, won 15, 4/4/44, Los Angeles; Luis Castillo,

KO 4, 9/12/44, Los Angeles; Castillo, KO 9, 11/14/44, Los Angeles; Bert White, KO 7, 1/26/45, San Diego. Army. Defended: Castillo, KO 13, 2/25/46, San Francisco; Lindsay, KO 5, 5/26/46, Hollywood; Jackie Jurich, KO 11, 6/10/46, San Francisco. Lost title, Harold Dade, 15, 1/6/47, San Francisco. Regained title, Dade, 15, 3/11/47, Los Angeles. Defended: David Kui Kong Young, won 15, 5/30/47, Honolulu; Tirso Del Rosario, won 15, 12/20/47, Manila. Memo Valero, KO 8, 7/4/48, Mexicali, Mex.; Dado Marino, won 15, 3/1/49, Honolulu. Lost title, Vic Toweel 15, 5/31/50, Johannesburg, S. Africa. To retirement, 4 KO, 6 lost, inactive 1954, last fight, Enrique Esqueda, lost 10, 12/10/55, Mexico City. Odd jobs. Broke when succumbed to liver ailment in San Diego Naval Hospital. Recap: bouts 122, KO 45, decision 47, draw 3, lost decision 26, KO by 1.

OTTO, YOUNG (Arthur Susskind) B. 10/12/86, New York, N.Y. 5'6". First fight, Bobby Flynn, won 6, 1903. Undefeated 1904–05 including 17 sraight KO. Avoided by name fighters, 93 ND, never title chance. Billy Papke, Leo Houck, ND. Undefeated 1907–08; 1912–15, 1917, 1919. Inactive. 1922: KO 7, decision 1, draw 1, lost 2. Last fight, Jimmy Gaudy, lost 8, 2/1/23, NYC. Boxing instructor NYC, referee, judge. Recap: bouts 197, KO 66, decision 22, draw 4, lost decision 8, KO by 4, ND 93.

OVERLIN, KEN B. 1910, Decatur, Ill. Irish. 5'8½", 160. First fight, Bill Brennan won 6, 1932. Won 8, lost Vince Dundee, 10. 1933: undefeated in 19. 1934: won 14, lost 2. 1935: undefeated in 12. 1936: undefeated in 15, lost 2, Teddy Yarosz, Kid Tunero. World middle title, Freddy Steele, KO by 4, 9/11/37, Seattle. Won NY title, Ceferino Garcia, 15, 5/23/40, NYC. Defended: Steve Belloise, won 15, 11/1/40, NYC; Belloise, won 15, 12/13/40, NYC. Lost title, Billy Soose, 15, 5/9/41, NYC. Undefeated to 1944, Ezzard Charles, won, draw; Al Hostak, won. Navy 1942. Last fight, R.J. Lewis, won 10, 9/26/44, Denver. Recap: bouts 147, KO 23, decision 103, draw 7, lost 12, KO by 1, no contest 1.

PACE, GEORGIE B. 2/2/16, Cleveland, Ohio. Negro. 5'5", 118. First fight, Nat Liftin, KO 1, 1936. To 1940, undefeated in 27, KO by Spider Armstrong, 6, 1937. NBA bantam title, Lou Salica, draw 15, 3/4/40, Toronto. NBA recognized Pace. N.Y. Commission bantam title, Salica, lost 15, 9/24/40, NYC. Fair record to 1942. Army. Last fight, Al Reasoner, lost 10, 8/1/43, New Orleans. Recap: bouts 42, KO 15, decision 18, draw 2, lost decision 5, KO by 1, ND 1.

PADDU, ANTONIO (Tonino) B. 1944, Cagliari, Italy. 135 lbs. One of Europe's most spectacular, 33 KO, 50 fights. A former plasterer, later police-man until size disqualified him, he turned full time to boxing. Won International Military Force Games light title, 1965. First pro fight, Ben Layesi, KO 2, 3/28/66, Modena, Italy. Undefeated first two years, including 9 KO, 3 decision. 1968: 5 straight KO to Carmen Coscia, KO by 7 (return, KO 2, 1972). Undefeated to 1972, 17 KO. Won Italian light title, Enrico Barlatti, KO 9, 9/5/70, Cagliari. Won European title, Claude Thomas, 15, 10/28/71, Rome. Defended European title: Jean Pierre, 15, 1/28/72, Milan; Enzio Petriglia, KO 11, 9/3/72, Sardinia; Dominique Azzaro, KO 1, 1973, Rome. Recap: bouts 50, KO 33, decision 13, won foul 2, draw 1, KO by 1.

PALMER, THOMAS (Pedlar; Little Box o' Tricks) B. 11/19/76, Canning Town, England. D. 2/13/49, London, England. 5'3", 115. First fight, won 11, 1891. Undefeated to 1899. Won British bantam title, Billy Plimmer, 14, 11/25/95, London. World bantam title, Terry McGovern, KO by 1,

9/12/99, Tuckahoe, N.Y. Vacated world bantam title. Harry Harris, lost 15, 3/18/01, London. British feather title, Ben Jordan, lost 15, 12/12/04, London. Lost British bantam title, Joe Bowker, 12, 3/20/05, London. George Dixon series: won three, draw one, lost one. Active to 1919, fair success. Last fight, Jem Driscoll, lost 4, 3/10/19, Hoxton, Eng. Recap: bouts 64, KO 2, decision 40, won foul 3, draw 4, lost decision 10, KO by 5.

PAPKE, BILLY (William Herman Papke) (Illinois Thunderbolt) B. 9/17/86, Spring Valley, Ill. D. 11/26/36, Newport, Calif. German. 5'8¾", 158–160. First fight, Battling Hurley, draw 6, 11/6/05, NYC. 1905–08: undefeated. World middle title, Stanley Ketchel, lost 10, 6/4/08, Milwaukee. Won title, Ketchel, KO 12, 9/7/08, Los Angeles. Title, Ketchel, lost 20, 7/5/09, Colma, Calif. 1910: claimed title after Ketchel death. Lost title claim, Cyclone Johnny Thompson, 20, 2/11/11, Sydney. Thompson vacated title, couldn't make weight. Papke claimed. Frank Mantell, lost 20, 2/22/12, Sacramento. Mantell claimed, but Papke continued generally recognized. Defended: Marcel Moreau, won 16, 6/29/12, Paris; Georges Carpentier, won foul, 17, 10/23/12, Paris; George Bernard, KO 7, 12/4/12, Paris. Lost title, Frank Klaus, foul 15, 3/15/13, Paris. Last fight, Soldier Bartfield, won 4, 4/8/19, San Francisco. Tragic end: destroyed himself and wife. Hall of Fame 1973. Recap: bouts 65, KO 29, decision 9, won foul 1, draw 7, lost decision 6, lost foul 2, KO by 1, ND 10.

PAPP, LASZLO B. 3/25/26, Hungary. 5'8½", 160. Legendary Hungarian athlete. Won three Olympic titles, London 1948, Helsinki '52, Melbourne '56. Undefeated as amateur and pro. First pro fight, Alois Brand, won 4, 5/18/57, Cologne, West Germany. To 1962, 8 KO, 9 dec., 1 draw. Tiger Jones, won 10, Vienna, 1962. Won European middle title, Christ Christensen, KO 7, 5/16/62, Vienna. Defended: Hippolyte Annex, KO 9, 11/19/62, Paris; George Aldridge, KO 15, 2/6/63, Vienna; Pete Muller, KO 4, 3/30/63, Dortmund, West Germany; Luis Folledo, KO 8, 12/6/63, Madrid; Christensen, KO 4, 7/2/64, Copenhagen; Mike Leahy, 15, 10/9/64, Vienna. Hungarian government ordered retirement 1965. Recap: bouts 29, KO 15, decision 11, draw 3.

PASTRANO, WILLIE (Wilfred Raleigh Pastrano) B. 11/27/35, Miami, Fla. Italian. 5'11¾", 175–180. First fight, Domingo Rivera, won 4, 9/10/51, New Orleans. 1951, 4 wins. 1952: 14 wins. Alvin Pellegrini, won, lost, draw. 1953–57; Undefeated in 32, lost 4, John Cesario, Del Flanagan, Italo Scortichini, Roy Harris. 1958–59: Brian London, KO by 5, won 10. Spotty (5 lost, 2 draw, 10 wins) until 1963. Wayne Thornton, lost, draw, win. Won world light heavy title, Harold Johnson, 15, 6/1/63, Las Vegas. Defended: Gregorio Peralta, KO 6, 4/10/64, New Orleans; Terry Downes, KO 11, 11/30/64, Manchester, Eng. Lost title, Jose Torres, KO by 9, 5/30/65, NYC. Retired. Recap: bouts 83, KO 14, decision 48, draw 8, lost decision 11, KO by 2.

PATERSON, JACKIE B. 9/5/20, Springfield, Ayrshire, Scotland. D. 11/19/66. First fight, Joe Kiely, won 10, 5/26/38, Greenock, Scotland. Impressive first 2 years: Won vacant British fly title, Paddy Ryan, KO 13, 9/30/39, Glasgow. Won vacant Empire fly title, Kid Tanner, 15, 3/11/40, Manchester. Defended both titles same time: Jim Stewart, KO 6, 11/13/40, Newcastle; Ryan, KO 8, 2/3/41, Nottingham. Won world flyweight title, Peter Kane, KO 1, 6/19/43, Glasgow. Defended: Joe Curran, won 15, 7/10/46, Glasgow. Lost title, Rinty Monaghan, KO by 7, 3/23/48, Belfast. British, Empire bantam titles, Jim Brady, lost 15, 7/16/41, Glasgow; return titles, Brady, lost 15, 9/12/45, Glasgow. Won European bantam title, Theo Medina, foul 8, 3/19/46, London. Lost European title, Medina, KO by 4, 10/30/46, Glasgow. Won British bantam title, Johnny King, KO 7, 2/10/47, Manchester. Defended: Norman Lewis, KO 5, 10/20/47, London. Lost title, Stan Rowan 15, 3/24/49, Liverpool. Last fight, Willie Myles, lost 8, 2/7/51, Dundee. Died, gunshot wounds. Recap: bouts 91, KO 41, decision 20, won foul 1, draw 3, lost decision 15, lost foul 1, KO by 10.

PATTERSON, FLOYD B. 1/4/35, Waco, N.C. Negro. 6', 182. 1952 Olympic middle title. Golden Gloves titles: 1951 middle, N.Y., Eastern, lost Inter-City to Richard Guerrero; 1952: light heavy, Inter-City title, N.Y. Open, Eastern titles. First pro bout, Eddie Godbold, KO 4, 9/12/52, NYC. To title, only loss, Joey Maxim, 8, 1934, 11 successive KO. Won vacant heavy title, Archie Moore, KO 5, 11/30/56, Chicago. (Youngest to win heavy title.) Defended: Tommy Jackson, KO 10, 7/29/57. NYC; Pete Rademacher, KO 6, 8/22/57, Seattle; Roy Harris, KO 12, 8/18/58, Los Angeles; Brian London, KO 11, 5/1/59, Indianapolis. Lost title, Ingemar Johansson, KO by 3 (floored 7 times), 9/26/59, NYC. Regained title, Johansson, KO 5, 6/20/60, NYC. (First heavy to rewin title.) Title, Johansson, KO 6, 3/13/61, Miami Beach. (First time 2 heavies fought 3 times for title.) Defended: Tom McNeeley, KO 4, 12/4/61, Toronto. Lost title, Sonny Liston, KO by 1, 9/23/62, Chicago. Return title, KO by 1, 7/22/63, Las Vegas. (Patterson advised not accept fight because of Liston's criminal record, affiliation with hoodlums.) 1964–65: 3 KO, 2 win. Title, Cassius Clay, KO by 12, 11/22/65, Las Vegas. WBA heavy title, Jimmy Ellis, lost 15, 9/14/68, Stockholm. 1969 inactive. 1970, 1 KO. 1971, 3 KO, 3 win, mediocre opposition. Recap.: bouts 60, KO 39, decision 14, lost decision 3, KO by 4.

153

PAUL, TOMMY B. 1907, Buffalo, N.Y. 5'4", 126. Active amateur. First pro bout, Freddie Griffiths, KO 4, 1927. Busy, impressive. Won over both Frankie Genaro, Jackie Britton twice. Phil Zwick, won; Freddie Miller, won, lost; Fidel LaBarba, twice. Won vacant NBA title, Johnny Pena, 15, 5/26/32, Detroit. Lost title, Miller, 10, 1/13/33, Chicago. Never regained title chance. From 1934, lost 10 of 14. Last fight, Holman Williams, lost 10, 3/22/35, Detroit. Recap: bouts 110, KO 28, decision 47, won foul 2, draw 9, lost decision 19, lost foul 3, KO by 2.

PEACOCK, BILLY B. 6/30/33, Los Angeles, Calif. 5'4", 118. 1951: National AAU bantam champ. First pro bout, Howard Curry, won 4, 10/25/51, Phila. Impressive early record, undefeated 1952. N. America bantam title, Pappy Gault, won 12, 8/17/53, Brooklyn. Defended: Johnny Ortega, KO 9, 12/22/53, Los Angeles. Lost title, Nate Brooks, KO by 8, 2/8/54, Brooklyn; return non-title, Brooks, KO 1, 1956. Undefeated 1955, including Chamrern Songkitrat, KO 9. Vacant California, bantam title, Frankie Campos, KO 8, 12/7/57, Hollywood. Defended: Ross Padilla, won 12, 1/18/58, Hollywood. Lost title, Boots Monroe, 12, 6/7/58, Hollywood. Last fight, Benny Casing, lost 10, 6/7/58, Stockton, Calif. Recap: bouts 79, KO 28, decision 24, draw 1, lost decision 21, KO by 5.

PELKEY, ARTHUR (Andrew Arthur Peletier) B. 10/27/84, Chatham, Ontario. D. 2/18/21, Ford City, Ontario. French-Irish. 6'1½", 210. First fight, Kent Salibury, draw 6, 12/8/10, Boston. Upset 1911, 2nd fight, George Christian, KO by 1. To 1914 undefeated: 12 KO, ND Tommy Burns, Jess Willard, Jim Coffey. White heavy title, Luther McCarty, KO 1, 5/24/13, Calgary, Alberta (McCarty collapsed, died in ring). Lost title, Gunboat Smith, KO by 15, 1/1/14, Daly City, Calif. After McCarty tragedy, never won. To 1920, 12 KO by. Last fight, Leo Gates, draw 10, 1920. Recap: bouts 50, KO 12, decision 9, draw 4, lost decision 1, KO by 13, ND 11.

PEP, WILLIE (William Papaleo) (Will o' the Wisp) B. 9/19/22, Middletown, Conn. Italian. 5'5½", 125. One of boxing's most remarkable, a name mentioned when greatest "pound for pound" discussed. Amateur, Connecticut state fly, bantam championships, 1938–39. First pro fight, Jim McGovern, won 4, 7/3/40, Hartford. Undefeated three years. Won world feather title, Chalky Wright, 15, 11/20/42, NYC. (Youngest boxer to win a title in 40 years.) Nontitle, Sammy Angott, lost 10, 3/19/43, NYC (first loss 42 fights). Defended: Sal Bartolo, won 15, 6/8/43, Boston. Navy, discharged 1944. Continued undefeated. Defended: Wright, won 15, 9/29/44, NYC; Phil Terranova, 15, 2/19/45, NYC; Bartolo, KO 12, 6/7/46, NYC; Jack

Leslie, KO 12, 8/22/47, Flint, Mich.; Humberto Sierra, KO 10, 2/24/48, Miami. Lost title, Sandy Saddler, KO by 4, 10/29/48, NYC. Regained title, Saddler 15, 2/11/49, NYC. Defended: Eddie Compo, KO 7, 9/20/49, Waterbury, Conn.; Charley Riley, KO 5, 1/16/50, St. Louis; Ray Famechon, won 15, 3/17/50, NYC. Lost title, Saddler, KO by 8, 9/8/50, NYC. Title, Saddler, KO by 9, 9/26/51, NYC. 1958, 11 straight wins until Kid Bassey, KO by 9, Sonny Leon, lost 10. Announced retirement 1/27/59. Comeback, won 5, KO 4, 1965. Last fight, Calvin Woodland, lost 6, 3/16/66, Richmond, Va. Hall of Fame 1963. Recap: bouts 241, KO 65, decision 164, draw 1, lost decision 5, KO by 6.

PERALTA, GREGORIO (Goyo) B. 5/8/35, San Juan, Argentina. 185–195. One of Argentine's great heavies. First fight, Rene Pereyra, KO 4, 4/5/58, Buenos Aires. Undefeated first year, five straight KO. First *major* setback, Mauro Mina, KO by 8, 1960. Undefeated 1961–62; won Argentine heavy title, Jose Giorgetti, 12, 8/4/62, Mar del Plata. Defended: Justo Benitez, 12, 9/19/62, Buenos Aires. Undefeated to 1964, including Willie Pastrano, won 10, 1963. CLAB proclaimed South American heavy champ 8/20/63. World light heavy title, Pastrano, KO by 6, 4/10/64, New Orleans. Defended S.A. title, Roberto Davila, 15, 7/18/64, Buenos Aires. Undefeated to Oscar Bonavena, lost 12, 1965; return, draw, 1969. Inactive 1966. Undefeated 1967–69, including 15 KO. Only loss 1970–71, George Foreman, 10, 1970; North American WBA heavy title, Foreman, KO by 10, 5/10/71, Oakland. To 1973, 11 KO; only loss, Ray Anderson, 10, 1972, Madrid. 1973: Bo Sounkalo, won 10; Ron Lyle, lost 10, Denver. Recap: bouts 105, KO 52, decision 34, won foul 2, won disq. 1, draw 8, lost decision 6, KO by 2.

PEREZ, PASQUAL B. 3/4/26, Tupungate, Mendoza, Argentina. Flyweight champion London Olympic Games 1948. First pro bout, Jose Ciorino, KO 5, 12/5/52, Gerli, Argentina. 18 straight KO, 1 win, 5 KO, to nontitle draw with Yoshio Shirai. Return, won flyweight title, 15, 11/26/54, Tokyo. Defended: Alberto Barenght, KO 3, 4/13/55, Buenos Aires; Shirai, KO 5, 5/30/55, Tokyo.; Leo Espinosa, won 15, 1/11/56, Buenos Aires; Oscar Suarez, KO 11, 6/30/56. Montevideo; Ricardo Valdez, KO 5, 8/3/56, Tandil, Argentina; Dai Dower, KO 1, 3/30/57, Buenos Aires; Young Martin, KO 3, 12/7/57, Buenos Aires; Ramon Arias, won 15, 4/19/58, Caracas, Venezuela; Dommy Ursua, won 15, 12/15/58, Manila; Kenji Yonekura, won 15, 8/10/59, Tokyo; Sadao Yaoita, KO 13, 11/5/59, Osaka. Lost title, Pone Kingpetch, 15, 4/16/60, Bangkok, Thailand. Return title, Kingpetch KO by 8, 9/22/60, Los Angeles. To 1963, creditable, never another title chance. Last fight, Eugenio Hurtado, KO by 6, 3/15/64, Panama City. Retired 4/11/64. Recap: bouts 91, KO 56, decision 27, draw 2, lost decision 4, KO by 2.

PEREZ, YOUNG (Victor Perez) B. 10/18/11, Tunis, Tunisia. D. 1942. First fight, Zerbib, draw 6, 2/4/28, Tunis. 1928–29: undefeated in 33, lost 1. French flyweight title, Kid Oliva, KO by 4, 2/8/30, Limoges, France. Won French title, Valentin Angelman, 15, 6/11/31, Paris. Won IBU world title, Frankie Genaro, KO 2, 10/26/31, Paris. Lost title, Jackie Brown, KO by 13, 10/31/32, Manchester, Eng. World bantam title, Al Brown, lost 15, 2/19/34, Paris. Spotty record to 1938. Last fight, Ernest Weiss, lost 10, 11/11/38, Berlin. Died in German prison camp. Recap: bouts 131, KO 26, decision 62, won foul 1, draw 16, lost decision 19, KO by 7.

PERKINS, EDDIE B. 3/3/37, Clarksdale, Miss. Negro. 5'5". First fight, Norm Johnson, lost 6, 12/27/56, Milwaukee. So-so early record. Undefeated 1960. NBA junior welter title, Duilio Loi, draw 15, 10/21/61, Milan. Won title, Loi, 15, 9/14/62, Milan. Lost title, Loi, 15, 12/15/62, Milan. Won vacant world junior welter title, Roberto Cruz, 15, 6/15/63, Manila. Defended: Yoshinori Takahashi, KO 13, 1/4/64, Tokyo; Bunny Grant, won 15, 4/18/64, Kingston. Lost title, Carlos Hernandez, won 15, 1/18/65, Caracas. To 1971 fair success, never another title chance. Last fight, Angel Espada, won 10, 10/18/71. San Juan. Recap: bouts 80, KO 18, decision 44, draw 2, lost decision 14, KO by 1, ND 1.

PETROLLE, BILLY (The Fargo Express) B. 1/10/05, Berwick, Pa. Italian. 5'7", 135. First fight, Star Rose, KO 2, 1924, Impressive early years, crowd pleaser. Fought ranking fighters third year, lost to Eddie Kid Wagner, Sid Terris, Louis Kid Kaplan; Ray Miller, draw. Fought six world champions: Kaplan; Sammy Mandell, ND; Jack Kid Berg, ND, lost; Jimmy Goodrich, won; Tony Canzoneri won, title, lost 15, 11/4/32, NYC; Jimmy McLarnin, won, lost twice; Battling Battalino, KO, won; Barney Ross, lost twice. Last fight, Ross, lost 10, 1/24/34, NYC. Retired, foundry business Duluth, Minn., later owned religious gift store there. Hall of Fame 1962. Recap: bouts 157, KO 63, decision 22, won foul 4, draw 10, lost decision 17, KO by 3, ND 37, no contest 1.

PINDER, ENRIQUE B. 8/7/47, Panama. First fight, Jorge Jacobs, KO 1, 8/20/47, Panama. Undefeated first 3 years. First U.S. fight, Carlos Zayas, won 8, 9/6/68, NYC. 1969–70: only loss, Orlando Amores, KO by 9, 1969. Won N. American bantam title, David Vansquez, 12, 10/3/71, NYC. Defended: Vansquez, won 12, 11/13/71, NYC. 1972: undefeated, won world bantam title, Rafael Herrera, 15, 7/30/72. Lost title, Romero Anaya, KO by 3, 2/73, Panama City. Recap: bouts 41, KO 14, decision 22, draw 2, KO by 3.

PLADNER, SPIDER (Emile Pladner) B. 9/2/06, Clermont-Ferrand, France. First fight, Boriello, won 10, 1926. Undefeated 28, then lost to Johnny Hill, 15, 1927. European fly title, lost Johnny Hill, 3/19/28, London. Nontitle, Hill, KO 6, 1929. Won world fly title, Frankie Genaro, KO 1, 3/2/29, Paris. (International Boxing Union regarded Pladner champ.) Lost title, Genaro, foul 5, 4/18/29, Paris. Lost European, French fly titles, Eugene Huat, KO by 15, 6/20/29, Paris. Impressive record thru mid-32, won French bantam title, Francis Biron, 12, 5/28/31, Paris. (Nontitle, Al Brown, KO by 1, 9/19/32; Brown, KO by 2, 11/14/32, Paris.) Defended French bantam title: Joseph Decico, won 12, 10/5/34, Paris. Creditable record to last fight, Salvador Lorzano, draw 10, 12/3/35, Barcelona. Recap: bouts 122, KO 34, decision 61, won foul 1, draw 10, lost decision 11, lost foul 2, KO by 3.

QUARRY, JERRY B. 5/15/45, Los Angeles, Calif. 6'1", 200. 1965 Golden Gloves champ. First pro fight, Gene Hamilton, won 4, 5/7/65, Los Angeles. Undefeated first year. First loss, Eddie Machen, 10, 1966. Undefeated, including Floyd Patterson, won; Thad Spencer, KO 12 (WBA title elimination) to WBA title, Jimmy Ellis, lost 15, 4/27/68, Oakland. Undefeated to N.Y. version heavy title, Joe Frazier, KO by 7, 6/23/69, NYC. George Chuvalo KO by 7, 1969. 1970–71: won 8, including Mac Foster, KO 6, Muhammad Ali, KO by 3. 1972: 3 bouts, KO, won, KO by Ali, 7. Upset Ron Lyle, 12, 1973, to regain third heavyweight ranking. Recap: bouts 53, KO 25, decision 19, draw 3, lost 2, KO by 4.

QUARRY, MIKE B. Los Angeles, Calif. Brother, heavy Jerry Quarry. First fight, Butch McCarthy, KO 2, 4/11/69, Woodland Hills, Calif. Undefeated first year, 8 KO, 9 dec. Undefeated 1970–71, including 22 dec., 11 KO; upset first-ranking Andy Kendall, 10. Won North America light heavy title, Jimmy Dupree, disq. 5, 10/30/71, Anaheim. World light heavy title, Bob Foster, KO by 4, 6/27/72, Las Vegas. 1973: dec. 2, KO 1, draw 1; Tom Bogs, lost 10. Recap: bouts 42, KO 13, decision 25, won disq. 1, draw 1, lost decision 1, KO by 1.

RADEMACHER, PETE B. 8/20/28, Grandview, Wash. 6'2", 202. Only amateur champ to fight first pro for heavy title, Floyd Patterson, KO by 6, 8/22/57, Seattle. Provided creditable opposition. Promoted by Jack Hurley, SRO, TV, and radio banned. Outstanding amateur, won Olympic title, three straight KO, 1956. Second pro fight, Zora Folley, KO by 4, 1958. Undefeated 1959, 3 KO, 2 dec. 1960: upset George Chuvalo, Willie Besmanoff; Brian London, KO by 7. 1961: 3 KO by, Doug Jones 5, George Logan 2, Archie Moore 6; won 1, KO 3. 1962: Karl Mildenberger, lost; Bobo Olson, won 10, 4/3/62, Honolulu, last fight. Recap: bouts 23, KO 8, decision 7, draw 1, lost decision 1, KO by 6.

RAMOS, MANDO (Armundo) B. (Date unavailable), Los Angeles, Calif. First fight, Berlin Roberts, won 4, 11/17/65, Los Angeles. Undefeated to 1967. Light title, Carlos Ortiz, lost 15, 9/28/68, Los Angeles. Won title, Carlos Cruz, KO 11, 2/18/69, Los Angeles. Defended: Yoshiaki Numata, KO 8, 10/4/69, Los Angeles. Lost title, Ismael Laguna, KO by 9, 3/3/70, Los Angeles. WBC title, lost, Pedro Carrasco, disq. 11, 11/5/71, Madrid. Recap.: bouts 36, KO 20, Decision 11, lost decision 3, lost foul 1, KO by 1.

RAMOS, SUGAR (Urtiminio Ramos Zaqueira) B. 12/2/41, Matanzas, Cuba. First fight, Rene Arce, KO 2, 10/5/57, Havana. 1957–63 undefeated. Won Cuban feather title, 1960. Won world feather title, Davey Moore, KO 10, 3/21/63, Los Angeles (Moore died of brain injuries). Defended: Rafui King, won 15, 7/13/63, Mexico City; Mitsunori Seki, KO 6, 3/1/64, Tokyo;

Floyd Robertson, won 15, 5/9/64, Accra, Gold Coast. Lost feather title, Vicente Saldivar, KO by 12, 9/26/65, Mexico City. Lightweight title, Carlos Ortiz, KO by 5, 10/22/66, Mexico City. Return title, Ortiz, KO by 5, 10/22/66, San Juan. Inactive 1968. Attempted comeback as lightweight, 3 KO, 1 win, 1 loss. Last fight, Mando Ramos lost 10, 8/7/70, Los Angeles. Recap: bouts 61, KO 39, decision 13, won foul 1, draw 3, lost decision 1, lost foul 1, KO by 3.

RENAULT, JACK B. 1/18/98, Chashem, Quebec. 6'1", 195. First fights started 1919, Canada, unrecorded. First U.S. fight, Harry Greb, ND 10, 3/16/21, Pittsburgh. Sturdy trial horse, met most of leading heavies. Undefeated first year, including Billy Miske, ND. Opponents included: Gene Tunney, NC; George Godfrey, KO, won, lost; Fred Fulton, won foul, KO; Johnny Risko, won; Bartley Madden, won. In typical stumbling block fights he lost to Jack Sharkey, Jack Delaney, Jim Maloney, Paolino Uzcudun, Ernie Schaaf, Tommy Loughran. Only 1 KO by, Miske, 13, 1922, to last fight. Crowd pleaser, part of the colorful heavy scene of 1920s. Last fight, Joe Crawford, KO by 2, 12/21/31, Peru, Ind. Recap: bouts 86, KO 32, decision 25, won foul 1, draw 1, lost decision 14, lost foul 2, KO by 2, ND 7, NC 2.

RICKARD, TEX (George L.) B. 1/2/70, Sherman, Tex. D. 6/5/29, Miami Beach, Fla. Promoter. Recognized as most renowned of fight promoters, Rickard is recalled as the "Man with the Midas Touch" and "Master of Ballyhoo." When history refers to "the first million-dollar gate," it has in mind the Rickard promotion of the Jack Dempsey–Georges Carpentier fight July 2, 1921, at Boyle's Thirty Acres, Jersey City.

An orphan at 10, he grew up on Cambridge, Tex., ranch and was a cowboy during early years. Young Tex was later town marshal of Henrietta, Tex., joined the Klondike gold rush in 1895. With another former cowboy lugged sleds 300 miles through Chilkoot Pass, struck it rich at the famous Bonanza strike.

Embracing a profit of $60,000, he established a gambling hall and saloon at Dawson. His venture folded when in a single night a group of miners wiped him out at the faro and roulette tables. Alongside novelist Rex Beach, he cut wood for $15 a cord for five months. He hiked to Nome in 1899, $35 in his pocket, set up another saloon. Four years later he was $500,000 richer, lost the bulk of it in barren gold claims, settled in Goldfield, Nev., with $60,000, established the Northern Hotel, including a saloon and gambling hall.

When the Chamber of Commerce considered possibilities of a promotion that would put the community in the limelight, Rickard was the name that came to mind. It coincided with his promotion ambitions.

His original idea was to feature an outstanding lightweight contender, Battling Nelson, and Jack Clifford. As the idea caught fire, he canceled out Clifford and convinced Joe Gans to defend his title against Nelson, Sept. 3, 1906. Among his ballyhoo gimmicks was a display of 1500 twenty-dollar gold pieces unguarded in his saloon window. His venture was a total success, grossing $69,715. Betting in Goldfield was estimated at $5 million. (Gans won foul, 42 rounds.)

Rickard was on his way, promoting fights that were to gross over $15 million. The Rickard-Dempsey-Kearns combination contributed substantially, including the Boyle's Acres $1,789,238 gate, and also helped establish the Golden Age of Boxing along the way.

He brought his promotional talents to the old Madison Square Garden, immediately started to promote a new Garden in which an estimated 600 millionaires invested. His promotions began to attract the "best people," including society women, and it was not unusual to observe several tuxedos at ringside. First fight, new Garden, Paul Berlenbach defended light heavy title, Jack Delaney, 15, 12/11/25; last fight, old Garden, Sid Terris decisioned Johnny Dundee, 12, 5/4/25.

Died at 60 from a peritonic infection, appendectomy aftermath. At the time he was contemplating a heavyweight elimination tournament, owned a dog racing track and extensive Florida real estate. His body lay in state at Madison Square Garden where the ring was usually placed.

RISKO, EDDIE (Henry Pylkowski) (Babe) B. 1911, Syracuse, N.Y. D. 3/7/57, Syracuse, N.Y. Polish-Lithuanian. 5'10", 160. First fight, Steve Wolanin, won 8, 3/16/34, Utica, N.Y. 1934: undefeated in 15. Teddy Yarosz, KO 7, 1/1/35, Scranton. Won American middle title, Yarosz, 15, 9/19/35, Pittsburgh. Nontitle, Jock McAvoy, KO by 1, 12/20/35, NYC. Defended: Tony Fisher, won 15, 2/10/36, Newark. Lost title, Freddie Steele, 15, 7/11/36, Seattle. Title, Steele, lost 15, 2/19/37, NYC. To 1939, KO by 8 of 17. Last fight, Lloyd Marshall, KO by 5, 5/17/39, Sacramento, Calif. Recap: bouts 51, KO 7, decision 20, draw 6, lost decision 9, KO by 9.

RISKO, JOHNNY (Cleveland Rubber Man) (The Spoiler) B. 12/18/02, Austria. D. 1/13/53, Miami Beach, Fla. 5'10½", 188. When contender neared title, Risko was a "must." Never title chance himself. Fought 12 champions: Gene Tunney, lost; Jack Sharkey, won, lost; Jack Delaney, won, lost; Paul Berlenbach, won; Tommy Loughran, won two, lost two; Jimmy Slattery, lost foul; Max Schmeling, KO by 8; Mickey Walker, won, lost twice; Max Baer, won, lost; Bob Olin, won; John Henry Lewis, lost, Mike McTigue, lost. Those whose title-bent careers he shortstopped: Jack Renault, Chuck

Wiggins, Lou Scozza, King Levinsky, Jim Maloney, Ernie Schaaf, Vittorio Campolo, Tuffy Griffith. Last fight, Tony Musto, KO by 3, 2/19/40, Miami Beach. Army. Opened tavern Cleveland. Recap: bouts 128, KO 21, decision 44, draw 5, lost decision 34, lost foul 7, KO by 2, ND 15.

RITCHIE, WILLIE (Gerhardt A. Steffen) B. 2/13/91, San Francisco, Calif. 5'6¼", 101–135. First fight, Eddie Steele, lost 2, 1907, Oakland, Calif. Through 1912, undefeated in 34, lost 5. Two oddities: Freddie Welsh, lost 20, 11/30/11, Los Angeles, substituted for Ad Wolgast from spectators; as spectator, took Packy McFarland's place in fight with Young Erne, ND 6, 2/7/12, Phila. Won lightweight title, Ad Wolgast, foul 16, 11/28/12, Daly City, Calif. (Weight limit raised to 135 lbs.) Defended: Joe Rivers, KO 11, 7/4/13. San Francisco. Tommy Murphy, won 28, 4/17/14, San Francisco. Lost title, Freddie Welsh, 20, 7/7/14, London. To 1918 undefeated in 18, lost 1, no title return. Army boxing instructor, Camp Lewis, Wash. Benny Leonard ND, KO by 8, 1919. Last fight, Dick Hoppe, won 6, 1927, Los Angeles. Boxing instructor, Calif. Hall of Fame, 1962. Recap: bouts 73, KO 8, decision 27, won foul 1, draw 4, lost decision 8, KO by 1, ND 24.

RIVERS, JOE (Jose Ybarra) B. 3/19/92, Los Angeles, Calif. D. 6/25/57, Inglewood, Calif. 5'5", 130. 1908–09 not recorded. First recorded fight, Billy Cappalle, won 10, 3/20/10, Los Angeles. Creditable early record, two light title chances: Ad Wolgast, KO by 13, 7/4/12, Vernon, Calif.; Willie Ritchie, KO by 11, 7/4/13, San Francisco. Wolgast nontitle return, ND. Leach Cross, won, ND, lost; Johnny Dundee, ND, lost, Joe Thomas, KO 2. Last fight, Pete McCarthy, KO 3, 4/3/23, Albuquerque, N. Mex. Recap: bouts 67, KO 15, decision 13, won foul 3, draw 8, lost decision 11, lost foul 1, KO by 5, ND 11.

ROBINSON, SUGAR RAY (Walker Smith) B. 5/3/20, Detroit, Mich. Negro. 5'11". Golden Gloves: 1939, N.Y. feather; 1940, N.Y. light, Inter-City titles. Among smoothest, all-round pound-for-pound greats of all time. First pro bout, Joe Echeverria, KO 2, NYC. Won 40 straight, then lost to Jake LaMotta, 10, 2/5/43, Detroit. Won return, 2/23/45. Won vacant world welter title, Tommy Bell, 15, 12/20/46, NYC. Defended: Jimmy Doyle, KO 8, 6/24/47, Cleveland (Doyle died from fight injuries); Chuck Taylor, KO 6, 12/19/47, Detroit; Bernard Docusen, won 15, 6/28/48, Chicago; Kid Gavilan, won 15, 7/11/49, Phila.; Charley Fusari, won 15, 8/9/50, Jersey City. Won world middle title, Jake LaMotta, KO 13, 2/14/51, Chicago. Lost middle title, Randy Turpin, 15, 7/10/51, London. (Relishing overseas high life, Sugar Ray not in condition.) Regained title, Turpin, KO 10, 9/12/51, NYC. Defended: Carl Bobo Olson, won 15, 3/13/52, San Francisco; Rocky Graziano, KO 3, 4/16/52, Chicago. World light heavy title, Joey Maxim,

KO by 14, 6/25/52, NYC. (Leading, but overcome by heat exhaustion.) Announced retirement 12/18/52. 1954: several exhs. 1955: 5 wins, 1 loss (Tiger Jones). Won middle title, Olson, KO 2, 12/9/55, Chicago. Defended: Olson, KO 4, 6/18/56, Los Angeles. Lost title, Gene Fullmer, 15, 1/2/57, NYC. Regained, Fullmer, KO 5, 5/1/57, Chicago. Lost title, Carmen Basilio, 15, 9/23/57, NYC. Regained, Basilio, 15, 3/25/58, Chicago. Lost title, Paul Pender, 15, 1/22/60, Boston. Title, Pender, lost 15, 6/10/60, Los Angeles. NBA middle title, Gene Fullmer, draw 15, 12/3/60, Los Angeles. NBA title, Fullmer, lost 15, 3/4/61, Las Vegas. Through 1965 never another title chance. Won most of fights. Last fight, Joey Archer, lost 10, 11/10/65, Pittsburgh. Won middle title unprecedented five times. Hall of Fame 1967. Bad investments dissipated fortune, restaurant-bar (Robinson doesn't drink, smoke), apartment houses, laundry, beauty shop. Hollywood 1968, movies, TV. Fighting-days trademark, a pink Cadillac. Established Sugar Ray Robinson Youth Foundation in Los Angeles, embracing some 20,000 youngsters, emanating from Holman United Methodist Church. Recap: bouts 202, KO 109, decision 66, draw 6, lost decision 18, KO by 1, ND 1, no contest 1.

RODAK, LEO B. 6/5/13, Chicago, Ill. Ukrainian. 5'5", 125. Amateur: 1931 Golden Gloves flyweight title, Inter-City title, CYO, lost finals. 1932: Golden Gloves bantam champ, Intersectional CYO feather title. 1933: Golden Gloves bantam champ, Inter-City feather title. First pro bout, Pete McGee, KO 4, 1933. Undefeated 1933–34. Tony Canzoneri, lost 10, 1935. Undefeated 1937. Sammy Angott, won, KO by, lost, 1938. Won vacant NBA feather title, Leone Efrati, 10, 12/29/38, Chicago. Lost title, Joey Archibald, 15, 4/18/39, Providence, R.I. (Elimination, Archibald N.Y. champ.) Up-down to marines. 1942, KOs by Henry Armstrong and Willie Joyce. Last fight, John Thomas, KO by 5, 11/12/46, Los Angeles. Recap: bouts 117, KO 6, decision 74, draw 10, lost decision 22, KO by 5.

RODRIGUEZ, LUIS B. 6/17/37, Camaguey, Cuba. 5'7". First fight, Lazaro Kessell, KO 3, 6/2/56, Havana. Undefeated to 1960, beat Virgil Akins twice, Issac Logart, Chico Vejar, Yama Bahama; lost to Emile Griffith, 1960. Curtis Cokes, won, lost, 1961. Won world welter title, Griffith 15, 3/21/63, Los Angeles. Lost title, Griffith, 15, 6/8/63, NYC. Title, Griffith, lost 15, 6/12/64, Las Vegas. Undefeated 1965. Impressive record to world middle title bout, Nino Benvenuti, KO by 11, 11/22/69, Rome. 1970–71: 6 KO, 5 win, 2 lost, 1 KO by. Recap: bouts 109, KO 47, decision 50, lost decision 8, KO by 3, no contest 1.

ROOT, JACK (Janos Ruthaly) B. 5/26/76, Austria. D. 6/10/63, Los Angeles, Calif. Bohemian. 5'10", 165. First champ of light heavy division. Had been top-ranking middleweight till 1903, when 175-lb. class born of idea

165

by Lou Houseman. First light heavy title bout, Kid McCoy, won 10, 4/22/03, Detroit. Lost title, George Gardner, KO by 12, 7/4/03, Fort Erie, Ont. (Fought Gardner 5 times, won foul; KO by 17, title, draw, won.) Marvin Hart, KO by 12, 7/3/05, Reno (Jim Jeffries, referee, announced bout was for his vacated heavy title). Last fight, Fred Russell, won 10, 2/26/06, Kalamazoo, Mich. Retired. Established theater chain. Millionaire. Hall of Fame 1961. Recap: bouts 53, KO 24, decisions 17, won foul 3, draw 5, KO by 3, ND 1.

ROSE, LIONEL B. (date unavailable). Australian. First fight, Mario Magries, won 8, Waragul, Australia. Won Australian bantam title, Noel Kunde, 15, 10/28/66, Melbourne. Defended: Rocky Gattellari, KO 13, Sydney. Won world bantam title, Fighting Harada, 15, 2/26/68, Tokyo. Defended world title: Takao Sakurai, 5/2/68, Tokyo; Chico Castillo, won 15, 12/6/68, Los Angeles; Alan Rudkin, won 15, 3/8/69, Melbourne. Lost title, Ruben Olivares, KO by 5, 8/22/69, Inglewood, Calif. Spotty record to 1971, WBC Jr. light title, Yoshiaki Numata, lost 15, Hiroshima. Recap: bouts 47, KO 11, decision 29, lost decision 4, KO by 3.

ROSENBERG, CHARLES PHIL (Charles Green) B. 8/15/02, New York, N.Y. Jewish. 5'4", 118. First fight, Charles Bengo, lost 4, 1921. Mediocre start. 1922–25: undefeated. Won world bantam title, Eddie Martin, 15, 3/20/25, NYC. Defended: Eddie Shea, KO 4, 7/3/25, NYC; George Butch, 10, 3/2/26, St. Louis. 1927, outgrew division. Last fight, Johnny Dundee, won 10. Army. Recap: bouts 64, KO 7, decision 28, won foul 1, draw 6, lost decision 14, lost foul 1, ND 7.

ROSENBERG, DAVE B. 5/15/01, New York, N.Y. Jewish. 5'8½", 160. New York State, National AAU welter champ 1918–19. Turned pro 1919; no available record through 1920. First recorded pro, Rudy Lundy, KO 3, 1921. Active, impressive 1st year: KO 6; won 21 including Zulu Kid, Phil Bloom, Jimmy Darcy; ND 2; lost 2, Mike Gibbons, Italian Joe Gans, return draw. Won N.Y. version world middle title, Phil Krug, 15, 8/14/22, NYC. Lost title, Mike O'Dowd, foul 8, 11/30/22, NYC. Never figured in final title showdown, won by Johnny Wilson. 1923: won; KO 2 including Soldier Bartfield, 4; lost Pat Walsh, return KO 4. Young Stribling, ND 12, 1924. Last fight, Pat McCarthy, lost 10, 4/24/25, Fall River, Calif. Recap: bouts 57, KO 9, decision 30, draw 4, lost decision 6, lost foul 3, ND 5.

ROSENBLOOM, MAXIE (Slapsie Maxie) B. 9/6/04, New York, N.Y. Jewish. 5'11", 165–170. First fight, Jack Rivers, KO 3, 1923. Roller coaster career led to 7 series: Jimmy Slattery, lost, 6, 8/22/25, Coney Island; lost,

10, 1926; lost, 10, 8/30/27, Hartford; won 10, lost 10, 1929; won 10, 6/25/30, Buffalo; NY light heavy title, won 15, 6/25/30, Buffalo. Other series: Leo Lomski, won 3, draw 2, lost 1; Lou Scozza, won 4, lost 1, won world light title, Scozza, 15, 7/14/32, Buffalo. John Henry Lewis, won 3, lost 2. Lee Ramage, 3 fights 35 days; 1934: 2 lost, 1 draw; 1937, won 10. Jim Braddock, won 1929, return 1931 provided incident without precedent—a light heavy champ and future heavy champ thrown out of ring for stalling. Veteran Minneapolis referee George Barton declared no contest, round 2. Defended: Slattery, Scozza; Al Stillman, won 10, 2/22/33, St. Louis; Adolph Beuser, won 15, 3/10/33, NYC; Bob Goodwin, KO 4, 3/24/33, NYC; Joe Knight, draw 15, 2/5/34, Miami. Lost title, Bob Olin, 15, 11/16/34, NYC. Closed out career with creditable record, beating King Levinsky, Lou Nova; draw, Bob Pastor. Last, Al Ettore, KO 3, 8/26/39, Hollywood. Colorful, unpredictable, a favorite for appearances on radio, TV, movies. Lives in Hollywood, semiretired. Hall of Fame 1973. Recap: bouts 288, KO 18, decision 185, won foul 5, draw 23, lost decision 33, KO by 2, ND 20, no contest 2.

ROSI, PAOLO (Paulo) B. 1/28/28, Rieti, Italy. 5'7½", 135. First fight, Nicola D'Amato, won 6, 1/18/51, Albano, Italy. To U.S. 1952. First fight, Jimmy Wilde, KO 3. Undefeated 1953, including Eddie Compo, won 8, return, KO 6. First U.S. setback, Orlando Zulueta, KO by 8, 1954. Only 1956 loss, Baby Vasquez, KO by 7; won return, 1957. Undefeated 1957–58, including Johnny Busso, won. 1959 to title match, Frankie Ryff, KO 3; Flash Elorde, won. World light title, Joe Brown, KO by 9, 6/3/59, Washington, D.C. 1961: won, Tommy Tibbs, Len Matthews; lost, Jackie Donnelly, return, KO 2; lost, Carlos Ortiz. Last fight, Carlos Hernandez, KO by 1, 6/16/62, NYC. Recap: bouts 47, KO 15, decision 20, won foul 1, draw 1, lost 5, KO by 5.

ROSS, BARNEY (Barnet David Rasofsky) B. 12/23/09, New York, N.Y. D. 1/17/67, Chicago, Ill. Jewish. 5'7", 145. Amateur: won Western Golden Gloves feather title. First pro bout, Virgil Tobin, KO 2, 1929. Undefeated in 21. Lost Roger Bernard 1931. Undefeated in 28. Won world light and junior welter titles, Tony Canzoneri, 15, 6/23/33, Chicago. Defended, Canzoneri, won 15, 9/12/33, NYC. Gave up title. Defended junior welter: Sammy Fuller, won 10, 11/17/33, NYC; Pete Nebo, won 12, 2/7/34, Kansas City, Mo.; Frankie Klick, draw 10, 3/5/34, San Francisco; Bobby Pacho, won 12, 12/10/34, Cleveland; Henry Woods, won 12, 4/9/35, Seattle. Won world welter title, Jimmy McLarnin, 15, 5/28/34, NYC. Lost title, McLarnin, 15, 9/17/34, nyc. regained welter title, McLarnin, 15, 5/28/35, NYC. Defended: Izzy Jannazzo, won 15, 11/27/37, NYC; Ceferino Garcia, won 15, 9/23/37, NYC. Lost title, Henry Armstrong, 15, 5/31/38, Long Island. Last fight. Stand against Armstrong in late rounds regarded as one of most courageous made by defending champ. Enlisted marines, wounded Guadalcanal, Silver Star. Dope addiction, service treatment connected, public relations agency, NYC. Movie *Monkey on My Back* with Cameron Mitchell depicted Ross's life. Cancer victim. Hall of Fame 1966. Recap: bouts 82, KO 24, decision 50, draw 3, lost decision 4, ND 1.

ROUTIS, ANDRE B. 7/16/1900, Bordeaux, France. 5'4", 118–130. Outstanding amateur, 1918. First pro fight, Vyes Gram, won 4, 2/2/19, Bordeaux. To mid-1926, impressive overseas. Won French bantam title, Charles Ledoux, 20, 1/22/24, Paris. Lost title, Kid Francis, 15, 10/27/25, Paris. To U.S. 1926. First fight, Eddie Anderson, won 10, 8/20/26, NYC. Tony Canzoneri, lost 12, 11/22/26. Won title, Canzoneri, 15, 9/28/28, NYC. Nontitle, Canzoneri, lost 10, 5/10/29. Defended: Buster Brown, KO 3, 5/27/29, Baltimore. Lost title, Battling Battalino, 15, 9/23/29, Hartford, Conn. Last fight, Davey Abad, lost 10, 11/5/29, St. Louis. Recap: bouts 86, KO 10, decision 33, won foul 11, draw 7, lost decision 17, lost foul 6, KO by 2.

RYAN, TOMMY (Joseph Youngs) B. 3/31/70, Redwood, N.Y. D. 8/3/48, Van Nuys, Calif. English-French. 5'7¾", 142–158. First fight, John Case, won 5, 1887. Undefeated in 32, 1887–94. Won world welter title, Mysterious Billy Smith, 20, 7/26/94, Minneapolis. Fought Smith 6 times, 3 draws, 1893–94–95, ND, won foul 1896. Claimed middle title when Bob Fitzsimmons vacated, 1895. Nonpareil Jack Dempsey, won 3, 1895. Lost welter title, Kid McCoy, KO by 15, 3/2/96, Maspeth, L.I. Geo. Green, won 18, 2/25/98, *San Francisco,* officially recognized as middle champ. Defended: Jack Bonner, won 20, 10/24/98. Coney Island. Frank Craig, won 10, 9/18/99, Coney Island. Tommy West, won 17, 3/4/01, Louisville; Kid Carter, KO 6, 9/15/02, Fort Erie, Ont. Retired undefeated from middle title 1907; last ring appearance, Battling Nelson, exh. 6, 8/4/07, South Bend, Ind. Recap: bouts 109, KO 48, decision 37, won foul 1, draw 9, lost decision 1, lost foul 1, KO by 1, ND 11.

SADDLER, SANDY (Joseph Saddler) B. 2/25/26, Boston, Mass. Negro. 5'8½", 127. Family moved to N.Y. 1929. Amateur: won 16 of 17. First pro fight, Earl Roys, won 8, 3/7/44, Hartford, Conn. Record studded with 103 KO, 28 in first 38 fights. Won world feather title, Willie Pep, KO 4, 10/29/48, NYC. Lost title, Pep, 15, 2/11/49, NYC. Won vacant junior light title, Orlando Zulueta 10, 12/6/49, Cleveland. Regained feather title, Pep, KO 8, 9/8/50, NYC. Defended: Pep, KO 9, 9/8/51, NYC (fought Pep 4 times, 3 KO, 1 loss); Teddy Davis, won 15, 2/25/55, NYC; Flash Elorde, KO 13, 1/13/56, San Francisco. Last fight, Larry Boardman, lost 10, 4/14/56, Boston. 1957, vision failing, due to auto accident, vacated titles, retired. Recap: bouts 162, KO 103, decision 41, draw 2, lost decision 14, lost foul 1, KO by 1.

SALAS, LAURO B. 1927, Mexico. 5'6", 130. First fight, Bobby Dykes, won 4, Corpus Christi, Tex. Pee Wee Swingler, lost 6, 6/17/47, Los Angeles, only defeat first year, 14 fights. Record up and down through 1951. World light title, Jimmy Carter, lost 15, 4/1/52, Los Angeles. Won title, Carter, 15, 5/14/52, Los Angeles. Lost title, Carter, 15, 10/15/52, Chicago. Fought nine years, never earned another title chance. Last fight, Bunny Grant, KO by 10, 3/4/61, Kingston, Ontario, Recap: bouts 148, KO 39, decision 44, draw 12, lost decision 44, lost foul 1, KO by 7, ND 1.

SALDIVAR, VICENTE (Vincente Samuel Saldivar Garcia) B. 5/3/43, Mexico City, Mex. First fight, Baby Palacios, KO 3, 2/18/61, Iguala, Mex. Undefeated to 1962, lost foul, Babe Luis, return KO 8. Undefeated to Mexi-

169

can light title, Juan Ramirez, KO 2, 2/8/64, Mexico City. Defended: Guerrero, won 15, 4/4/64, Manila. Won world light title, Sugar Ramos, KO 12, 9/26/64, Mexico City. Defended: Fino Rosales, KO 11, 12/6/64, Leon, Mex.; Raul Rojas, KO 15, 5/7/65, Los Angeles; Howard Winston, won 15, 9/7/65, London; Floyd Robertson, KO 2, 2/12/66, Mexico City; Mitsunori Seki, won 15, 8/7/66, Mexico City; Seki, KO 7, 1/29/67, Mexico City; Winstone, won 15, 6/15/67, Cardiff; Winstone, KO 12, 10/14/67, Mexico City. Retired, vacated title. Comeback. Jose Legra, won 10, 1969. Regained title, Johnny Famechon, 15, 5/9/70, Rome. Lost title, Kuniaka Shibata, KO by 13, 12/11/70, Tijuana. 1971, Frankie Crawford, won 10. Recap.: bouts 38, KO 25, decision 10, won foul 1, lost foul 1, KO by 1.

SALICA, LOU B. 7/26/13, New York, N.Y. Italian. 118. Outstanding amateur, Won Metropolitan AAU flyweight title, 1931–32, won NY Golden Gloves, defeated Steve Enekes, Olympic champ. First pro fight, Lew Franklin, won 4, 1/5/33, NYC. To 1935, undefeated in 28, lost 2—Midget Wolgast, Speedy Dado. Won NBA bantam title, Sixto Escobar, 15, 8/26/35, NYC. Lost title, Escobar, 15, 11/15/35, NYC. Title, Escobar, lost 15, 2/21/37, San Juan, Puerto Rico. NBA vacant bantam title, Georgie Pace, draw 15, 3/4/40, Toronto. Won NY bantam title, Pace, 15, 9/24/40, NYC. Won world bantam title, Tommy Forte, 15, 1/13/41, Phila. Defended: Lou Transparenti, won 15, 4/15/41, Baltimore; Forte, won 15, 6/15/41, Phil. Lost title, Manuel Ortiz, 12, 8/7/42, Hollywood. Title, Ortiz, KO by 11, 3/10/43, Oakland, Calif. Last fight, Harry Jeffra, lost 10, 3/27/44, Baltimore. Recap: bouts 90, KO 13, decision 49, draw 11, lost decision 16, KO by 1.

SALVARRIA, ERBITO B. 1/20/48, Manila, Philippines. First fight, Pablito Seldo, KO 4, 9/14/63, Quezon City. Creditable record 1963–66 to Philippine fly title, Rick Magramo, lost 12, 10/14/67, Araneta. Won Philippine fly title, Magramo, 12, 8/17/68, Araneta. Won Oriental fly title, Takeshi Nakamura, KO 12, 10/10/69, Manila. Defended Orient: Witaya Plernjit, 12, 6/21/70, Manila. Won world fly title, Chartchai Chionoi, KO 2, 12/7/70, Bangkok, Thailand. Defended: Susumu Hanagata, won 15, 4/30/71, Manila; Betulio Gonzalez, draw 15, 11/20/71, Caracas, Venezuela. Recap: bouts 41, KO 8, decision 24, draw 3, lost decision 5, KO by 1.

SANCHEZ, CLEMENTE B. 7/9/47, Monterrey, Mexico. 1962 Golden Gloves feather champ. First pro bout, Tony Herrera, won 6, 3/23/63, Monterrey. Impressive early record. 1968: 9 bouts, 7 KO, lost, Rogelio Lara, twice. 1969–71: 20 KO, 1 draw, 1 lost, Migel Riasgo. Won world feather title, Kuniaki Shibata, KO 3, 5/19/72, Tokyo. Jose Legra, KO by 10, 12/16/72,

Monterrey. Vacated title over weight dispute. Recap: bouts 51, KO 27, decision 12, draw 3, lost decision 8, KO by 1.

SANDS, DAVE (David Ritchie) B. 2/4/26, Australia. D. 8/11/52, Newcastle, New South Wales, Australia. 5'10", 158. Many predicted world champ till untimely death. First fight, Leo Corregan, KO 1, 1943. First year, 18 straight KO; George Cook, lost, won return. Impressive record 1944–46: 34 bouts, 22 KO; won Australian middle title, Jack Kirkhorn, KO 12, 5/11/46, Sydney. Defended: Kirkhorn, KO 5, 6/7/46, Sydney. Won Australian light heavy title, Jack Johnson, KO 4, 8/24/46, Sydney. Defended: Johnson, KO 1, 10/12/46, Melbourne; Alf Gallagher, KO 3, 11/30/46, Sydney. 1947–48, only loss, Emory Jackson; won return. Won British Empire middle title, Dick Turpin, KO 1, 9/6/49, London. Bobo Olson, won, 1950, 1951. Won vacant Australian heavy title, Alf Gallagher, 15, 9/4/50, Sydney. Only career KO by Yolande Pompey, 7, 1951, London. Undefeated 1952, four straight KO: defended Australian light heavy title, Chub Keith, KO 14, 3/31/52, London; won British and Australian middle titles, Al Bourke, KO 5, 5/9/52; defended Australian light heavy title, Jim Woods, KO 4, 6/9/52, Wagga Wagga, New South Wales; Ron Toohey, KO 10. Died, auto accident, peak of career. Recap: bouts 104, KO 62, decision 31, draw 1, lost decision 7, KO by 1, no contest 2.

SANGCHILLI, BALTAZAR (Baltazar Belenguer Hevoas) B. 10/15/11, Valencia, Spain. 5'3", 118. First fight, Casanova, KO 2, 4/29/29, Valencia, 1930–31: undefeated. Won Spanish bantam title, Carlos Flix, 12, 4/22/33, Valencia. Defended: Flix, draw 12, 2/6/34, Madrid. Won world bantam title, Al Brown, 15, 6/1/35, Valencia. Lost title, Tony Marino, KO by 14, 6/29/36, NYC. (All fights overseas to 1936. First U.S. fight, Jimmy Martin, KO 8, 5/16/36, Brooklyn.) Last two years, lost 5. Last fight, Peter Kane, lost 10, 4/3/39, London. Recap: bouts 77, KO 24, decision 33, won foul 2, draw 5, lost decision 11, lost foul 1, KO by 1.

SARRON, PETEY B. 1918, Birmingham, Ala. Syrian. 5'4", 126. Amateur: 120 bouts, competed Olympic Games, Paris. Pro, 1926, broke hand, inactive two years. First comeback, Pinky May, draw 10, 1928, Savannah. Slow starting, through 1931, 11 KO, 15 wins, lost 7. 1932: undefeated. To 1936 contender. World feather title, Freddie Miller, lost 15, 3/2/36, Miami. Won title, Miller, 15, 5/11/36, Washington, D.C. Defended: Baby Manuel, won 15, 7/22/36, Dallas. Nontitle, Miller, lost 10, 1937. Title, Miller, won 12, 9/4/37, Johannesburg, South Africa. Lost title, Henry Armstrong, KO by 6, 10/29/37, NYC. Through 1939: 11 wins, 1 loss. Last fight, Sammy Angott, lost 10, 7/17/39, Pittsburgh. Army. Recap: bouts 103, KO 18, decision 56, won foul 1, draw 8, lost decision 15, lost foul 3, KO by 1, ND 1.

SATTERFIELD, BOB B. 11/9/23, Chicago, Ill. Heavy. "In and outer," potentially great heavy, upsetting top rankers, losing to mediocrities. First fight, Young Mitchell, KO 1, 3/19/45, Chicago. First year: 11 KO, 1 draw; Mike Parshay, KO by 1. To 1953, erratic record, 10 KO, including Lee Oma; 6 decisions, including Harold Johnson; KO by Johnson, Jake LaMotta, Archie Moore, Clarence Henry, Bob Foxworth, Sam Baroudi, Henry Hall, Rex Layne. 1953, four fights, all KO, including Bob Baker 1. 1954, 5 KO, including Julio Mederos 2, Cleveland Williams 3, John Holman twice; Ezzard Charles, KO by 2; Marty Marshall, KO by 2 (won return, 1955). To 1958, fair record: KO 5, dec. 8, draw 1, lost 6, KO by 1. Series: Johnson, won, lost, KO by; Harold Carter, draw, lost, KO by; Mederos, won, lost, KO by. Last fight, Harold King, won 10, 11/21/57, Oakland. Recap: bouts 77, KO 35, decision 15, draw 3, lost decision 12, KO by 12.

SAXTON, JOHNNY B. 7/4/30, Newark, N.J. Negro. 5'9", 145. First fight, Jimmy Swan, KO 3, 5/9/49, Phila. To 1953, undefeated in 40, then lost Gil Turner, 10, and Del Flanagan, 10. Won welter title, Kid Gavilan, 15, 10/20/54, Phila. Lost title, Tony DeMarco, KO by 14, 4/1/55, Boston. Regained title, Carmen Basilio, 15, 3/14/56, Chicago. Lost title, Basilio, KO by 9, 9/12/56, Syracuse. Title, Basilio, KO by 2, 2/22/57, Cleveland. Last fight, Willie Green, KO by 3, 12/15/58, Providence. Recap: bouts 66, KO 21, decision 33, won foul 1, lost decision 4, draw 2, KO by 5.

SCALZO, PETEY B. 8/1/17, New York, N.Y. Italian. 5'6", 130. First fight, Demasco Seda, KO 1, 6/29/36, NYC. Undefeated two years, first loss Mike Belloise, 8, 1938. Nontitle, Joey Archibald, KO 2, 1938. (Archibald refused to defend against Scalzo; NBA declared him champ. N.Y. and Maryland continued to recognize Archibald.) Defended: Bob Poison Ivy, KO 15, 7/10/40, Hartford; Phil Zwick, won 15, 5/19/41, Milwaukee. Lost title, Richie Lemos, KO by 5, 7/1/41, Los Angeles. 1942: lost 7 of 10. Army. Last fight, Bob Montgomery, KO by 6, 10/25/43, Phila. Recap: bouts 111, KO 46, decision 43, draw 6, lost decision 12, KO by 3, ND 1.

SCANLON, BOBBY B. 1/2/36, Buffalo, N.Y. 5'6", 135. First fight, Gene Donaldson, won 4, 5/31/54, NYC. Undefeated four straight years, including Lauro Salas, won 10, 1957. Spotty record to 1960: won four including Orlando Zulueta; lost 3, Johnny Gonsalves twice. Inactive 1961. Undefeated 1962, including Alfredo Escobar, won 10. 1963–65, won two, lost six. 1966, two fights, Andy Gonzales, won 10; last fight, Luis Molina, KO 9, 5/25/66, San Jose. Recap: bouts 56, KO 12, decision 31, draw 1, lost 10, KO by 2.

SCHAAF, ERNIE (Ernest Frederick Schaaf) B. 9/27/08, Elizabeth, N.J. D. 2/13/33, New York, N.Y. German-American. First fight, Sgt. Jim Harvey, KO 2, 1925. Undefeated 1926, 15 straight KO. 1927, only loss, Yale Okun; returns, won 10, ND. 1929 impressive, including Johnny Risko, won 10; lost return, 10, 1929. Tommy Loughran series: lost 10, 1929; returns, won twice 1930, lost 1931. Max Baer, won 1930. 1931, Jim Braddock, won; Jim Mahoney, KO twice; Tuffy Griffith, won. 1932 impressive; won, Young Stribling, Tony Galento, Paolino Uzcudun; lost Baer return, 10. Primo Carnera, KO by 13, 2/10/33, NYC. Died few days later, never coming to. Brain injury generally attributed to a thunderous right in the Baer fight, 8/31/32, Chicago. Recap: bouts 111, KO 46, decision 43, draw 6, lost decision 12, KO by 3, ND 1.

SCHMELING, MAX (Maximilian Schmeling) (The Black Uhlan) B. 9/28/05, Klein-Luckaw (Brandenburg), Germany. 6'1", 198. German middle, light heavy and heavy champ. First recorded fight, Czapp, KO 6, 8/2/24, Dusseldorf. Early record spotty: KO by Max Diekmann, Larry Gaines; lost Jack Taylor. Returns won, Diekmann, Gaines. Won German light heavy title, Fernard Delarge, KO 14, 6/19/27, Dortmund, Ger. Won European light heavy, Hein Domgoerger, KO 7; won German heavy title, Franz Diener, 15, 4/4/28, Berlin. To U.S., Joe Monte, KO 5, 11/23/28, NYC. 1929; Joe Sekyra, won 10; Pietro Corri, KO 1; Johnny Risko, KO 9; Paolino Uzcudun, won 15, setting stage for Tunney's vacated title. Won world heavy title, Jack Sharkey, foul 4, 6/12/30, NYC. (Only heavy to win title on floor.) Defended: Young Stribling, KO 15, 7/3/31, Cleveland. Lost title, Sharkey, 15, 6/21/32, NYC. Mickey Walker, KO 8, 9/26/32, Lond Island; Max Baer, KO by 10, 6/8/33, NYC. 1934–35: 5 fights: Steve Hamas, lost, return, KO 2; Uzcudun, draw, return, win; Walter Neusel, KO 8. Joe Louis, KO 12, 6/19/36, NYC, an all-time upset. Despite loss, Louis matched with Braddock for title—gate, potential reason. Title, Louis, KO by 1, 6/22/38, NYC. Joined German army 1941, parachute troops, injured. Comeback 1947: 5 fights, lost 2. Last fight, Richard Vogt, lost 10, 10/31/48, Berlin. Likened to Dempsey in style, looks. Referee, boxing instructor. Hall of Fame 1970. Recap: bouts 71, KO 39, decision 14, won foul 3, draw 5, lost decision 5, KO by 5.

SCHMIDTKE, RUDI (Ruediger) B. 2/9/43, Germany. 173. Part-time clothes model. 1966–68: 13 bouts, KO 5, dec. 5, draw 1, lost 2. Undefeated 1969. Won German light heavy title, Arno Prick, 12, 1/23/70, Frankfurt. Defended: Conny Velensek, 12, 4/16/70 Offenbach. European light heavy title, Piero Del Papa, lost 15, 9/11/70, Frankfurt; won nontitle return, 10, 1972. Undefeated to Chris Finnegan, won European light heavy title, KO 12, 11/14/72, London. Lost title, John Conteh, KO by 12, 4/73, Wembley, Eng. Successful businessman in Frankfurt, besides boxing talent. Recap: bouts 31, KO 10, decision 16, draw 3, lost decision 1, KO by 1.

SCHWARTZ, CORPORAL IZZY B. 10/23/02, New York, N.Y. Jewish. 5'1". First fight, Billy Stone, KO 4, 1922. Creditable record thru 1927. Won vacant NY fly title recognition, Newsboy Brown, 15, 12/16/27, NYC. Defended: Routier Parra, won 15, 4/9/28, NYC; Frisco Grande, won foul 4, 7/20/28, NYC; Frenchy Belanger, won 12, 3/12/29, Toronto. World bantam title, Bushy Graham, lost 15, 5/23/28, Brooklyn. (Schwartz eliminated in confusion of title claimants.) Lost last 4 fights. Last, Eugene Huat, lost 10, 11/4/29, NYC. Gave up fly title. Recap: bouts 117, KO 7, decision 51, won foul 1, draw 12, lost decision 27, KO by 1, ND 18.

SERVO, MARTY B. 11/9/19, Schenectady, N.Y. D. 2/9/69, Pueblo, Colo. Italian. Amateur: won 91, lost 4: 1937 won Golden Gloves feather title; 1938 Diamond Belt feather; 1938: lost in finals AAU championship. First pro bout, George Hall, won 6, 1/8/38, Washington D.C. Through 1941 undefeated in 45. 1942: Lew Jenkins, won 10, Ray Robinson lost 10. Coast Guard. Won world welter title, Freddie Cochrane, KO 4, 2/1/46, NYC. Nontitle, Rocky Graziano, KO by 2; Jimmy Anest, KO 5; Bobby Lakin, ND 10; Bobby Singleton, KO 2. Last fight, Joe DeMartino, KO by 1. Retired because of nose injury. Never defended title. Recap: bouts 56, KO 15, decision 34, draw 2, lost decision 2, KO by 2, ND 1.

SHADE, DAVE B. 1902, Vallejo, Calif. Irish. 5'8". Light, welter, middle. 1918–21—bouts not recorded. George Ward, won 16, 1921, NYC. Mickey Walker, KO by 8, ND, 1921. Active, mostly successful (Pete Latzo, draw; Jimmy Slattery, KO) to world welter title bout, Mickey Walker, lost 15, 9/21/25, NYC (last title fight). To 1935, fought Lou Scozza, draw; Maxie Rosenbloom, lost twice; Jack McVey, draw; Ace Hudkins, won; Ben Jeby, draw, won. Undefeated 1933. Last fight, Al Gainer, lost 10, 2/4/35, New Haven. Recap: 149, KO 10, decision 83, draw 12, lost decision 15, lost foul 1, KO by 1, ND 26, no contest 1.

SHARKEY, JACK (Giovanni Cervati) (Little Jackie) B. 6/20/98, Bologna, Italy. 5'3", 118. First fight, Billy Murphy, KO 6, 1915. Impressive 1915–20, NDs: Pete Herman, three; Johnny Buff, one; Memphis Pal Moore, six; Frankie Burns, four; Joe Lynch, ND, draw 15, KO by 15, 12/2/20, NYC.

174

1921, Midget Smith series: draw, lost, won. World bantam title, Buff, lost 15, 11/10/21, NYC. Undefeated to junior light title bout, Johnny Dundee, lost 15, 6/6/22, NYC. Slippery road to 1925 retirement, KO 1, won foul 1, ND 2, lost 6, KO by 3. Last fight, Jim Lynch, draw 4, 7/2/25, NYC. Recap: bouts 168, KO 4, decisions 8, won foul 2, draw 15, lost decision 15, KO by 9, ND 115.

SHARKEY, JACK (Joseph Paul Zukauskas) (Big Skee) B. 10/6/02, Binghamton, N.Y. Lithuanian. 6', 196, Shoe factory. Construction. Navy 1920, served 3 years, 8 months. Several service fights, lost one, Jim Crawley (Sharkey dislocated shoulder). Adopted his name from two idols, Tom Sharkey and Jack Dempsey. Pro 1924: 3 KOs; Eddie Record, lost 10, return, KO 7; Romero Rojas, KO by 8; Jimmy Maloney, lost 10. 1925–27: won 11, KO 5, won foul 3, lost 2, until Jack Dempsey, KO by 7, 7/21/27, NYC (Sharkey claimed foul, turned head, KO'd). 1928–29: lost only to Johnny Risko; wins: Jack Delaney, K.O. Christner, Leo Gates, Arthur Dekuh, Young Stribling, Tommy Loughran; draw, Tom Heeney. Phil Scott, KO 3, Feb. 1930, Miami. Vacant world heavy title, Max Schmeling, lost foul 4, 6/12/30, NYC. 1931: Mickey Walker, draw 15; Primo Carnera, won 15. Won title, Schmeling, 15, 6/21/32, NYC. Lost title, Carnera, KO by 6, 6/29/33, NYC. Same year, lost, King Levinsky, Loughran. Last fight, Joe Louis, KO by 3, 8/18/36. Cocky, erratic, he was mostly popular with fans. Regarded as a sound boxer, fair hitter. Saved his money, retired to Boston. Recap: bouts 55, KO 15, decision 20, won foul 3, draw 3, lost decision 8, lost foul 1, KO by 4, ND 1.

SHARKEY, TOM (Thomas J. Sharkey) B. 11/26/73, Dundalk, Ireland. D. 4/17/53, San Francisco, Calif. 5'8½", 185. Fought 3 heavy champs, regarded by some as an uncrowned champ. First fight, J. Gardner, KO 4, 3/17/93, Honolulu. 20 successive KO wins, mostly Honolulu. 1896: 3 successive fights, Jim Corbett, draw 4; John L. Sullivan, ND; Bob Fitzsimmons, won foul, 8. Undefeated 1897. Jim Jeffries, lost 20, 1898. Corbett, won foul, 9, 1898. World heavy title, Jeffries, lost 25, 11/3/99, Coney Island. 1900: 6 KO; Gus Ruhlin, lost 15; Fitzsimmons, KO by 2. Last fight, Jack Munroe, ND 6, 2/27/04, Phila. Exh., Frank Shields, 1923. Opened bar NYC, joined Jeffries in vaudeville, worked at California race tracks. Hall of Fame, 1959. Recap: bouts 54, KO 37, decision 1, won foul 2, draw 5, lost decision 3, lost foul 1, KO by 2, ND 3.

SHAVERS, ERNIE B. 1946, Warren, Ohio. 1969 AAU heavy champ. First pro fight, Red Howell, KO 2, 11/6/69, Akron. First year, 5 KO, 1 lost. 1970–72: remarkable KO record, 6 straight KO; 1 KO by (Ron Stander, 5),

1970; 24 straight KO, 2 dec., 2 KO to 1973. No name opponents. 1973: Joe Young, KO 1; Harold Carter, KO 1; Jimmy Ellis, upset KO 1, NYC. Promising career. Recap: bouts 43, KO 40, decision 1, lost decision 1, KO by 1.

SHAW, BATTLING B. October 1910, Laredo, Mexico. 5'8½", 138. First fight, Ray Kiser, lost 10, 2/22/32. Mediocre record, lost three in first year. Won junior welter title, Johnny Jadick, 10, 2/20/33, New Orleans. Lost title, Tony Canzoneri, 10, 5/21/33, New Orleans. Lost all five remaining fights. Last, Young Peter Jackson, KO by 7, Los Angeles. Recap: bouts 23, KO 4, decision 9, draw 7, KO by 3.

SHIBATA, KUNIAKI B. 3/29/47, Japan. First fight, Seiichi Iizuka, KO 1, 3/6/65, Tokyo. To mid-1968, undefeated. Dwight Hawkins KO by 7, 1968. Orient feather title, Hubert Kang, KO by 6, 1/15/69, Tokyo. Undefeated to world feather title, Vincente Saldivar, KO 13, 12/11/70, Defended: Ernesto Marcel, draw 15, 11/10/71, Matsuyama. Recap: 41 bouts, KO 22, decision 14, draw 3, KO by 2.

SHIRAI, YOSHIO B. 11/23/23, Tokyo, Japan. 5'6". 1946–47 pro fights not recorded. First recorded fight, T. Hanada, lost 10, 1948, Tokyo. Won Japanese fly title, Hanada, KO 5, 1/28/49, Tokyo. Won Japanese bantam title, Hiroshi Horiguchi, 10, 12/15/49, Tokyo. Lost bantam title, Nagashima, 8, 3/3/51, Tokyo. Rewon title, Nagashima, 10, 9/20/51, Tokyo. Defended: Horiguchi, KO 6, 10/28/51, Tokyo. Won world flyweight title, Dado Marino, 15, 5/19/52, Tokyo. Defended: Marino, won 15, 11/15/52, Tokyo; Tanny Campo, won 15, 5/18/53, Tokyo; Terry Allen, won 15, 10/27/53, Tokyo; Leo Espinosa, won 15, 5/23/54, Tokyo. Lost title, Pascual Perez, 15, 11/26/54, Tokyo. Last fight, title, Perez, KO by 5, 5/30/55, Tokyo. Recap: bouts 42, KO 15, decision 20, draw 1, lost decision 4, KO by 2.

SHUGRUE, YOUNG JOE (Jersey Bobcat) B. 9/11/94, Jersey City, N.J. D. 5/11/61, Jersey City, N.J. Irish. 5'6", 130. First fight, Banty Lewis, won 4, 7/23/10, Newark. Undefeated to mid-1913: Benny Leonard, KO 4; Johnny Dundee, ND twice; Charley White, ND twice; Jim Coffey, ND twice; Leach Cross ND. 1914: Owen Moran, KO 7; Freddy Welsh, ND twice; Charley White, ND; Jimmy Murphy, ND; Ted (Kid) Lewis, lost. 1915 series: Dundee, ND four, lost; White, ND three; Cross, ND three. Last fight, Murphy, ND 6, 11/1/15, Phila. Career started at 16, regarded as sensational for age. Failing vision forced retirement at 21. Recap: bouts 88, KO 15, decision 6, draw 1, lost decision 5, ND 61.

SIKI, BATTLING (Louis Phal) (Singular Senegalese) B. 9/16/97, Senegal, West Africa. D. 12/15/25, New York, N.Y. Negro. 5'11", 176. First fight, Jules Perroud, KO 8, 1913. Won light heavy title, Georges Carpentier, KO 6, 9/24/22, Paris. Lost title, Mike McTigue, 20, 3/17/23, Dublin (St. Pat's Day). Spotty career to 1925. Last fight, Les Anderson, lost 12, 11/13/25, Baltimore. Shot to death in tavern brawl. Recap: bouts 74, KO 29, decision 25, draw 1, lost decision 10, lost foul 1, KO by 1, ND 6, no contest 1.

SINGER, AL B. 9/6/07, New York, N.Y. D. 4/20/61, New York, N.Y. Jewish. 5'4½". First fight, Jim Reilly, KO 2, 1927. Impressive early years: Tony Canzoneri, draw, 1928; Bud Taylor, won foul 4, won 10; Kid Chocolate, lost 12; Pete Nebo, KO 1, all 1929. Won world light title, Sammy Mandell, KO 1, 7/17/30, NYC. Non-title, Jimmy McLarnin, KO by 3, 1930. Lost title, Tony Canzoneri, KO by 1, 11/14/30. NYC. Bat Battalino, KO by 2, 1931. Inactive to 1935, 3 KO, 1 win. Army 1942. Retired. Recap: bouts 70, KO 24, decision 34, won foul 2, draw 2, lost decision 4, KO by 4,

SLATTERY, JIMMY B. 8/25/04, Buffalo, N.Y. Irish. 5'11", 165. First fight, Joe Burns, KO 1, 1921. Series of prelim wins through 1923. First loss, Joe Eagan, 6, Boston, 1924. 1925: Harry Greb, lost 6; Jack Delaney, won 6; Eagan, KO 1; Dave Shade, KO by 3; Maxie Rosenbloom, won 6. Won light heavy title, Paul Berlenbach, KO by 11, 9/11/25, NYC. Rosenbloom (NBA title), won 10, 8/30/27, Hartford. Lost title, Tommy Loughran, 15, 12/12/27. Won N.Y. Commission light heavy title, Lou Scozza, 15, 2/10/30, Buffalo. Lost title, Rosenbloom, 15, 6/25/30, Buffalo. Last fight, Jack Gibbons, KO by 3, 8/28/35, Minot, N. Dak. Regarded smooth boxer. Nicknamed "Silk Shirt Jim" for habits, clothing. Recap: bouts 128, KO 45, decision 62, won foul 2, draw 1, lost decision 9, KO by 5, ND 2, no contest 2.

SMITH, GUNBOAT (Edward J. Smyth) B. 2/17/87, Philadelphia, Pa. Irish. 6'2", 185. Started boxing in Navy. One of most colorful heavies, fought all comers, upset champs—Jess Willard, Sam Langford, Battling Levinsky. First fight, Chuck Carleton, KO 3, 7/4/06, Bremerton, Wash. To 1910 undefeated, won Pacific Fleet heavy title, Matt Turner, KO 5, 6/3/09, Seattle Harbor. 1911–14: Jack Geyer only losses, (KO by 9, L 10). 25 KO, beat Willard, Langford, Frank Moran. Won white heavy title, Arthur Pelkey, KO 15, 1/1/14, Daly City, Calif. Lost title, Georges Carpentier, foul 6, 7/16/14, London. Series: Jack Dempsey: ND, lost, KO by twice; Levinsky: won, draw, ND three, lost. Creditable record to 1920 including Harry Greb, Jack Dillon, Billy Miske, Carl Morris, Jack Moran, Kid Norfolk. 1921: KO by four straight, retired. Last fight, Harry Wills, KO by 1, 10/10/21, Havana. Recap: bouts 131, KO 40, decision 15, won foul 1, draw 7, lost decision 8, lost foul 1, KO by 11, ND 48.

SMITH, JEFF (Jerome Jefferds) (The Globetrotter) B. 4/23/91, New York, N.Y. 5'9", 158. A natural middle, he fought several light heavies and heavies. Regarded as one of the great underrated. First fight, Ray Hatfield, won 4, 3/7/10, Newark. Undefeated 3½ years including Jimmy Clabby, ND; Mike Gibbons, ND; George Chip, won; Frank Mantell, draw. Georges Carpentier, lost 20, 1913. Series: Harry Greb, ND five, draw, lost; Mike Gibbons, ND three; Mike McTigue, ND, won, lost. 1917: army boxing instructor. Undefeated from 1916 to Mike O'Dowd, lost, 1920. To 1927, fair record: Tommy Loughran, ND twice; Gene Tunney, ND. Last fight, George Manley, lost 10, 6/11/27, Denver. Eye condition, retired. School physical instructor, Bayonne, N.J. Recap: bouts 178, KO 46, decision 51, won foul 2, draw 3, lost decision 8, lost foul 1, KO by 1, ND 65, no contest 1.

SMITH, MIDGET (William Joseph Smith) B. 12/3/99, New York, N.Y. Irish. 5', 118. Regular army (stationed Panama, 1917–19) division bantam champ. First pro bout, Bill Baker, KO 8, 1920. Johnny Buff, only loss in 1920. Fought ranking fighters second year: Jackie Sharkey, won, draw, lost; Joe Burman, ND twice, lost; Young Montreal, won; Pal Moore, ND; upset Pete Herman, 15. World bantam title, Joe Lynch, lost 15, 12/22/22, NYC; return, ND. 1924–25: fought three world champs—Bud Taylor, ND; Kid Williams, lost; Eddie Martin, lost. Inactive 1926. Last fight, Taylor, ND 10, 2/15/27, Indianapolis. Recap: bouts 79, KO 5, decision 28, won foul 1, draw 4, lost decision 19, lost foul 1, ND 21.

SMITH, MYSTERIOUS BILLY (Amos Smith) B. 5/15/71, Eastport, Me. D. 10/15/37, Portland, Oreg. Irish. 5'8½", 145–50. Welter division, between light and middle loosely created 1880, weight first set 142 lbs. later raised to 145. Paddy Duffy claimed title early 80s, later vacated. Smith won title, Danny Needham, KO 14, 12/14/92, San Francisco. First fight, Spider Kelly, draw, 1891, San Francisco. Defended title: Tom Williams, KO 2, 4/17/93, Coney Island. Lost title, Tommy Ryan, 20, 7/26/94, Minneapolis. Title, Ryan fight stopped by police, 5/27/95, Coney Island. Title, Ryan, won foul 9, 11/25/96, Maspeth, L.I. Defended: Matty Matthews, won 25, 8/25/98. NYC; Charley McKeever, won 25, 10/7/98, NYC; Joe Walcott, won 20, 12/6/98, NYC; McKeever, draw 20, 6/30/99, NYC. Lost title, Rube Ferns, foul 21, 1/15/1900. Balance of career spotty: Walcott, lost 2, lost foul 1; Ryan, KO by 4. Last fight, Jim Cameron, lost foul 3, 7/21/11, San Francisco.

Operated hotel, Tacoma, Wash. Recap: bouts 81, KO 13, decision 15, won foul 2, draw 28, lost decision 4, lost foul 10, KO by 3, ND 6.

SMITH, SOLLY B. 1878, Los Angeles, Calif. D. 1929. 5'4", 122. Something of a lost statistic in most record books. First dated fight, Dan Mahoney, KO 15, 10/3/91, Los Angeles. Undefeated in 25 (10 draws), only loss, George Dixon, 7. Claimed feather title, Dixon, won 20, 10/4/97, San Francisco. To 1899, won foul, 1; draw, 4; lost, 2; KO by 1; lost foul, 1, Last fight, Jack McClelland, lost foul 6, 10/2/99, Pittsburgh, Recap: bouts 35, KO 6, decision 7, won foul 1, draw 14, lost decision 3, lost foul 1, KO by 1, ND 2.

SMITH, WALLACE (Bud) B. 4/2/29, Cincinnati, Ohio. D. 7/10/73, Cincinnati, Ohio. 5'6½", 123. Outstanding amateur, won AAU light championship 1948. First pro fight, Torpedo Tensley, KO 1, 11/29/48, Cincinnati. To 1955, so-so record. Won world light title, Jimmy Carter, 15, 6/29/55, Boston. Defended: Carter, 15, 10/19/55, Cincinnati. Lost title, Joe Brown, 15, 8/24/56, New Orleans. Title, Brown, KO by 11, 2/13/57, Miami Beach. Last fight, Gomeo Brennan, KO by 5, 4/1/58, Miami Beach. Shot, killed while acting as peacemaker between man and woman in street quarrel. Recap: bouts 59, KO 18, decision 14, draw 6, lost decision 15, KO by 6.

SOOSE, BILLY B. 8/2/17, Farrell, Pa. Hungarian. 6'½", 165–170. First fight, Johnny Dean, KO 4, 3/15/38, Los Angeles; First year, undefeated in 10, lost 2. 1939: 7 wins, 1 loss to George Abrams. 1940: 11 won including Tony Zale; Abrams, lost 10. Won NY middle title, Ken Overlin, 15, 5/9/41, NYC. Never defended, vacated Nov. 1941 to fight as light heavy. Last fight, Jimmy Bivins, lost 10, 1/13/42, Cleveland. Navy, 1942. Recap: bouts 41, KO 13, decision 21, draw 1, lost 6.

STANLEY, DIGGER (George Stanley) B. 2/28/83, Norwich, England. 5'6½", 118. First recorded fight, Owen Moran, won 20, 6/17/01. Birmingham, Eng. Impressive to 1904, including George Dixon, won, lost; Moran return, won; Jimmy Walsh, won, draw. 1904: Joe Bowker outgrew world bantam title, vacated. Stanley claimed title, recognized in Eng.; Walsh also claimed, recognized in U.S. Walsh, won recognized world title, 15, 10/20/05, Chelsea, Mass. (Both outgrew class, return, draw 15, 5/24/09, London.) Undefeated 1908–11, including Bowker, KO 8, 1910. Only 3 U.S. fights, Walsh title, 1905; Frankie Burns, Tommy O'Toole, NDs, 1911. English bantam title, Bill Benyon, lost 20, 6/2/13, London; return, won title, 20,

12/27/13, London. Last fight, Charley Walker, lost foul, 13, 1914, London. Recap: bouts 56, KO 6, decision 36, lost decision 10, lost foul 1, KO by 1, ND 2.

STEELE, FREDDIE B. 12/18/12, Tacoma, Wash. Irish. 5'10½", 158. First fight, Jimmy Farrar, KO 3, 1930. 1930–37: 89 fights, 87 undefeated; Tommy Herman, lost 4, return, Herman, won 6. Won NBA middle title, Babe Risko, 15, 7/11/36, Seattle. Defended: Gorilla Jones, won 10 1/1/37, Milwaukee; Risko, won 15, 2/19/37, NYC; Frankie Battaglia, KO 3, 5/11/37, Seattle; Ken Overlin, KO 4, 9/11/37, Seattle; Carmen Barth, KO 7, 2/19/38, Cleveland. (Nontitle, Fred Apostoli, KO by 9, 1/7/38. NYC.) Lost title, Al Hostak, KO by 1, 7/26/38, Seattle. Last fight, Jimmy Casino, KO by 5, 5/23/41. Recap: bouts 95, KO 38, decision 46, draw 5, lost decision 2, KO by 3, no contest 1.

STERLING, BUNNY B. 4/4/48, England. 160. First fight, Joe Devitt, lost 6, 9/13/66, London. Spotty early record. Undefeated 1970. Won British and Empire middle titles, Mark Rowe, KO 4, 9/8/70, London. Defended Empire title: Kahu Mahanga, 15, 11/13/70, Melbourne. 1971: undefeated, including wins, Tommy Bogs and Luis Rodriguez; draw, Tommy Mundine; to Jean-Claude Bouttier, KO by 14. Lost Empire title, Mundine, KO by 15, 4/14/72, Milton, N.S.W. Defended British title: Phil Matthews, KO 5, 9/19/72, Manchester; Don McMillan, KO 11 3/73; Rowe, 15, 5/73. Recap: bouts 41, KO 9, decision 19, draw 3, lost decision 8, KO by 2.

STRIBLING, YOUNG (William Lawrence Stribling) (King of Canebrakes; Georgia Peach) B. 12/26/04, Bainbridge, Ga. D. 10/2/33, Macon, Ga. 5'11½", 172. Handsome, busy fighter, impressive KO record, 126 of 286 fights, bantam to heavy. Son of circus family, managed by father. First fight, Kid Dunn, won 4, 1/17/21, Atlanta. Fought 9 champs: Mike McTigue, draw 1923, ND 1924; Jimmy Slattery, lost 1924, won 1928; Tommy Loughran, won 1924, won 1925, lost 1927; Paul Berlenbach, lost 1924, lost light heavy title 10, 6/10/26, NYC; Battling Levinsky, ND 10, 11/11/26; Maxie Rosenbloom, won 10, 1927; Jack Sharkey, lost 10, 1929; Primo Carnera, won foul, lost foul, 1929; heavy title, Max Schmeling, KO by 3, 7/3/31, Cleveland. Thru 1933, 9 KO, 7 wins, 2 lost, 1 no contest. Last fight, Rosenbloom, won 10, 9/22/33, Houston. Sports writer Grantand Rice: "He was born with so much inborn ability, he was never called on to fight when the chips were down, thus no title. . . ." Motorcycle accident. Recap: 286, KO 126, decision 93, won foul 3, draw 14, lost decision 9, lost foul 2, KO by 1, ND 36, no contest 2.

SUGGS, CHICK (Edward Murray Suggs) B. 10/9/01, Washington, D.C. Negro. 5'5½", 118–126. Busy trial horse, averaged over fight a month, 1924–26 almost two monthly. 1917–23: spotty record. Undefeated 1924, 23 bouts including, won: Joey Sangor, Young Montreal; ND: Benny Bass. 1925: undefeated 20, including Sammy Fuller, won; Johnny Datto, draw; lost 3, Bushy Graham, Honeyboy Finnegan, Babe Herman, won return. Last three years, trial horse for champ aspirants, lost Al Singer, Kid Chocolate, Pancho Villa, Lew Massey; KO by Bud Taylor, Tony Canzoneri, Fuller. Last fight, Mike Dundee, KO by 2, 11/12/29, Chicago. Recap: bouts 168, KO 37, decision 72, won foul 2, draw 10, lost decision 31, lost foul 4, KO by 4, ND 8.

SULLIVAN, JACK (Twin) B. 9/23/78, Cambridge, Mass. D. 9/4/47, Cambridge, Mass. Irish. 5'9", 160–70. First fight, Jack Fitzpatrick, won 3, 1898, Boston. To 1904, impressive (1902 undefeated). 1904: Hugo Kelly, won, draw, lost; Kid McCoy, lost 20; Philadelphia Jack O'Brien, KO by 3 (ND, lost 1903, draw 1905). Fought two heavy champs: Tommy Burns, draw, won, 1905; Marvin Hart, lost foul, 1908. Series: Frank Mantell, draw, ND, lost; Jim Flynn, ND, won foul, draw two, lost. Closing years impressive. Last fight, Tom Cotter, won 10, 9/8/22, Boston. Fought unprecedented 40 draws. Twin brother of welter champ Mike (Twin) Sullivan. Recap: bouts 137, KO 20, decision 32, won foul 1, draw 40, lost decision 10, lost foul 2, KO by 6, ND 26.

SULLIVAN, JOHN L. (John Lawrence Sullivan) (Boston Strong Boy) B. 10/15/58, Roxbury, Mass. D. 2/2/18, Abington, Mass. Irish. 5'10½", 190. 1878: bare-knuckle theater bouts. First important fight, Jack Stewart, Canadian champ, KO 2, 1/3/81, Boston. Last of bare-knuckle champions, won heavy title, Paddy Ryan, KO 9, 2/7/82, Mississippi City, Miss. Charley Mitchell, English champ, won 3 (police stopped), 5/14/83, NYC. Ryan, police, 50 seconds, 1/19/85, NYC. Ryan, KO 3, 11/13/86, San Francisco. Mitchell, draw 39, 3/10/88, Chantilly, France (Mitchell down 39 times, Sullivan not off feet). Jake Kilrain, KO 75, 7/8/89, Richburg, Miss. (last of bare-knuckle championship fights). Jim Corbett, exh., 6/26/91, San Francisco. Lost title, Corbett, KO by 21, 9/7/92, New Orleans—first championship fight with padded gloves, under Marquis of Queensberry rules. Tom Sharkey, ND 3, 8/31/96, NYC. Last fight, Jack McCormick, KO 2, 3/1/05, Grand Rapids, Mich. Recognized as first of modern-era heavyweight champions. In several stage plays, including *Honest Hearts and Willing Hands* and *East and West with Parson Davies,* 1890s. Successful movie of his life, *The Great John L.,* with Greg McClure. Notorious for drinking and tavern brawls. Later abjured drinking, became temperance exponent. Hall of Fame 1954. Recap: bouts 75, KO 16, decision 14, draw 3, KO by 1, ND 41.

SULLIVAN, MIKE (Twin) B. 9/23/78, Cambridge, Mass. D. 1937. Irish. 5'10", 133. First fight, Billy Thrower, KO 5, 1901. Undefeated in 32, lost 1 until Joe Gans, KO by twice, 15, 10, 1906 (draw, Gans, 1905). Won welter title, Honey Mellody 20, 4/23/07, Los Angeles. Nontitle, Stanley Ketchel, KO by 1, 1908. Outgrew division. (Title was up for grabs several years until Ted Lewis and Jack Britton.) Undefeated through 1913. Last fight, Roddie MacDonald, KO by 4, 2/14/14, Canada. (Twin brother Jack, middleweight, creditable record, never had chance at title.) Recap: bouts 69, KO 18, decision 17, draw 14, lost decision 3, KO by 4, ND 13.

SULLIVAN, STEVE (Stephen J. Tricamo) (Kid) B. 5/21/97, Brooklyn, N.Y. Italian. 5'5", 130. First fight, Young Kenny, KO 3, 1911. Impressive record through 1917. Inactive 1918–20. Return spotty. Won junior light title, Johnny Dundee, 10, 6/20/24, Brooklyn. Defended: Mike Ballereno, KO 5, 10/15/24, NYC. Lost title, Ballerino, 10, 4/1/25, Phila. Last fight, Tod Morgan, KO by 6, 6/3/26, Brooklyn. Recap: bouts 111, KO 13, decision 18, won foul 2, draw 10, lost decision 13, lost foul 1, KO by 4, ND 50.

TAYLOR, BUD (Charles B. Taylor) (Terre Haute Terror) B. 5/8/03, Terre Haute, Ind. D. 3/8/62, Los Angeles, Calif. 5'6", 118. First fight, Walter Gorring, KO 3, 1920. Undefeated to Jimmy Kelly, KO by 6, 1922 (followed by 2 Kelly ND). Impressive record to 1927, including Jimmy McLarnin, won 10, lost foul 2, won 10. Tony Canzoneri, draw 10, 1927. Won vacant NBA bantam title, Canzoneri, 10, 6/24/27, Chicago. Vacated title, weight, 8/21/28. Fair record to last fight, Lew Massey, disq. 8, 3/6/31, Phila. Effective righthand puncher, hand trouble most of career. Manager, promoter. Recap: 157, KO 35, decisions 33, won foul 1, draw 6, lost decision 16, lost foul 3, KO by 4, ND 59.

TAYLOR, HERMAN B. 5/1/88. Promoter. No prominent personality has devoted more active years to boxing than Herman Taylor, the sometimes controversial Philadelphia promoter who celebrated his 85th birthday May 1, 1973, marking over 65 years association with the sport.

One birthday, his 80th in 1968, provided display of the respect with which Taylor is regarded by sock society. Attending were 12 former champions: Jack Dempsey, Jimmy Braddock, Ray Robinson, Rocky Graziano, Willie Pep, Tommy Loughran, Billy Conn, Joey Giardello, Bob Montgomery, Ike Williams, Benny Bass, Pete Latzo, most of whom were featured one or more times in Taylor promotions.

Taylor, an outspoken individualist, experienced troubled rounds during his years. In 1949 there was a much-publicized tax battle over amusement receipts, and in 1948 he had launched a blast against TV, claiming that promoters "lost when they should have made money. . . . I refuse to lose my money for the benefit of TV sponsors who should be forced to cooperate with promoters so that we will be insured against loss. . . ."

He cited the Ike Williams–Beau Jack lightweight title fight (Williams won, KO 6, 7/12/48), reporting that he lost $10,000 when he should have made $50,000. Adding that he would never allow another telecast under his promotion, Taylor pointed out that the fight drew a disappointing gate of $83,787, and nontelevised Williams–Bob Montgomery (Williams won, KO 6, 8/4/47) attracted $200,000 in Philadelphia.

However, Taylor's anti-TV campaign didn't last forever. A TV event, Harold Johnson–Julio Mederos (Mederos won, KO 2, 5/6/55) promoted by Taylor, indirectly caused his voluntary two-year retirement.

When Johnson surprisingly folded in the second round, charges of "fake" prompted investigation by the Pennsylvania Athletic Commission. Doctors testified that Johnson had been drugged by a barbiturate. The commission charged Johnson, matchmaker Pete Moran, four others with "sham and a collusive contest," completely clearing Taylor.

This prompted a full-blown investigation of boxing during which it was recalled that a magazine article had accused Taylor with managing a New Jersey middleweight named George Johnson. Promoters managing fighters is taboo, and Taylor's license was suspended during the 10 investigative sessions. Findings exonerated the promoter who could have had his license renewed at any time. However, he chose to retire for two years.

But the call of the ring was too much. Taylor returned and was promptly granted license renewal.

Taylor's troubled times were compensated by the respect in which boxing regards him. The 12 former world champs attending his 80th birthday some 10 years later is evidence of this.

TENDLER, LEW B. 9/28/98, Philadelphia, Pa. Jewish. 5'5". Bantam to welter. First fight, Mickey Brown, ND 6, 1913. Seven successive years undefeated. Johnny Noye, lost foul, 1919, return, KO 2. Undefeated to 1921: Rocky Kansas, lost 15. To 1928 highlights: Benny Leonard, ND, lost; Pinkey Mitchell, won; Mickey Walker, lost; Jack Zivic, KO by, return won; Joe Dundee, draw; Ace Hudkins, lost twice. Last fight, Nate Goldman, KO 5, 6/18/28, Phila. Hotel, restaurant. Hall of Fame 1961. Recap: bouts 167, KO 37, decision 22, draw 2, lost decision 7, lost foul 3, KO by 1, ND 94, no contest 1.

TERRANOVA, PHIL B. 9/4/19, New York, N.Y. Italian. 5'5". First fight, Marty Kopp, KO 1, 7/14/41, NYC. Mostly success to title including nontitle, Jackie Callura, KO 3, 1943. Won NBA feather title, Callura, KO 8, 8/16/43, New Orleans. Lost title, Sal Bartolo, 15, 3/10/44, Boston. Title, Bartolo, lost 15, 5/5/44, Boston. Title, Willie Pep, lost 15, 2/19/45, NYC. 1946, undefeated including Sandy Saddler, won 10. To 1949 fair success. Last fight, Guillermo Gimenez, lost 8, 7/13/49, NYC. Recap: bouts 99, KO 29, decision 38, draw 11, lost decision 18, KO by 3.

TERRELL, ERNIE B. 4/4/39, Chicago, Ill. Negro. 6'6", 224. First fight, Norman Bolden, won 4, 5/15/57, Chicago. Creditable early years: Zora Folley, won; Bob Foster, KO; Cleveland Williams, KO by 7, won return. Won vacant WBA heavy title, Eddie Machen, 15, 3/5/65, Chicago. Defended: George Chuvalo, won 15, 11/1/65, Toronto; Doug Jones, won 15, 6/28/66, Houston. World title, Cassius Clay, lost 15, 2/6/67, Houston. Lost 2, retired 1968–69. Sonny Moore, won 10, 12/15/70, Milwaukee. Comeback, Jeff Merritt, KO by 1, 9/10/73, NYC. Recap: bouts 47, KO 18, decision 21, lost decision 6, KO by 2.

TERRIS, SID B. 9/27/04, New York, N.Y. Jewish. 5'10", 133. Undefeated as amateur, won N.Y. State, Metropolitan, International championships. First pro fight, Tommy Hayes, KO 3, 1922. Remarkable early record. First two years: 1 loss, 1924; Eddie Kid Wagner, KO by 6, return won, undefeated in rest. 1925: Sammy Mandell only loss; Pal Moran ND, won; Johnny Dundee, won twice; Ace Hudkins, won. 1926: undefeated, Billy Petrolle, won. 1927: Ruby Goldstein, KO 1; Phil McGraw, won twice, lost foul; Hilario Martinez, lost. To 1931: career spotty, KOs by Jimmy McLarnin, Ray Miller. Last fight, Johnny Gaito, lost 6, 5/7/31, Yonkers. Recap: bouts 107, KO 12, decision 70, won foul 3, draw 4, lost decision 7, lost foul 1, KO by 4, ND 6.

THIL, MARCEL B. 5/4/04, Saint-Dizier, France. D. 8/14/63, Cannes, France. 5'10", 160. First fight, Klauss, KO 1, 11/8/25, Cherbourg, France. 1926–27: record mediocre, lost 9 of 23. 1928: undefeated in 13, won France middle title, Marcel Thuru, KO 1, 10/12/28, Paris. Won middle title of Europe, Leone Jacovacci, 15, 3/27/29, Paris. Lost Europe title, Mario Bosisio 15, 11/23/30, Milan. Undefeated in 15. Won NBA middle title, Gorilla Jones, foul 11, 6/11/32, Paris. Defended: Len Harvey, won 15, 7/4/32, London; Kid Tunero, won 15, 10/2/33, Paris (had lost nontitle to Tunero, 12, 1/16/33, Paris); Ignacio Ara, won 15, 2/26/34, Paris; Gustave Roth, won 15, 5/3/34, Paris; Carmelo Candel, draw 15, 10/15/34, Paris; Ara, won 15,

6/2/35, Madrid; Candel, won 10, 6/28/35, Paris; Lou Brouillard, won foul 4, 1/20/36, Paris (defeated Brouillard, 12, nontitle, 1935); Brouillard, won foul, 6, 2/15/37, Paris. Won light heavy title of Europe, Martinez Alfara, foul 13, 3/26/34, Paris. Defended: Jock MacAvoy, won 15, 1/14/35, Paris. Last fight, Fred Apostoli, KO by 10, 9/23/37, NYC. N.Y. Commission refused to approve bout unless stipulated that no championship was at stake. Apostoli didn't claim title, Thil vacated title. Retired. Died from car accident. Recap: bouts 96, KO 34, decision 40, won foul 4, draw 4, lost decision 12, KO by 2.

THOMAS, JOE (Joseph Daly) B. 8/30/86, Beverly, Mass. D. 2/1/26, Boston, Mass. Irish. 5′8″, 154. First fight, Jack Moriarty, KO 3, 1904. Undefeated 1905–06. Stanley Ketchel, draw 20, 1907. Vacant world middle title, Ketchel, KO by 32, 9/2/07, San Francisco. Return title, Ketchel, lost 20, 12/12/07, San Francisco. KO by 2, 1908. Had peaked in Ketchel fights. To 1921: KOs by Hugo Kelly, Billy Papke, Jack Dillon. Frank Klaus, ND; Other ND opposition mediocre. Inactive 1913–20. Last fight Jack (Twin) Sullivan, KO by 3, 2/19/21, Boston. Recap: bouts 50. KO 17, decision 7, draw 3, lost decision 5, KO by 6, ND 12.

THOMPSON, CYCLONE JOHNNY B. 6/20/76, Ogle County, Ill. D. 5/28/51, Sycamore, Ill. Danish. 5′4″, weight: fought from lightweight to light heavy. First fight, 1892, early fights not recorded. Has dubious distinction as least recognized middle champ. When Stanley Ketchel was shot, Billy Papke claimed title, generally recognized. Thompson beat Papke, 20, for title, 2/11/11, Sydney, Australia. Vacated title next year, couldn't make weight, no recorded defenses. Papke reclaimed title. Few familiar names in 22-year up-and-down record: Battling Nelson, lost twice; Packey McFarland, lost; Frank Klaus, ND; Frank Mantell, draw. Last fight, Gunboat Smith, ND 6, 9/28/14, Pittsburgh. Recap: bouts 139, KO 47, decision 34, won foul 3, draw 20, lost decision 18, lost foul 5, KO by 1, ND 11.

THOMPSON, YOUNG JACK (Cecil Lewis Thompson) B. 1904, San Francisco, Calif. D. 4/9/46, Los Angeles, Calif. Negro. 5′8″, 145. First fight, Frankie Turner, KO 8, 1926. To title fight: bouts 35, 20 KO, 9 win, 3 draw, 3 lost. World welter title, Jackie Fields, lost 10, 3/25/29, Chicago. Return title, Fields, won 15, 5/9/30, Detroit. Lost title, Tommy Freeman, 15, 9/5/30, Cleveland. Regained title, Freeman, KO 12, 4/14/36, Cleveland. Lost title, Lou Brouillard, 15, 10/23/31, Boston. Last fight, Leonard Bennett, won 6, 5/25/32, Seattle. Recap: bouts 66, KO 31, decision 15, draw 3, lost decision 16, ND 1.

TIBBS, TOMMY B. 7/23/34, Lancaster, Ohio. 5'4", 135. One of the most tireless campaigners, 18 years facing top lights. First fight, Little Chief, won 4, 1/2/50, Columbus. Sluggish early career, name opponents mostly lost: Lauro Salas, Ike Chestnut, Bobby Bell, George Araujo, Larry Boardman. Series: Tommy Edwards, won, draw, lost twice; Harold Gomes, KO twice, won one, lost three; George Monroe, won, lost twice. 1957–60 winning years: won New England light title, Gene Butler, 12, 14/24/57, Boston; Salas, won, draw; Paul Armstead, won, lost; Lulu Perez, won. 1958, Willie Pep, won. Lost title, Tommy Garrow, 10, 1/26/59, Providence; regained title, Garrow, 12, 6/29/59, Providence. Defended: Nick Previti, 10, 12/14/59, Boston. 1960 undefeated, including returns, won, Boardman, Chestnut. 1961–67, rocky years; title, Dick DeVola, lost 10, 10/31/63, Boston; lost 10 straight, including two KO by. Last fight, Renaldo Victoria, lost 10, 2/6/67, Boston. Recap: bouts 135, KO 14, decision 42, draw 4, lost decision 68, KO by 7.

TORRES, ALACRAN (Efren) B. (date unknown), Guadalajara, Mexico. First recorded fight, Felix Padilla, won 10, 10/7/61, Guadalajara. 1961–62 impressive. 1963: 9 straight KO. Won Mexican fly title, Carlos Gomez, KO 6, 7/6/63, Mexico City. Defended: Fabian Esquiver, KO 1, 11/30/63, Mexico City; Cuervo Salinas, won 12, 8/5/64, Guadalajara; Octavio Gomez, KO 5, 4/29/67, Mexico City. WBA fly title, Horacio Accavallo, lost 15, 12/10/66, Buenos Aires. World fly title, Chartchai Chionoi, KO by 13, 1/28/68, Mexico City. Won title, Chionoi, KO 8, 2/23/69, Mexico City. Lost title, Chionoi, 15, 3/20/70, Bangkok, Thailand. 1971: lost 1, KO by 1. Recap: bouts 56, KO 29, decision 17, draw 1, lost decision 6, KO by 3.

TOWEEL, VIC B. 1/12/29, Benoni, South Africa. Outstanding amateur; 190 bouts, won 160 KO, lost 2. First pro bout, John Landman, KO 2, 1/21/49. Johannesburg. Impressive overseas record. Won South African bantam title, Jimmy Webster, foul 3, 3/26/49, Johannesburg. Won South African feather title, Tony Lombard, 12, 8/6/49, Johannesburg. Defended S.A. feather title: Lombard, won 12, 9/30/49, Johannesburg. Won British Empire bantam title, Stan Rowan, 15, 11/12/49, Johannesburg. Defended British bantam title, Fernando Gagnon, won 15, 4/8/50, Johannesburg. Won world bantam title, Manuel Ortiz, 15, 5/31/50 (won title after 18 months as pro, shortest ever), Johannesburg. Defended: Danny O'Sullivan, KO 10, 12/2/50, Johannesburg. Defended S.A. feather title: Fanie van Graan, KO 2, 6/16/51, Johannesburg. World title: Luis Romero, won 15, 11/17/51, Johannesburg; Peter Keenan, won 15, 1/26/52, Johannesburg. Defended: S.A. feather: Lombard, KO 8, 3/24/52, Cape Town. Lost world bantam title, Johnny Carruthers, KO by 1, 11/15/52, Johannesburg. Title, Carruthers, KO by 10, 3/21/53, Johannesburg. Last fight, Harry Walker, KO 8,

11/6/54, Johannesburg. Recap: bouts 32, KO 14, decision 13, won foul 1, draw 1, lost decision 1, KO by 2.

TUNNEY, GENE (James Joseph Tunney) (The Fighting Marine) B. 5/25/97, New York, N.Y. Irish. 6'½", 190. First fight, Bobby Dawson, KO 7, 7/2/15, NYC. Enlisted U.S. Marines, 5/2/18. 15 fights prior to winning AEF (American Expeditionary Forces) light heavy title 1919; then defeated Bob Martin, AEF heavy champion, 4. Nov. 919–21: 22 fights, no defeats, 16 KO. Won American light heavyweight championship, Battling Levinsky, 12, 1/13/22, NYC. Lost title, Harry Greb, 15, 5/23/22, NYC (Tunney's only defeat). Regained title, Greb, 15 2/23/23, NYC. Fought Greb, three more times, won one, two ND (reporters gave Tunney edge). Georges Carpentier, KO 15; Tommy Gibbons, KO 12. Won heavyweight title, Jack Dempsey, 10, 9/23/26, Phila. Defended: Dempsey, won 10, 9/22/27, Chicago. ("Long count" fight. Dave Barry referee. Dempsey didn't return to neutral corner after scoring knockdown. Tunney floored 14 seconds at least. Regarded as most controversial incident in boxing history. Prompted 278-page book, *The Long Count,* Mel Heimer.) Last fight, Tom Heeney, KO 11, 7/26/28, NYC. Retired. Not popular with gym crowd; chided for interest in classics; quoted Shakespeare. Compared with Corbett's style, habits, public reaction. Married socialite Polly Lauder. Three sons—one, John V., U.S. senator from Calif. Comdr., navy, World War II. Several business ventures. Has homes in N.Y., Calif. Hall of Fame 1955. Recap: bouts 76, KO 41, decision 14, won foul 1, draw 1, lost decision 1, ND 17, no contest 1.

TURNER, GIL B. 10/9/30, Philadelphia, Pa. Welter. Remarkable first two years; KO record: 13 fights, 13 KO, first year; 9 KO, 5 dec., second year. First fight, Jimmy Verne, KO 1, 5/1/50, Phila. KO inc. Beau Jack 8, Ike Williams 10, Charley Fusari 11. World welter title, Kid Gavilan, KO by 11, 7/7/52, Phila. 1953, won, Bobby Dykes, Johnny Saxton; Ramon Fuentes, KO 5; lost, Joey Giardello, Rocky Castellani. Gene Fullmer series: won one, lost two. Yama Bahama, lost 1956, won 1957. Only 1957 loss, Isaac Logart; won, Virgil Akins. 1958, lost four—Vince Martinez, Mickey Crawford, Ralph Dupas, Del Flanagan—draw, Sugar Hart; won, Stefan Redl. Last fight, Flanagan, lost 10, St. Paul. Recap: bouts 77, KO 35, decision 21, draw 2, lost 15, KO by 4.

TURPIN, RANDY (Randolph Adolphus Turpin) B. 6/7/28, Lemington, England. D. 6/17/66, Warwickshire, England. 5'10", 160. First fight, Gordon Griffiths, KO 1, 9/17/46, London. 1946–48: undefeated in 20, KO by 1, lost 1; 1949–50: undefeated in 15. Won British middle title, Albert Finch, KO 5, 10/17/50, London. Won vacant European middle title, Luc van Dam,

KO 1, 2/27/51, London. Won world middle title, Ray Robinson, 15, 7/10/51, London. Lost title, Robinson, KO by 10, 9/12/51, NYC. Won British Empire light heavy title, Don Cockell, KO 11, 6/10/52, London. Won vacant British Empire middle title, George Angelo, 15, 10/21/52, London. Won European middle title, George Humez, 15, 6/9/53, London. Vacant world middle title, Bobo Olson, lost 15, 10/21/53, NYC. Lost European middle title, Tiberio Mitri, KO by 1, 5/2/54, Rome. Won British Empire light heavy title, Alex Buxton, KO 2, 4/26/55, London. Won vacant British light heavy title, Buxton, KO 5, 11/26/56, Leicester. To 1966: four KO, one win, KO by one. Last fight, Charles Seguna, KO 2, Malta. Some British reporters observed that Turpin could have been one of the great English boxers of all time if it weren't for his not infrequent disdain for training. Recap: bouts 73, KO 43, decision 17, won foul 4, draw 1, lost decision 3, KO by 5.

URTAIN, JOSE B. 5/14/43, Spain. First fight, Tony Rodri, KO 1, 7/24/68, Villafranca. 1968–70: 30 straight KO, 11 in 1st round. Won European heavyweight title, Peter Weiland, KO 7, 4/3/70, Madrid. Defended: Jurgen Blin, won 15, 6/22/70, Barcelona. Lost title, Henry Cooper, KO by 9, 11/10/70, London. Won Spanish title, Benito Canal, KO 2, 5/8/71, Bilbao. George Peralta, KO by 8, 1971, Madrid. European title, Blin, lost 15, 6/9/72, Madrid. 1973: 1 won, 1 KO. Recap: bouts 49, KO 39, decision 3, won disq. 1, draw 1, lost decision 2, lost foul 1, KO by 2.

UZCUDUN, PAOLINO (Basque Woodchopper) B. 5/3/99, Regil, Spain. 5'11½", 200. First fight, Touroff, KO 3, 9/16/23, Paris. Outstanding record early years. Came to U.S. 1927, Homer Smith, KO 7, Tampa; Tom Heeney, won, draw; Harry Wills, KO. Rugged, fought most of ranking fighters including 7 champs. Heavy title, Primo Carnera, lost 15, 10/22/33, Rome; Max Baer, won; Jack Delaney, lost foul; Max Schmeling, draw, lost twice; Tommy Loughran, lost; Mickey Walker, lost. Last fight, Joe Louis, KO by 4, 12/13/35, NYC. Returned Spain, successful real estate. Recap: bouts 70, KO 34, decision 16, draw 3, lost decision 14, lost foul 2, KO by 1.

VEJAR, CHICO B. 9/5/31, Stamford, Conn. 160 lbs. After only one loss first two years, predicted as future champ, but never had title shot. First fight, Danny Rubino, KO 2, 5/25/50, Brooklyn. Undefeated first year (1950), 14 KO. 1951: 8 KO, 7 decision, 1 loss (Eddie Campo, 10). Impressive 1952–53: 7 KO, 10 decision, 1 loss, 1 KO by (Chuck Davey); Vince Martinez, won, lost. Army 1953. Undefeated 1954. 1955: Billy Graham, decisioned twice; Tony DeMarco, KO by 1. 1956–57: 12 wins, lost big ones—Kid Gavilan, Tiger Jones, Joey Giambra, Joey Giardello, Gene Fullmer. Spotty 1958: 5 KO, 4 decision, 5 lost. Last fight, Rudell Stitch, lost 10, 12/29/58, Louisville. Recap: bouts 103, KO 39, decision 45, draw 2, lost decision 14, KO by 3.

VELENSEK, CONNY B. 3/1/42, Holland. Yugoslavian, naturalized German. 175 lbs. Early fights unrecorded; 1966–69: 19 bouts, won 11, lost 6, draw 2. First recorded fight, Hans Koschina, KO 5, 1/24/70, Berlin. First loss, German light heavy title, Rudi Schmidtke, 12, 4/16/70, Offenbach, W. Germany. Won European light heavy title, Piero del Papa, 15, 1/22/71, Berlin. Defended: Chris Finnegan, draw 15, 5/5/71, Berlin. Lost title, Finnegan, 15, 12/1/72, Nottingham. 1972: Gregorio Peralta, KO by 4; Jan Lubbers, decision. 1973: Pierre Fourie, lost 10; Jose Madrid, won 10. Recap: bouts (excluding early record)19, KO 7, decision 7, draw 1, lost decision 3, KO by 1.

VILLA, PANCHO (Francisco Guilledo) B. 8/1/01, Iloilo, Philippines. D. 7/14/25, Oakland, Calif. 5'1", 110. First pro, Kid Castro, won 4, 1919. Spectacular record to 1922 in Philippines. First U.S. bout, Abe Attell, ND

12, 6/7/22, NYC. Won U.S. flyweight title, Johnny Buff, KO 11, 9/14/22, NYC. Lost U.S. title, Frankie Genaro, 15, 3/1/23, NYC. Won world flyweight title, Jimmy Wilde, KO 7, 6/18/23, NYC. Defended: Frankie Ash, won 15, 5/30/24, Brooklyn. Jimmy McLarnin, lost 10, 7/4/25 (nontitle), Oakland. Died from blood poisoning caused by infected tooth resulting from McLarnin fight. Regarded as one of Orient's greatest. Hall of Fame 1961. Recap: bouts 103, KO 22, decision 49, draw 4, lost decision 4, lost foul 1, ND 23.

VILLAFLOR, BEN B. Philippines. First fight, Tony Jumaoas, won 10, 6/25/70, Quezon. Undefeated career. To junior lightweight title, 5 KO, 3 decisions. Won title Alfredo Marcano 15, 4/25/72, Honolulu. Nontitle, Jimmy Robertson, won 10, 1972. Juan Collado, won 10, 1973. Recap: bouts 14, KO 6, decision 7, draw 1.

WAJIMA, KOICHI B. Japan. First fight, Hileo Kusanigi, KO 9, 6/12/69, Tokyo. Won Japanese junior welter title, Noriyasu Yoshimura, KO 4, 9/4/69, Nagoya. Nontitle, Pedro Adigue, KO by 1, 1969. Japanese junior middle title, George Carter, lost 10, 2/5/70, Tokyo. Won title, Carter, 10, 4/9/70. Tokyo. Defended: Tetsuo Hoshino, KO 5, 9/10/70, Tokyo; Raizo Kajima, KO 3, 10/30/70, Tokyo; Hisao Minami, KO 7, 1/8/71, Tokyo; Hoshino, KO 2, 5/28/71, Tokyo. Undefeated 1971–72, 11 KO, 2 decision. Won WBA junior middle title, Carmelo Bossi, 10, 10/31/71, Tokyo. Defended: Domenico Tiberia, KO 1, 5/7/72, Fukuoka City.; Miguel De Oliveire, draw 15, 1/73. Recap: bouts 19, KO 14, decision 2, draw 1, lost 1, KO by 1.

WALCOTT, JERSEY JOE (Arnold Raymond Cream) B. 1/31/14, Merchantville, N.J. Negro. 6', 194. Overcame poverty of huge family, lack of education, death of father. Oldest man to win heavy title. First fight, Cowboy Wallace, KO 1, 9/9/30, Vineland, N.J. 1933–35: eight straight KOs, then Al Ettore, KO by 8, 1/21/36, Camden, N.J. 1936–46; spotty. 1947: beat Joey Maxim twice. Heavyweight title, Joe Louis, lost 15 (split dec.), 12/5/47, NYC. Title, KO by Louis, 11, 6/25/48. Title bouts, Ezzard Charles (NBA), lost 15, 6/22/49, Chicago; Charles, lost 15, 3/7/51, Detroit; Charles, won title, KO 7, 7/18/51, Pittsburgh. Rematch, Charles, won 15, 6/5/52, Philadelphia. Lost title, Rocky Marciano, KO by 13, 9/23/52, Philadelphia. Title, Marciano, KO by 1, 5/15/53, Chicago. Retired. Parole officer. Participated in youth activity. Elected sheriff, Camden County, N.J., Nov. 1971. Hall of

Fame 1970. Recap: bouts 67, KO 30, decision 18, won foul 1, draw 1, lost decision 11, KO by 6.

WALCOTT, JOE (Barbados Demon) B. 4/7/72, Barbados, West Indies. D. 1935, buried Dalton, Ohio. Negro. 5'1½", 142. To U.S. 1887. At 15 worked passage as cabin boy to Boston. Amateur boxer, wrestler, won New England lightweight title, both sports. First fight, Tom Powers, KO 2, 2/29/90. Boston. Through 1893: undefeated in 22, lost 2, also barnstormed with sideshow, facing all comers. 1894: 6 KO, 5 wins. 1895–97: impressive, lost two sensationals to Kid Lavigne. World welter title, Billy Smith, draw 25, 4/14/98, Bridgeport. Return title, Smith, lost 20, 12/6/98, NYC. Won world welter title, Jim Ferns, KO 5, 12/18/01, Fort Erie, Ont. Defended: Tommy West, won 15, 6/23/02, London. Lost title, Dixie Kid, foul 20, 4/30/04, San Francisco. Title, Dixie Kid, draw 20, 5/12/04, San Francisco. Dixie Kid outgrew division, vacated 1904. Walcott claimed. Lost title, Honey Mellody, 15, 10/16/06, Chelsea, Mass. Return nontitle, Mellody, lost 12. Last fight, Henry Hall, ND 6, 11/13/11, Eastport, Me. Hall of Fame 1955. Played part of trainer in *The Harder They Fall.* Victim of car accident. Recap: bouts 150, KO 34, decision 45, won foul 2, draw 30, lost decision 17, lost foul 3, KO by 4, ND 15.

WALKER, MICKEY (Toy Bulldog) B. 7/13/01, Elizabeth, N.J. Irish. 5'7", 145–170. Studied architecture. Rejected by army, too small, World War I, worked in shipyards. First fight, Phil Delmont, KO by 1, 1919, finished year, 6 KO, 5 ND. 1920–22: undefeated in 33, lost foul 2, lost 2. Won world welter title, Jack Britton, 15, 11/1/22, NYC. Defended: Lew Tendler, won 10, 6/2/24, Philadelphia. World middle title, Harry Greb, lost 15, 7/2/25, NYC. Defended welter title: Dave Shade, won 15, 9/21/25, NYC. Lost welter title, Pete Latzo, 10, 5/20/26, Scranton. Joe Dundee, KO by 8, next fight. Won world middle title, Tiger Flowers, 10, 12/3/26, Chicago, a disputed verdict. Defended: Tommy Milligan, KO 10, 6/30/27, London; Ace Hudkins, won 10, 6/21/28, Chicago. Light heavy title, Tommy Loughran, lost 10, 3/28/29, Middle defense: Hudkins, won 10, 10/29/29, Los Angeles. 1929–30: campaigned with success in light heavy, heavy divisions. Relinquished middle title 6/19/31. 1932: Johnny Risko, lost 12; Max Schmeling, KO by 8. Light heavy title, Maxie Rosenbloom, lost 15, 11/3/33, NYC. Return, defeated Rosenbloom, 10 (Max had previously lost title). Bids for heavier titles faded. Paul Pirrone, KO by 11, 1934; John Anderson, lost 8, 1935. Last fight, Eric Seelig, KO by 7, 11/29/35, NYC. Retired, operated taverns in Los Angeles, NYC. Recognized as a primitive art painter. Possibly the most colorful of a colorful division. Hall of Fame 1953. Recap: bouts 148, KO 58, decision 35, draw 4, lost decision 11, lost foul 2, KO by 5, no decision 32, no contest 1.

WALSH, JIMMY B. 1886, Newton, Mass. Irish. 5'2", 115. First fight, Young Schindler, won 3, 10/23/01, Boston. Undefeated in 40 to mid-1904, then lost to Digger Stanley, 15. Return, Stanley, draw 15, both 1904. Undefeated through 1905 to vacant world bantam title fight, Stanley, won 15, 10/20/05, Chelsea, Mass. Nontitle, Abe Attell, lost 15, KO by 8. Outgrew division 1907. To 1915 mostly successful feather career, fought Attell three times, Young Britt, Pal Moore, Johnny Kilbane three times, Pete Herman. Last fight, Johnny Ertle, ND 8, 2/25/15, Milwaukee. Recap: bouts 120, KO 12, decision 39, won foul 1, draw 18, lost decision 8, KO by 1, ND 41.

WARD, GEORGIE B. 7/7/01, Niagara Falls, N.Y. 5'10½", 142. First fight, Joe McNally, KO 3, 1919. Undefeated first year. Upset Phil Bloom, 10, 1920. Creditable record to 1924, including Mickey Walker, ND twice; Soldier Bartfield, won; Pete Latzo, ND twice, lost twice; Dave Shade, ND one, lost three; Benny Leonard, lost; Eddie Shevlin, lost, won three returns. Undefeated 1925. Despite impressive record, never title match. Last fight, Freddie Polo, KO by 3, 6/9/29. Newark. After retirement, on police force, Cranford, N.J. Recap: bouts 113, KO 26, decision 15, won foul 1, draw 1, lost decision 14, lost foul 1, KO by 3, ND 51, no contest 1.

WEBB, SPIDER (Ellsworth Webb) B. 11/20/31, Tulsa, Okla. 5'9½", 158. NCAA middle champ 1951–52. Olympics 1952, lost finals to Laszlo Papp, Hungary. First pro fight, Johnny Johnson, KO 2, 6/1/53, Chicago. Impressive first year, six KO, two dec., one lost. 1954 undefeated, four straight KO. Army 1955. Undefeated 1956, including Holly Mims, Rory Calhoun, Charlie Cotton. 1958, only loss, Charley Joseph; won return. 1958, Calhoun, KO 4; Joey Giardello, KO 7; Terry Downes, KO 8; dec., Dick Tiger; lost, Gene Fullmer, Mims. KO Bobby Boyd, Neal Rivers to NBA middle title, Fullmer, lost 15, 12/4/59, Logan, Utah. 1960, one fight— Calhoun, won. Announced retirement. Comeback. Last fight, Tiger, KO by 6, 4/15/61, NYC. Recap: bouts 40, KO 19, decision 15, lost decision 5, KO by 1.

WEILL, AL B. 1894. D. 10/21/69, Miami, Fla. Manager. "Master of his trade," said Arthur Daley, *New York Times* sports editor, recalling Weill, manager of four world champions and Madison Square Garden matchmaker.

He wasn't a front runner in popularity contests, but he was respected by those in the ring, corners, gyms and behind the front-office desks. As Daley further commented, ". . . even his enemies admitted he was a master, and that added up to high praise from an awful lot of people. His few friends said the same, thereby making it unamimous." And historians concede that all were correct because his background substantiates that he was a superior manipulator of fighters. He was a relic of a bygone era.

Another noted sports writer, Dan Parker, contributed to the Weill legend, establishing the "Vest" as a nickname. Parker's explanation, "The Vest gets all the gravy." The gravy included his split of the ring earnings of Rocky Marciano, whom Weill guided to the heavy title with timely and astute matchmaking.

Others who won championships with the assist of the Vest's unique talents were welterweight Marty Servo, lightweight Lou Ambers and featherweight Joey Archibald. None was accorded the deserved historical stature of Marciano, but his guidance of Ambers in four title fights is recalled with respect by the sideliners.

Ambers, who is fairly categorized as "an average champion," was involved in title fights with two of the all-time greats, Tony Canzoneri and Henry Armstrong. In his first light title bout (5/10/35, NYC), he lost 15 to Canzoneri, but a verbal and fistic buildup earned him a return title bout two years later (5/7/37, NYC), when he won the title from the fading champ. Lost title, 15, to Armstrong (8/17/38, NYC), regained title, 15 (8/22/39, NYC), when Armstrong was mostly busy defending welter crown.

When Weill died at 75 in a nursing home, he was a wealthy man.

WEINERT, CHARLEY (Newark Adonis) B. 10/22/95, Budapest, Austria-Hungary. 5'11", 185. First fight, Frank Joseph, KO 2, 1913. Undefeated, first year, including Battling Levinsky, ND 10. To 1917, only setback Jack Dillon, KO by 2, 1914, return ND, 1915. Series: Levinsky, won one, ND three; Billy Miske, ND three; Gunboat Smith, won foul one, ND 2; Fred Fulton KO by 2, lost foul 2, 1917. Undefeated to 1921, then lost to Harry Greb, 15, 11/4/21, NYC. Entered navy 1918. 1922: Gene Tunney, ND 12, KO by 4. 1923: undefeated, including Martin Burke, Chuck Wiggins to Luis Firpo, KO by 2. Firpo return, ND 12, 1924. Jack Sharkey, ND 12, 1924, won return, 10, 1925. Harry Wills, KO by 2, Jimmy Maloney, KO by 3, otherwise undefeated to last fight, Murray Gittlitz, ND 10, 2/28/29, Newark. Unpredictable trial horse, potential greater than accomplishment. Operated Newark tavern. Recap: bouts 78, KO 23, decision 9, won foul 4, draw 1, lost decision 1, lost foul 1, KO by 7, ND 32.

WEIR, IKE O'NEIL (Belfast Spider) B. 2/5/67, Belfast, Ireland. D. 9/12/08, Charleston, Mass. 5'5¾", 118. After 1885, success in England. To Boston 1886, first fight, William Snee, won 4, 5/28/86, Boston. To 1889, undefeated. Vacant feather title, Frank Murphy, draw 80, 3/31/89, Kouts,

Ind. Billy Murphy, KO 14, 1/13/90, Los Angeles. Murphy claimed title. To Australia 1890, returned U.S. 1891. Last fight, Young Griffo, lost 3, 3/17/94, Chicago. Recap: bouts 41, KO 12, decision 17, draw 8, lost decision 2, KO by 1, ND 1.

WELLS, BILLY (Bombardier) B. 8/31/87, London, England. D. 1967. 6'3", 186. Legendary English boxer. Won All-India heavy title 1909. First recorded fight, Gunner Joe Mills, won 6, 6/8/10, London. First year, five straight KO. 1911, first KO by, Gunner Moir, 3; started reputation of glass jaw. Won British heavy title same year, Ian Hague, KO 6, 4/24/11, London. 1912–13: KO by four, Georges Carpentier twice, Al Palzer, 3 (first U.S. fight), Gunboat Smith; KO five, including title defense, Packey Mahoney, KO 13, 6/30/13, London. Undefeated 1914: four KO, two dec. 1915: four KO; Frank Moran, KO by 10. 1916: four straight KO, including title defense, Dan Voyles, KO 2, 12/18/16, London. Lost title, Joe Beckett, KO by 5, 2/27/19, London. Inactive 1921. 1922, three bouts—KO one, KO by two (Frank Goddard, Jack Bloomfield). 1924, two bouts—two KO. Last fight, Jack Stanley, KO by 3, 4/30/25, London. Never lost decision. Recap: bouts 49, KO 33, decision 4, KO by 11, lost foul 1.

WELLS, MATT B. 12/14/86, London, England. D. 7/8/53, London, England. 5'4", 140. Outstanding British amateur, won light title 1904–07. First pro fight, Gunnar Hart, KO 5, 1909. Undefeated 1909–11, including Phila. Pal Moore, won; Leach Cross, ND; NDs, Abe Attell, Dick Hyland. Won British light title, Freddie Welsh, 20, 2/27/11, London; lost title, Welsh, 20, 11/11/12, London. U.S. campaign 1915–17; lost first, Mike Glover, 12, Boston. Mostly impressive, including Charley White series, won one, ND two, lost one, KO by one, no contest; Eddie Murphy, won; NDs, Bryan Downey twice, Phil Bloom. Returned to England 1919; Ted (Kid) Lewis, KO by 12, 12/26/19. Spotty record to last fight, Jack Hart, won 15, 5/12/22, London. Boxing coach, referee. Recap: bouts 75, KO 7, decision 18, won foul 2, draw 2, lost decision 13, lost foul 1, KO by 3, ND 28, no contest 1.

WELSH, FREDDY (Frederick Hall Thomas) (The Welsh Wizard) B. 3/5/86, Pontypridd, Wales. D. 7/29/27, New York, N.Y. 5'7", 133. First fight, Kid Allen, KO 3, 1905. To 1910, undefeated in 70, lost 1—Packey McFarland, 10; return, draw. To title only loss Matt Wells, 20; return, won 20. Won world light title, Willie Ritchie, 20, 7/7/14, London. Defended: Ad Wolgast, KO 8, 11/2/14, NYC; Charley White, won 20, 9/4/16, Colorado Springs. Lost title, Benny Leonard, KO by 9, 5/28/17, NYC. Army captain World War I. 1920–22: KO three, won one, draw one. Last fight, Archie Walker, lost 10, 4/5/22, Brooklyn. Active, physical education. Lectured.

Operated "health farm." Hall of Fame 1960. Recap: bouts 166, KO 23, decision 50, won foul 3, draw 7, lost foul 3, KO by 1, ND 79.

WEPNER, CHUCK B. Bayonne, N.J. Heavy. First fight, George Cooper, KO 3, 8/5/64, Bayonne. Undefeated first year. 1965–67, mostly impressive; setbacks: Buster Mathis, KO by 3, 1966; Jerry Tomasetti, KO by 5, 1967 (return, KO 1, 1968). Undefeated 1968. 1969–70, moved into fast company —KO by George Foreman, 3; Sonny Liston, 10; Joe Bugner, 3. Undefeated 1972. American heavy title, awarded disputed dec. (12) over Ernie Terrell 6/23/73, Atlantic City. Commissioner Abe Greene directed rematch "within short order," following investigation of ref's decision. (N.J. allows dec. by ref. alone. Harold Valan scored 7–5 Wepner.) Recap: bouts 37, KO 9, decision 17, draw 2, lost decision 3, KO by 6.

WHITE, CHARLEY (Charles Anchowitz) B. 3/25/91, Liverpool, England. 5'6", 133. First fight, Marty Kane, won 6, 1906. Undefeated, 1906–07. 1908: undefeated to Abe Attell, lost 8, 12/6/09, Memphis. Impressive: Joe Mandott, draw, lost; NDs, Attell, Freddie Welsh, Johnny Dundee, Ad Wolgast, Leach Cross, Ted (Kid) Lewis; Joe Thomas, KO twice; Jack Shugrue, KO, ND two. World light title, Welsh, lost 20, 9/4/16, Colorado Springs. 1917–20: Earned title match, Benny Leonard, KO by 9, 7/5/20, Benton Harbor. Creditable to retirement, including Johnny Dundee, won, ND twice, draw, lost. Last fight, Henry Perlick, KO by 2, 2/21/30, Chicago. Recap: bouts 170, KO 52, decision 28, won foul 1, draw 8, lost decision 13, KO by 3, ND 65, no contest 1.

WILDE, JIMMY (Mighty Atom) B. 5/15/92, Pontypridd, Wales. 5'2½", 108. First fight, Lewis Williams, KO 3, 1911. Undefeated through 1914, then Tommy Lee, KO by 17, 1915. Undefeated to Zulu Kid, won vacant flyweight title, KO 11, 12/18/16, London. Pal Moore, lost 3, 12/12/18, London (final bantams, Inter-Allied Kings Trophy competition). Undefeated through 1920. Pete Herman, KO by 17, 1/13/21, London. Lost title, KO by 7, Pancho Villa, 6/18/23, NYC. Newspaper reporter. Hall of Fame 1959. Recap: bouts 138, KO 77, decision 47, draw 1, won foul 1, lost decision 1, KO by 3, ND 8.

WILLARD, JESS (Pottawatomie Giant) B. 12/29/81, Pottawatomie County, Kans. D. 12/15/68, Los Angeles, Calif. 6'6", 250. Cowboy. First fight, Louis Fink, lost foul 10, 2/15/11, Sapulpa, Okla. 1912–14: 13 KO, won 1, ND 3; lost, Gunboat Smith, Tom MacMahon; Charley Miller, draw. Won heavy title, Jack Johnson, KO 26, 4/5/15, Havana. (Rumor fight was fixed; cite photo of Johnson on back being counted out while shading eyes with hand.) Defended: Frank Moran, ND 10, 3/25/16, New York. Lost title, Jack Dempsey, KO by 3 (floored 7 times in 1st round), 7/4/19, Toledo, Ohio. Last fight, Luis Firpo, KO by 11, 5/12/23, Jersey City. Retired to Calif. Supermarket. Well respected. Recap: bouts 36, KO 20, decision 4, draw 1, lost decision 3, lost foul 1, KO by 2, ND 5.

WILLIAMS, CLEVELAND B. 6/30/33, Griffin, Ga. Heavy. First fight, Lee Hunt, KO 2, 12/11/51, Tampa. Undefeated to 1953, 20 KO, 1 dec. First loss, Sonny Jones, 4, 1953; return, KO 7 (1954). Bob Satterfield, KO by 3, 1954. Army 1955. Undefeated 1956–58, including six straight KO. Sonny Liston, KO by 3, 1959, KO by 2, 1960. Undefeated 1961–62, including Ernie Terrell, KO 7 (lost return, 1963); Wayne Bethea, won; Eddie Machen, draw. Undefeated 1964. Inactive 1965. Two KO, 2 dec. to title, Muhammad Ali, KO by 3, 11/14/66, Houston. Announced retirement 1967. Returned 1968; KO four, dec. one; lost, Bob Cleroux, 10. 1969, three straight KO by—Al Jones, 8; Mac Foster twice, 5, 3. To 1973, KO three, decision four, lost two, KO by 1. Recap: bouts 92, KO 59, decision 18, won disq. 1, draw 1, lost decision 5, KO by 8.

WILLIAMS, IKE B. 8/2/23, Brunswick, Ga. Negro. 5'6", 130. First fight, Carmen Fatta, won 4, 3/15/40, New Brunswick. 1940–41, creditable record. Undefeated 1942–43, 14 KO. 1944: Bob Montgomery, KO by 12; Sammy Angott, won twice. Won NBA lightweight title, Juan Zurita, KO 2, 4/18/45, Mexico City. Defended: Ronnie James, KO 9, 9/4/46, Cardiff, Wales; Montgomery, KO 6, 8/4/47, Phila.; Enrique Bolanos, won 15, 5/25/48, Los Angeles; Beau Jack, KO 6, 7/12/48, Phila.; Jesse Flores, KO 10, 9/23/48, NYC; Bolanos, KO 4 7/21/49, Los Angeles; Fred Dawson, win 15, 12/5/49, Phila. Lost title, James Carter, KO by 14, 5/25/51, NYC. Last fight, Jack, KO by 9, 8/12/55, Augusta. Recap: bouts 154, KO 60, decision 65, draw 5, lost decision 18, KO by 6.

WILLIAMS, KID (Johnny Gutenko) B. 12/5/93, Copenhagen, Denmark. D. 1/18/63, Baltimore, Md. 5'1", 117. First fight, Shep Farren, KO 5, 7/18/10, Baltimore. Undefeated through 1916, except lost foul, Johnny Ertle, 1915. Won world bantam title, Johnny Coulon, KO 3, 6/9/14, Vernon, Calif. Defended: Frankie Burns, draw 20, 12/6/15, New Orleans; Pete Herman, draw 20, 2/7/16, New Orleans. Lost title, Herman, 20, 1/9/17, New Orleans. To 1929: record mostly impressive, never another title chance. Last fight, Bobby Burns, KO by 2, 1929. Frustrated comeback 1935. Rugged campaigner, met all challenges. Hall of Fame 1970. Recap: bouts 204, KO 48, decision 53, won foul 6, draw 7, lost decision 8, lost foul 6, KO by 3, ND 73.

WILLS, HARRY (Black Panther) B. 5/15/92, New Orleans, La. D. 12/21/58, New York, N.Y. Negro. 6'2", 220. First fight, Kid Navarro, KO 1, 1910. Fought during period when difficult for Negro fighters. Unrecorded estimates 22 fights with Sam Langford; records show 15, KO 2, decision 3, ND 8, KO by 2, Won Negro heavy title, Langford, 15, 11/5/19, Tulsa. Lost title, Bill Tate foul 1, 1/1/22. Return Tate, draw 10, 1/6/22, Portland. Challenged Jack Dempsey several times, never met, causing enlivened controversy. Luis Firpo, ND, 1924; Jack Sharkey, lost foul, 1926, Paolino Uzcudun, KO by 4, 1927. Last fight, Vinko Jankassa, KO 2, 1932, Staten Island. Retired, real estate business. Hall of Fame 1970. Recap: bouts 102, KO 45, decision 17, draw 2, lost decision 1, lost foul 3, KO by 4, ND 27, no contest 3.

WILSON, JACKIE (Jack Benjamin Wilson) B. 1909, Arkansas. Negro. 5'5". First recorded fight, Pat Flaherty, lost 10, 1931. Undefeated 1933, including wins over Eddie Shea, Tommy Paul, Johnny Pena. To 1941: fought tops in feathers and lights, Freddie Miller, Leo Rodak, Sammy Angott, Harry Jeffra, Chalky Wright. Won NBA feather title, Richie Lemos, 12, 11/18/41, Los Angeles. Return title, Lemos, won 12, 12/16/41, Los Angeles. Lost title, Jackie Callura, 15, 1/18/43, Providence, R.I. Return title, Callura, lost 15, 3/18/43, Boston. Record began fading. Last two years (1946–47) lost 15 of 17. Recap: bouts 120, KO 17, decision 55, won foul 2, draw 5, lost decision 33, lost foul 1, KO by 5, ND 1, no contest 1.

WILSON, JOHNNY (John Panica) B. 3/23/93, New York, N.Y. Italian. 158. First fight, George Cunningham, KO 2, 1911. 1912–20: erratic record to title. Won world middle title, Mike O'Dowd, 12, 5/6/20, Boston. Defended: George Chip, ND 10, 1/17/21, Pittsburgh; return, O'Dowd, won 15, 3/17/21, NYC; Bryan Downey, ND 12, 9/5/21, Jersey City. Lost title, Harry Greb, 15, 8/31/23, NYC. Title, Greb, lost 15, 1/18/24, NYC. 1924–26: Tommy Loughran, lost 10; Tiger Flowers, KO by 3; Greb, lost 10; Maxie Rosenbloom, lost 12. Last fight, Rosenbloom, lost 12, 10/4/26, Pittsburgh. Retired. Recap: bouts 122, KO 43, decision 20, won foul 1, draw 2, lost decision 17, lost foul 2, KO by 2, ND 34, no contest 1.

WINSTONE, HOWARD B. 4/15/39, Merthyr Tydfil, Wales. Outstanding amateur, won 84 of 86. 1958, won Welsh, British ABA, Empire bantam titles. First pro fight, Bill Graydon, won 5, 2/24/59, London. Undefeated to 1962. Won British feather title, Terry Spinks, KO 10, 5/2/61, London. Defended: Derry Trenor, KO 10, 4/10/62, London; Harry Carroll, KO 6, 5/30/62, Cardiff; John Morrissey, KO 11, 1/31/63, Glasgow. Nontitle upset, Leroy Jeffery, KO by 2, 1962. Won European feather title, Alberto Serti, KO 14,

7/9/63, Cardiff. Defended: British, European title, Billy Calvert, won 15, 8/20/63, Porthcawl, Wales; John O'Brien, 15, 12/19/63, London. 1964, nontitle Don Johnson, lost 10; won return, 1965; won disq., 4, 1966. Defended European title: Lino Mastellaro, KO 8, 5/12/64, London; Yves Desmarets, 15, 1/22/65, Rome. World feather title, Vicente Saldivar lost 15, 9/7/65, London. Defended European title: Andrea Silanos, KO 15, 3/7/66, Sassari; Jean DeKeers, KO 3, 9/6/66, London. Defended British, European title: Lenny Williams, KO 8, 12/7/66, Aberayron, Wales. World title, Saldivar, lost 15, 6/15/67, Cardiff; return title, Saldivar, KO by 12, 10/14/67, Mexico City. Joe Legra, KO by 5, 1968. 1969, relinquished titles to campaign as jr. light. Inactive. Recap: bouts 67, KO 27, decision 33, won disq. 1, lost decision 3, KO by 3.

WOLGAST, AD (Adolphus Wolgust) (Michigan Wildcat) B. 2/8/88, Cadillac, Mich. D. 4/14/55, Camarillo, Calif. German. 5'4¼", 122–126. First fight, Kid Moore, won 6, 6/10/06, Petosky, Mich. Undefeated to 1910, won lightweight title, Battling Nelson, KO 40, 2/22/10, Richmond Point, Va. Defended: Joe Rivers, KO 13, 7/4/12, Vernon, Calif. Lost title, Willie Ritchie, foul 16, 11/28/12, Daly City, Calif. 1913–17: spotty record. 1918–19, inactive. Last fight, Lee Morrissey, draw 4, 9/6/20, San Bernardino, Calif. Retired, mental problem, hospitalized. Recap: bouts 134, KO 38, decision 21, won foul 1, draw 14, lost decision 6, lost foul 4, KO by 2, ND 48.

WOLGAST, MIDGET (Joseph Robert Loscatzo) B. 7/18/10, Philadelphia, Pa. D. 10/19/55, Philadelphia, Pa. Italian. 5'3½", 112. First fight, Willie Davies, won 10, 11/3/27, NYC. Impressive third year. Won N.Y. Commission flyweight title, Black Bill, 15, elimination, 3/21/30, NYC. Defended: Willie La Morte, KO 6, 5/16/30, NYC. NBA title, Frankie Genaro, draw 15, 12/26/30, NYC. Defended N.Y. title: Ruby Bradley, 15, 7/13/31, Brooklyn. Undefended to mid-1935, not recognized as world champ. Lost American title, Small Montana, 10, 9/16/35, Oakland, Calif. Never another title chance. Last fight, Bill Morris, lost 6, 3/14/40, Lancaster, Eng. Recap: bouts 147, KO 11, decision 85, draw 15, lost decision 29, KO by 6, ND 1.

WRIGHT, CHALKY (Albert Wright) B. 2/10/12, Durango, Mexico. D. 8/12/57, Los Angeles, Calif. 5'7½". First fight in 1925—fought thrice. 1928–29 not recorded. Hungry early years. 1930–35: lost 4, KO by 1, won 1. Next four years fair: KO by Henry Armstrong, lost twice to Lew Feldman. 1941: series of KOs, wins, led to world feather title fight, Joey Archibald, KO 11, 9/11/41, Washington, D.C. Defended: Harry Jeffra, KO 11, 6/19/42, Baltimore; Lulu Constantino, won 15, 9/25/42, NYC. Lost title, Willie Pep,

15, 11/20/42, NYC. Title, Pep, lost 15, 9/29/44, NYC. Nontitle, Pep, lost 10, 12/5/44, KO by 3, 11/27/46. Last fight, Ernie Hunick, KO by 3, 3/9/48, Salt Lake City. Recap: bouts 140, KO 57, decision 45, draw 5, lost decision 27, KO by 5, no contest 1.

YANGER, BENNY (Frank Angone) (Tipton Slasher) B. 2/18/82, New York, N.Y. D. 4/15/58, Chicago, Ill. Italian. 5'5½", 133. First fight, Dusty Miller, KO 6, 6/10/99, Chicago. Undefeated nearly five years. Early fights in Chicago. Creditable early record: George Dixon, won; Joe Bernstein, won twice; Abe Attell, KO 19, 1902; Kid Broad, draw, won, ND. First setback, Eddie Hanlon, lost 20, 1903. To 1907: creditable record, never title chance. To 1909 mostly won; KO by Aurelio Herrera, Rube McCarty, Tommy Murphy, Packey McFarland. Last fight, Harry Cutch, ND 10, 5/19/09, NYC. Recap: bouts 83, KO 25, decision 25, won foul 1, draw 20, lost decision 5, KO by 4, ND 3.

YAROSZ, TEDDY B. 6/24/10, Pittsburgh, Pa. Polish. 5'10", 158. First fight, Jack McCarthy, KO 2. Undefeated 1926–32. First loss, Eddie Kid Wolfe, 10, 1/23/33; return, draw 10, 2/27/33. Young Terry, lost 10. Undefeated 1934. Won NBA middle title, Vince Dundee, 15, 9/11/34, Pittsburgh. Nontitle, Babe Risko, KO by 7, 1/1/35. Lost title, Risko, 15, 9/19/35, Pittsburgh. 1936: undefeated 5, including Risko, won 10 (Risko had lost title). 1937: won two, Solly Krieger, 10, Lou Brouillard, 10; lost, Billy Conn twice, 12, 15. Carmelo Candel, lost, 10. 1938: Conn, won 12, lost 7 of 18, 1939–41, including Ezzard Charles, lost 10. Last fight, Joe Muscato, lost 8, 2/12/42, Rochester, N.Y. Recap: bouts 127, KO 16, decision 90, draw 3, lost decision 17, KO by 1.

205

ZALE, TONY (Anthony Florian Zaleski) (Man of Steel) B. 5/29/13, Gary, Ind. Polish. 5'8". 160–65. Indiana Golden Gloves welter champ, 1931. Chicago Golden Gloves, lost welter finals, 1932. 95 amateur fights: KO 50, decision 37, lost 8. First pro, Eddie Allen, won 4, 6/11/34. Chicago. To 1939, bouncy record. In 1939–40, lost first fight, Nate Bolden 10, then 9 KO, 2 wins. Won NBA middle title, Al Hostak, KO 13, 7/19/40, Chicago. Nontitles, Billy Soose, lost 10; Fred Apostoli, won 10, 1940. Defended: Steve Mamakos, KO 14, 2/21/41, Chicago; Hostak, KO 2, 5/28/41, Chicago. Won vacant world middle title, George Abrams, 15, 11/28/41, NYC. 1942, Billy Conn, lost 20. Navy, 4 years. 1946: 7 straight KO, including title defense, Rocky Graziano, KO 6, 9/27/46, NYC. (First of most sensational three-fight series in history.) 1947: 5 straight KO; lost title, Graziano, KO by 6, 7/17/47, Chicago. Regained title, Graziano, KO 3, 6/10/48, Newark. Lost title, Marcel Cerdan, KO by 12, 9/21/48, Jersey City. Hall of Fame 1958. Recap: bouts 88, KO 46, decision 24, draw 2, lost 12, KO by 4.

ZIVIC, FRITZIE B. 5/8/13, Pittsburgh, Pa. Croatian. 5'9", 135–45. Five fighting brothers in family: Eddie, Joe, Pete, Jack, Fritzie. First fight, Al Reddinger, KO 1, 1931. 1932: won 6, lost 2. 1933–34: undefeated in 21, Laddie Tonnelli, KO by 3. Spotty through 1935–36. 1937–40: undefeated in 57, lost 7; won world welter title, Henry Armstrong, 15, 10/4/40, NYC. Defended: Armstrong, KO 12, 1/17/41, NYC. Lost title, Fred Cochrane, 15, 7/29/41, Newark. Busy, erratic through 1944: Lew Jenkins, KO 10; Norman Rubio, KO 9; beat Cochrane, Jake LaMotta; KO by Ray Robinson; lost,

Robinson, Tony Morisi, Rubio, Armstrong, Shiek Rangel, Beau Jack twice, LaMotta, Bob Montgomery, Ralph Zanelli, Freddie Archer, Tommy Bell. Army. 1944–49, up-down: won 54, lost 25. Last fight, Eddie Steele, won 10, 1/17/49, Augusta, Ga. Regarded as one of great journeyman boxers. Hall of Fame 1973. Recap: bouts 230, KO 80, decision 74, won foul 1, draw 10, lost decision 61, KO by 4.

ZURITA, JUAN B. (Date unavailable), Guadalajara, Mexico. 5'3", 122. First fight, Rudolfo Camacho, won 6, 1933. Early fights, Mexico City, mostly won. Midget Wolgast series: lost 3, 1935; KO 5, won 10, 1936. Henry Armstrong, KO by 4, 1936; KO by 2, 1942. Won NBA lightweight title, Sammy Angott, 15, 3/8/44, Hollywood. Lost title, Ike Williams, KO by 2, 4/18/45, Mexico City, last fight. Recap: bouts 85, KO 22, decision 50, draw 1, lost 9, KO by 3.